THE PROFICIENT PILOT
II

ALSO BY BARRY SCHIFF

* *in collaboration*

An AOPA Book

THE PROFICIENT PILOT
II

Barry Schiff

AN ELEANOR FRIEDE BOOK

MACMILLAN PUBLISHING COMPANY   *New York*

COLLIER MACMILLAN PUBLISHERS   *London*

Macmillan Publishing Company
866 Third Avenue, New York, N.Y. 10022
Collier Macmillan Canada, Inc.

Library of Congress Cataloging-in-Publication Data
Schiff, Barry J.
  The proficient pilot.
  "An AOPA book."
  "An Eleanor Friede book."
  Includes index.
  1. Airplanes—Piloting. I. Title
TL710.S293   1987   629.132'52   87-7893
ISBN 0-02-607151-7

Macmillan books are available at special discounts for bulk purchases for sales promotions, premiums, fund-raising, or educational use. For details, contact:

  Special Sales Director
  Macmillan Publishing Company
  866 Third Avenue
  New York, N.Y. 10022

10 9 8 7 6 5 4 3 2 1

Printed in the United States of America

An AOPA Book

THE PROFICIENT PILOT II

Barry Schiff

AN ELEANOR FRIEDE BOOK

MACMILLAN PUBLISHING COMPANY   *New York*

COLLIER MACMILLAN PUBLISHERS   *London*

Macmillan Publishing Company
866 Third Avenue, New York, N.Y. 10022
Collier Macmillan Canada, Inc.

Library of Congress Cataloging-in-Publication Data
Schiff, Barry J.
    The proficient pilot.
    "An AOPA book."
    "An Eleanor Friede book."
    Includes index.
    1. Airplanes—Piloting.   I. Title
TL710.S293   1987   629.132'52   87-7893

ISBN 0-02-607151-7

Macmillan books are available at special discounts for bulk purchases for sales promotions, premiums, fund-raising, or educational use. For details, contact:

    Special Sales Director
    Macmillan Publishing Company
    866 Third Avenue
    New York, N.Y. 10022

10 9 8 7 6 5 4 3 2 1

Printed in the United States of America

CONTENTS

ACKNOWLEDGMENTS

People acquire most of their knowledge from others. In this respect no man is an island. Similarly, what has been written on these pages consists primarily of a distillation of flying wisdom gleaned from others during my aviation career. Crediting each of these individuals is not possible because they consist of virtually everyone with whom I have shared a cockpit. In one way or another each has contributed to my aeronautical education. And for this I am genuinely grateful.

My deepest appreciation is extended to those directly involved with the creation of this book: Bart Everett, Hal Fishman, Eleanor Friede, Mischa Hausserman, Thomas Horne, Robert Said, Norman Schuyler, and Edward Tripp. Their efforts on my behalf have been invaluable.

—BARRY SCHIFF

Los Angeles, California

FOREWORD

AOPA *Pilot* is a monthly magazine provided as a benefit to the 260,000 members of the Aircraft Owners and Pilots Association. Virtually all of our members are active pilots, many of whom own their own aircraft. This is a sophisticated, upscale crowd that demands hard information on pilot technique from their asssociation's magazine. We give it to them.

Trouble is, it can be difficult to find a knowledgeable pilot endowed with writing skills, or, conversely, an accomplished author with an extensive piloting background. It is the lament of every editor of special-interest publications, particularly those with large circulations. An animated enthusiast may paint the most colorful, informative and entertaining verbal picture. But his prose is apt to be almost illiterate chicken scratch—another addition to the pile of unsolicited manuscripts that accretes on an editorial assistant's carrel.

Some promising pilot/authors—if they are energetic, disciplined and so inclined—try to land staff positions with aviation publications. Others crave flying so much that they make a living of it and work as freelance writers on the side.

Barry Schiff is one of the best. Since 1967 he has been a contributing editor for AOPA *Pilot*, publishing more than 200 feature articles and technical reviews. *The Proficient Pilot II* (an earlier edition was published in 1985) is a compilation of some of his most significant work.

Schiff's background makes him a uniquely qualified author. For all of you who believe that airline captains somehow spring, full-rated, into the cockpit of a Transport-category airplane, you should know that nearly half of his 20,000 hours of pilot-in-command time has been spent in light general aviation aircraft. He began flying at age 14, then quickly moved into flight instruction (which accounts for some 4,000 hours of his flight time) before signing on with Trans World Airlines in 1964. He is qualified as captain on the Boeing 707, 727, 747 and 767, and the Lockheed L-1011. In his off-hours he flies his single-engine Citabria 7GCAA.

There is more: Schiff holds ratings for all but one class of aircraft ("Except for airships . . . there are awfully few of them"), and he is a designated Federal Aviation Administration flight examiner. He also holds numerous aviation records and has been the recipient of several important awards for his many contributions to aviation safety.

One of them is in your hands. *The Proficient Pilot II* consists of topics that will appeal to the entire pilot spectrum. Whether you fly for fun or for profit, the information in these pages will have considerable value. Anyone who flies knows that the learning process should never end; there is always a need to review the basics and to probe new fields of knowledge. Schiff's easy writing style and breadth of experience makes this an easy task indeed.

AOPA, Eleanor Friede Books and the Macmillan Publishing Company are proud to make this contribution to aviation knowledge, yet another in the AOPA series of aviation publications. This is a book that belongs on every pilot's bookshelf and that will serve as a valuable and entertaining reference source for years to come. Those who are familiar with Barry Schiff's work already know that. Those who do not are about to discover.

—Thomas A. Horne
Editor, *AOPA Pilot*
Vice President, AOPA Publications Division

1

FLIGHT DYNAMICS

BEYOND THE BLUEPRINTS

Being a proficient pilot is more than just developing the necessary piloting skills. It also is having some appreciation of the major factors involved in aircraft design because these ultimately determine performance and handling qualities.

When an aircraft is conceived, its designer must mentally wrestle with a variety of variables. These include airframe weight, fuel capacity, range, payload, takeoff and landing speeds, cruise and climb performance, power, manufacturing cost, and operating economy.

Juggling these factors is a frustrating business because optimizing one almost always has a detrimental effect on another. Consequently, a designer must sacrifice certain elements to achieve a goal. The result invariably is a compromise between desire and pragmatism. Not one airplane performs, behaves, and handles the way its designer would have preferred. Creating an acceptable mix of variables is the designer's art and probably is as much intuitive as scientific.

Before finalizing a specific configuration, a lightplane designer makes a performance forecast to verify that priorities have been satisfied. This is done by analyzing certain variables. The most significant of these include power loading, wing loading, aspect ratio, and wetted area.

The first item, power loading, helps determine if an airplane is underpowered or overpowered. Power loading is determined by dividing the maximum allowable takeoff weight by the total rated horsepower of all engines. (In the case of turbofans and turbojets, power loading is expressed as pounds of weight per pound of engine thrust.)

A Mooney 201, for instance, has a maximum gross weight of 2,740 pounds and is powered by a 200-hp engine. Its power loading, therefore, is 13.7 (pounds per horsepower). Figure 1 shows the range of power loadings for different classifications of general aviation airplanes.

Like other design variables, power loading seldom can be used in isolation to make valid performance predictions. Other factors need to be combined with it to obtain meaningful information. Generally, however, low power loading is associated with high performance.

Power loading can be used to determine initial takeoff acceleration. It is, after all, the inverse of the power-to-weight ratio used to calculate the acceleration of drag racers. Everything else being equal, the vehicle with the greatest power-to-weight ratio (or the lowest power loading) has the best acceleration.

Figure 1 shows that a Cessna 152, with a power loading of 15.2, has the highest power loading of the general aviation aircraft. Although it is no surprise that this aircraft has the poorest takeoff acceleration, this is not as negative a characteristic as it may appear. Since the 152 does not require a high lift-off speed, it does not necessarily need more takeoff distance than other singles do. The 36-hp Aeronca C-3 (known as the "Flying Bathtub") had a power loading of 28 pounds per horsepower, but since it had to accelerate only to little more than jogging speed, takeoff distance was not excessive.

Runway length requirements are determined by acceleration

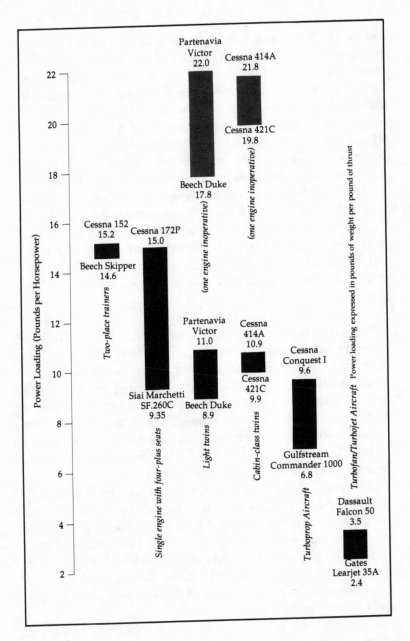

FIGURE 1

3

and by lift-off speed. If acceleration is constant, takeoff distance increases in proportion to the square of the lift-off speed. This means that every additional knot consumes more distance than the preceding knot. Stretching takeoff distance even farther is aircraft drag, which increases during the roll and reduces acceleration. This explains why manufacturers of STOL (short takeoff and landing) aircraft and modification kits rejoice with every knot that can be trimmed from the lift-off speed. A 5-percent speed reduction reduces takeoff distance by more than 10 percent.

Power loading also indicates how well (or how poorly) engine power can be relied upon to overcome aircraft inertia in flight. Everything else being equal, the airplane with the least power loading is best able to accelerate out of mushing flight and into a safe climb. This is perhaps best illustrated by referring to the power loadings of piston-powered twin-engine airplanes.

Notice from Figure 1 that power loadings vary from 11 for a Partenavia Victor to 8.9 for a Beechcraft Duke. (This is a relatively narrow range, indicating that light-twin designers remain within established guidelines.) It is obvious that twins have a substantial power advantage when compared to singles. But look what happens to power loading when a twin loses half of its horsepower: power loading doubles. It is apparent that the power loading of *any* twin with an inoperative piston engine exceeds that of a Cessna 152, which helps to explain why a crippled twin has such marginal performance.

Designers obviously prefer low power loadings but usually cannot justify the necessary sacrifices. Adding horsepower increases fuel consumption, inflates operating and manufacturing costs, and may decrease range and useful load. Power loading also can be improved by reducing gross weight, but this might require sacrificing fuel capacity, range, payload, and even airframe strength. Instead, the designer weighs priorities and makes the necessary compromises.

Although additional power substantially improves takeoff and climb performance, it does not increase cruise speed as much as you might expect (because drag increases in proportion to the square of the airspeed). For those who enjoy number crunching with a calculator, a rule of thumb states that cruise speed increases in approximate proportion to the cube root of the result obtained by dividing the horsepower of the new engine by the horsepower of the engine being replaced. For example, if a 300-hp aircraft with a 200-knot cruise were retrofitted with a 350-hp engine, the new speed would be approximately 211 knots. Although this 17 percent power boost results in only a 5 percent speed increase, takeoff and climb performance would improve dramatically.

Pilots should note that in operational practice, power loading is a variable. It decreases with a reduction of useful load and increases in proportion to the power loss (of naturally aspirated engines) associated with high density altitudes. This is just a fancy way of saying that aircraft performance varies with gross weight and available power.

One point of confusion to some is the difference between power and thrust. Power is the ability to perform work. One horsepower, by definition, is the power required to exert 550 pounds of force for a distance of one foot in one second. Thrust, however, is the force used to overcome drag and is measured in pounds.

Power and thrust are related by the following formula: Thrust = Horsepower × 260 ÷ Knots of True Airspeed (KTAS). (This formula assumes that the propeller converts horsepower into thrust with 80 percent efficiency, a crude average for light-planes in cruise flight.)

For instance, if an engine is producing 215 hp at a time when the airplane is stabilized in cruise at 200 KTAS, the force of thrust is 280 pounds. Since thrust equals drag at such a time, the drag of this particular airplane at 200 knots also is 280 pounds. Engineers sometimes use this technique to estimate total airframe drag, and pilots can do the same. It is an interesting way to compare the aerodynamic cleanliness of one airplane with another (at a given density altitude).

Just as power loading indicates how heavily an engine is burdened by weight, wing loading indicates the extent to which a wing is burdened. Wing loading is calculated by dividing the maximum allowable takeoff weight by wing area. A Beech V35B Bonanza, for instance, has a maximum takeoff weight of 3,400 pounds and a wing area of 181 square feet, resulting in a wing loading of 18.8 pounds per square foot. This result, however, is only an average because some areas of a wing lift more efficiently than others.

Confusing the issue somewhat is the definition of wing area, which includes more than the lifting surface. Wing area also includes the area between the wing roots (as outlined by extending the leading and trailing edges toward the airplane's longitudinal axis) as well as those areas of the wing covered by engine nacelles (on most multiengine aircraft). These nonlifting areas are included in the calculation of wing area because of tradition and engineering convention. (An argument can be made to justify this definition of wing area because of the nature of the pressure distribution in the vicinity of a wing.)

Figure 2 shows the range of wing loadings for several aircraft. For single-engine airplanes, for example, they vary from 10.5 pounds per square foot for a Cessna 152 to 22.9 for a Cessna P210N.

Some interesting wing-loading extremes also are worth noting. A Schweizer 1-26E sailplane has a wing loading of 4.4, which means that each square *inch* of wing produces only one-half ounce of lift. In contrast, each square foot of the Boeing 747-100's 5,500-square-foot wing must lift 133 pounds, or almost a pound per square inch. The wing loading of Rockwell International's B-1B bomber is an astonishing 239 pounds per square foot. Such a massive quantity of lift is possible—in part—because of the speed at which the B-1B moves through the air. For a given wing at a given angle of attack, lift increases in proportion to the square of the airspeed. This partially explains why two airplanes with the same wing area may have different wing loadings. The Northrop F-5A Tiger and the Aeronca Champ

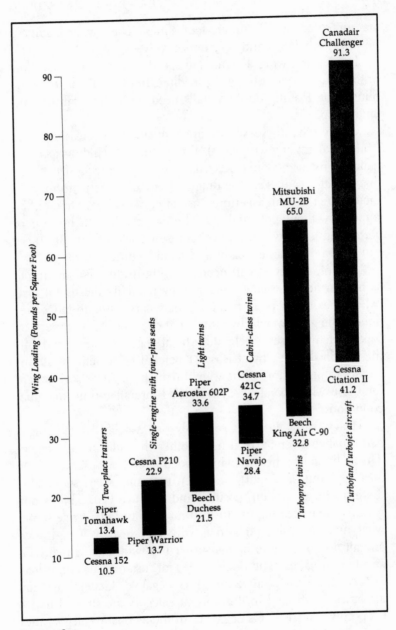

FIGURE 2

are supported by 170-square-foot wings. Their wing loadings, however, are 119.3 and 7.2, respectively.

For a given wing design, stall speed increases in proportion to the square root of the wing loading. In other words, quadrupling wing loading doubles stall speed, as well as takeoff and landing speeds.

Conversely, these speeds are reduced by decreasing wing loading (increasing wing area). But cutting the landing speed in half, for instance, would necessitate quadrupling wing size. Since this would create excessive drag and erode cruise performance, the designer of a high-performance aircraft may have to sacrifice some slow-flight potential. Or, he can reach into his bag of aerodynamic tricks and pull out an exotic set of flaps. But these can increase airframe weight and manufacturing cost.

A pilot, however, can decrease wing loading just as simply as he can decrease power loading: by reducing the useful load (when maximum performance is necessary). For instance, reducing the gross weight by 10 percent decreases takeoff speed by 5 percent, increases acceleration by at least 9 percent, and cuts the takeoff distance by at least 21 percent. Also, climb rate increases in proportion to the weight reduction. A message is here for those who operate heavily loaded aircraft during marginal conditions.

Heavy wing loading generally is associated with high-performance aircraft. It also smoothes the ride in turbulence. This is because a heavily wing-loaded aircraft exposes less wing area (per unit of weight) to a given gust and is less susceptible to vertical acceleration (positive and negative Gs). This is one reason why increasing useful load makes a turbulent ride somewhat more tolerable. It also is why very heavily wing-loaded aircraft do not have to be constructed to withstand as many Gs as other airplanes. The Boeing 747, for instance, has limit load factors of 2.5 Gs positive and 1 G negative. General aviation airplanes certificated in the normal category are stressed to 3.8 Gs positive and 1.52 Gs negative. In the aerobatic category they are stressed to 6 Gs positive and 3 Gs negative.

The lowest wing loadings are found on ultralight aircraft. This explains why ultralights are so sensitive to even the slightest gust.

A third factor used to predict aircraft performance is the wing's aspect ratio, which expresses the slenderness or stubbiness of the wings (or propeller blade or stabilizer). Mathematically, aspect ratio is found by dividing wingspan by mean chord length. Sailplanes have extraordinarily long, slender, high aspect-ratio wings. In other words, the ratio of span to chord is large.

In general, increasing aspect ratio reduces induced drag and improves climb, glide, and high-altitude performance. Lockheed's U-2 "spyplane" is a classic example of how high aspect ratio wings improve aerodynamic efficiency. A designer, however, cannot arbitrarily increase aspect ratio without accepting a penalty. Lengthening a wing moves the center of lift farther outboard and necessitates beefing up the wing-root structure. This can add substantially to airframe weight and manufacturing cost. Although slenderizing the wings often improves roll stability, it usually dampens roll rate.

Determining aspect ratio is not always as simple as dividing span by chord because the length of the mean chord is difficult to measure unless the wing has a rectangular planform. But an alternate method is available. Aspect ratio also is equal to the square of the wingspan divided by wing area.

The wingspan of a Cessna 421C is 41.1 feet and its wing area is 215 square feet, resulting in an aspect ratio of 7.9. The span is almost eight times as long as the chord. (By comparison, the Schweizer 1-35 sailplane has an aspect ratio of 23.3.) Dividing wingspan by aspect ratio results in the length of the mean chord, which—in the Cessna 421C—is 5.2 feet.

Another piece of the designer's puzzle is wetted area, or the total surface area of an airplane. It is the number of square feet that would get wet if a watertight airframe were immersed in a tank of water. Since wetted area for a given configuration can be used to estimate parasite drag, the designer is given added insight into the performance of his creation.

A safe, efficient airplane is the fruit of a designer's labor. But the final product often belies the blood, sweat, and tears that were spent in the design process. It may appear to the casual observer that the only talent necessary is the artistic flair used to sketch the eye-pleasing form. But the road from conception to production is strewn with mind-boggling obstacles that can be overcome only by a blend of applied mathematics, aerodynamic analysis, educated guesswork, imagination, perseverance . . . and a little luck.

GROUND EFFECT

High above the Pacific, the Boeing 377 Stratocruiser droned along the great-circle route from Honolulu to San Francisco. Thus far, the flight had been routine. Not much to report other than a minor hydraulic leak.

The clouds below drifted by with metronomic regularity and Aircraft Commander Tyson was becoming weary. He glanced casually at the matrix of instruments before him, yawned compulsively, and took mental note of how difficult it was to stay awake. But Tyson didn't have time to consider how delicious such boredom can be.

Without warning, the four-bladed propeller separated from the number 2, 28-cylinder engine and spun away toward infinity—but not before smashing into its companion engine on the same side. With "two turning and two burning," the heavily laden Stratocruiser began to descend. Tyson applied METO (maximum except takeoff) power to the two remaining engines on the right wing and eased back on the control yoke. But this wasn't sufficient to arrest the alarming sink rate. The calm waters of the Pacific were rising steadily.

All aboard struggled into their Mae Wests and prepared nervously for the mid-Pacific ditching. But when the crippled Boeing was within striking range of a reasonably healthy shark, Tyson noticed a strange turn of events. The sink rate began to decrease and Tyson found that he was able to at least postpone what had appeared to be an inevitable swim.

Struggling against powerful, unbalancing forces, Tyson managed to avoid the continuously threatening stall. After hundreds of miles just mere feet above the water, sufficient fuel had been consumed to lighten the airplane and allow the flight to continue at not so precarious an altitude.

The dramatic discovery Tyson made about the performance characteristics of an aircraft at extremely low altitudes was so profound that the phenomenon was named after him: the T-effect. But once the subject had been fully investigated and accurately explained, it became known by its current name, ground effect.

The average pilot probably would not cherish the opportunity to experiment with ground effect during an oceanic crossing, but he does encounter it at least twice during every flight—when taking off and landing. The "ground cushion," as it is sometimes called, can have significant influence during these operations.

Many pilots believe that ground effect is the result of air being compressed between the wing and the ground. Presumably, this increased air density creates a cushion beneath the wing and improves performance. This seems plausible, but is incorrect. Unfortunately, the Federal Aviation Administration (FAA) perpetuated this myth in its VFR Exam-O-Gram No. 47. So let's set the record straight. Air is not compressed between wing and ground.

Figure 3 shows the airflow about a wing. The streamlines separate at the leading edge and follow the upper and lower

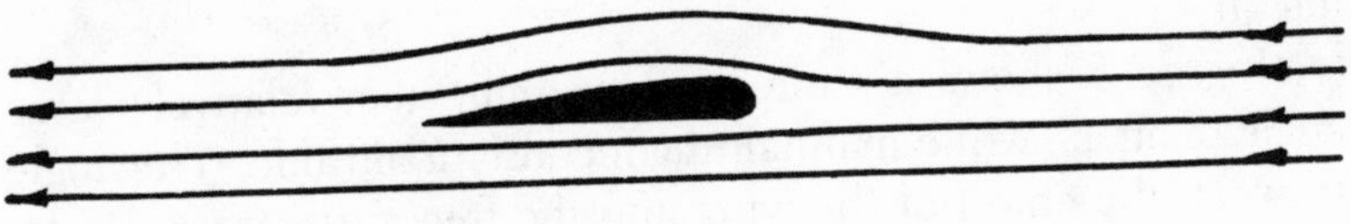

FIGURE 3

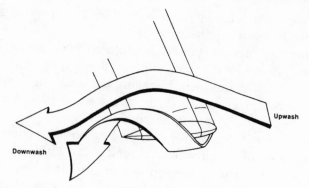

Upwash

Downwash

FIGURE 4

wing surfaces. This model is used almost universally to teach how a wing develops lift. But the diagram is too simplistic. It shows only an "airfoil section," a cross-sectional sliver of a wing. To better understand lift, the airflow about the entire wing must be investigated.

From the view shown in Figure 4, it can be seen that high-pressure air from beneath the wing attempts to curl over the tip toward the low-pressure region above the wing. This curling combines with the relative wind to produce a tornado of air— the wingtip vortex (wake turbulence).

During slow flight, when the angle of attack is larger, the difference in pressure between the lower and upper wing surfaces is obviously greater and results in a stronger vortex. (This explains why wake turbulence is more intense behind a slow aircraft than a fast one.)

The effect of the vortices is to induce considerable "upwash" to air approaching the wing and "downwash" to the air flowing aft.

Figure 5 shows a wing in slow flight at a relatively large angle of attack while maintaining a constant altitude. The angle between the chord of the wing and the free airstream is 16 degrees. This is the wing's angle of attack. But because of the upwash coming from ahead of the wing, the *average* or *local*

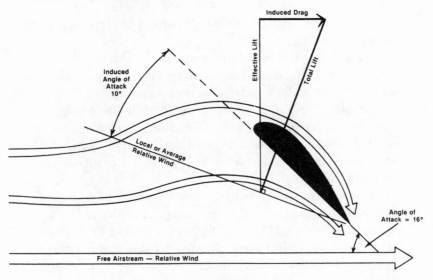

FIGURE 5

relative wind doesn't come from the same direction as the free airstream. The wing "feels" a relative wind induced by the immediately surrounding airflow which, at slow speeds, results in a smaller angle of attack than might be otherwise expected.

In this case, the "induced" angle of attack felt by the wing is only 10 degrees. Since lift acts perpendicular to the induced relative wind (not the free airstream), it can be seen that wing lift acts slightly rearward. The horizontal component of this rearward-acting lift is a retarding force called induced drag, an unavoidable by-product of lift. Induced drag has the same detrimental effects as the more familiar parasite drag (skin friction, form drag, and interference drag). An increase in either induced or parasite drag requires additional power to maintain a constant airspeed. But while parasite drag increases with airspeed, induced drag lessens.

Conversely, induced drag increases rapidly as airspeed decreases. At just above stalling speed, for example, induced drag may account for more than 80 percent of the total drag acting on an airplane. The remaining 20 percent (or less) is parasite drag (air resistance).

Parasite drag can be reduced somewhat by cleaning the wings, substituting flush-mounted antennas for those that protrude, and making other minor aerodynamic improvements.

Absolutely nothing can be done about induced drag. It is the constant companion to lift (something most pilots are unwilling to sacrifice). But if induced drag *could* be reduced substantially, aircraft performance at large angles of attack would improve dramatically.

One way to reduce induced drag would be to decrease the amount of upwash ahead of the wing. And the only way to accomplish this would be to fly the wing very close to the ground. The degree of upwash would decrease because air preceding the wing wouldn't have enough room to develop any significant vertical motion. Also, the wing would produce less downwash. Air flowing from the trailing edge would be forced more parallel to the ground. Figure 6 shows the airflow about a wing being flown in and above ground effect.

Those are the basics. Ground effect is caused by a reduction

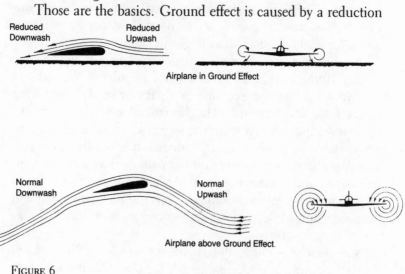

Reduced Downwash   Reduced Upwash

Airplane in Ground Effect

Normal Downwash   Normal Upwash

Airplane above Ground Effect.

FIGURE 6

of induced drag, not a compression of air beneath the wings. (Wingtip vortices also are reduced when the wing is flown very close to the ground. This is because the ground interferes with vortex formation. Reducing vortex diameter also reduces induced drag, creating the same effect as increasing the wing's aspect ratio.)

Ground effect does not have any measurable influence unless the wing is flown at a height no greater than its span— which is very close to the surface (see Figure 7). A Cessna P210, for example, has a wing span of 38.8 feet. To benefit from ground effect, the wing must be flown at less than 38.8 feet above the ground. At a height of 19.4 feet (a height equal to half the wing span), 8 percent of the induced drag is eliminated. When at only 9.7 feet (25 percent of the span), induced drag is reduced by 24 percent. When the wing is within three feet of the run-

Ratio of Wing Height (agl) to Wing Span	Percent Reduction of Induced Drag
.1	48%
.2	29%
.3	19%
.4	13%
.5	8%
.6	6%
.7	4%
.8	3%
.9	2½%
1.0	2%

FIGURE 7

way, more than half the induced drag disappears, but this is not a worthy goal because it would mean a gear-up landing.

It's evident, therefore, that low-wing aircraft usually are more influenced by ground effect than high-wing aircraft simply because a low wing can be flown closer to the ground. Nevertheless, high-wings are influenced by ground effect *almost* as noticeably. The reduction of induced drag enhances aircraft performance considerably. At times, embarrassingly so.

Consider the takeoff. As the hapless pilot urges his heavily laden aircraft along the runway, he notes reaching the minimum "unstick" speed and abruptly rotates the nose skyward. Since he desires to impress his passengers with a maximum-angle climb, he maintains the airspeed barely above stall. But as the aircraft leaves the influence of ground effect, induced drag increases dramatically and the pilot finds that his machine has a will of its own. It does not want to climb at all.

The speed that enabled the wing to climb at four feet isn't enough at 40. The pilot gets that uneasy feeling in the pit of his stomach as the ship begins to settle. But by now the runway has been left behind. Plane and pilot are about to land in the weeds.

The pilot's mistake was simple. He tried to fly out of ground effect without sufficient airspeed and power to cope successfully with an inevitable 100-percent increase in induced drag.

This type of accident occurs most frequently at airports at a high density altitude. Simply because an airplane has enough airspeed to get off the ground does not mean that it can climb above the influence of ground effect. A few feet of altitude can make a dramatic difference.

The point to remember is that additional power is required to compensate for increases in drag that occur as an airplane leaves ground effect. But during a takeoff climb, the engine is already developing maximum available power. If pilots climb at the ragged edge without sufficient airspeed, they may be unable to cope with the inevitable increase in drag.

Those who fly retractable-gear aircraft should be particularly careful. Numerous accidents are caused annually by pilots who prematurely raise the landing gear. Settling back to the runway with the wheels in the wells is of benefit only to aircraft sheet-metal workers and their families. When takeoff and initial climb performance is marginal, delay raising the gear until safely above the influence of ground effect.

Although ground effect can lead the unsuspecting pilot astray, it also can be used to advantage. Since slow-speed performance is improved while in ground effect, why be in a hurry to leave it? The proficient pilot will take off, lower the nose slightly, and maintain altitude just a few feet above the runway (particularly when departing an airport at a high density altitude). This is because an airplane accelerates more rapidly in ground effect than above it.

A skillful pilot literally aims the aircraft at the obstacle over which he wishes to climb, seemingly in sheer defiance. Once a safe climb speed has been attained he raises the nose gingerly and soars over the trees with the maximum possible safety margin. This technique is considerably more efficient than *forcing* an aircraft into a premature climb.

After a heavily loaded takeoff from a critically short runway at a high density altitude, an airplane *may* climb satisfactorily to the upper limits of ground effect at minimum speed, but as induced drag steadily increases, the airplane may reach a point where it will climb no more. FAA files bulge with accident reports describing how pilots have mushed headlong into obstacles when acceleration in ground effect might have provided the performance necessary to climb safely.

Ground effect also is influential during landings. As an aircraft descends into ground effect at a constant attitude, induced drag decays rapidly and is made noticeable by a floating sensation. As a result, the aircraft often won't land until well beyond the original touchdown target. If the runway is too short, abort the landing and try again. More than one pilot has just sat there occupying space while waiting for the wheels to touch only to discover that the runway had receded behind him.

If a pilot is approaching the runway with excessive airspeed, he might consider reducing airspeed while *above* the influence of ground effect. This is where induced drag is most powerful and causes maximum deceleration. Or, if a pilot is caught short with his airspeed down, he might lower the nose and descend into ground effect where he can expect a drag reduction and a slightly prolonged glide. This is recommended only as an emergency measure and when the terrain preceding the runway is flat and unobstructed.

But if the touchdown target is halfway down a long runway, such as during a spot-landing contest where a premature landing doesn't smart so badly, then this playing with ground effect can impress the judges. Knowing precisely what ground effect can and cannot do for a particular aircraft, however, takes practice, and lots of it.

After landing, some pilots prefer to keep the nose high and use aerodynamic braking to slow the aircraft. This is most effective when the wing is partially stalled. But because of the large reduction of induced drag caused by the wing being so close to the ground, aerodynamic braking is not as effective as using conventional brakes to decelerate (for most aircraft).

Another point to consider about ground effect is its influence on longitudinal or pitch stability. Remember the downwash of air that flows from the trailing edge of a wing? Normally, this descending air strikes the top of the horizontal stabilizer (except on T-tailed aircraft) and helps to keep the tail down.

As an aircraft enters ground effect, downwash is reduced and the tail wants to rise. Unless the fuselage bends in the process, this causes the nose to drop slightly. This explains why an aircraft becomes slightly more nose-heavy immediately prior to touchdown. Experienced pilots expect this or simply react subconsciously; students learn the hard way and wonder why they tend to land nosewheel first. This is also why it is difficult to make a "hands-off" landing. As an airplane gets to within five or 10 feet of the runway, it tends to pitch nose down.

Conversely, as a pilot climbs out of ground effect and downwash from the wing is restored, the tail becomes heavier and the nose wants to pitch up. This is of no help to a pilot climbing on the verge of a stall and emphasizes the foolishness of minimum-speed climbs.

This nose-up tendency is especially critical when flying an aircraft loaded at or beyond the rearward center-of-gravity limit. The aircraft might behave quite normally as the wheels leave the tarmac, but the pilot may be in for quite a surprise when the aircraft leaves the influence of ground effect and he has difficulty holding the nose down.

Ground effect also causes local increases in static pressure, which cause the airspeed indicator and altimeter to indicate slightly less than they should. For the same reason, the rate-of-climb indicator usually indicates a descent during the take-off roll.

Whether or not pilots are aware of it, ground effect plays a key role during every takeoff and landing. The proficient pilot, however, is aware of how to use this phenomenon to advantage.

CRUISE CONTROL

Aviation abounds with popular myths and misconceptions. Some are amusing and cause little harm; but believing others can lead to disaster. One such fallacy is that range can be extended when flying against a headwind by increasing cruise airspeed. Although there are extreme conditions under which this principle applies, such a practice usually has the opposite effect—range decreases.

Disproving this commonly held notion unfortunately requires some circuitous reasoning. A fringe benefit is that some fascinating lessons can be learned along the way. Considering the cost of fuel and the occasional need to make every drop count, long-range cruise control is a technique few can afford to ignore.

Since diving headlong into aerodynamic theory can be la-

borious, let's pave the way with some relatively simple fundamentals.

Figure 8 is a curve that relates sink rate to airspeed during
gliding flight. Notice that the minimum possible sink rate in
this hypothetical airplane occurs at point B (50 knots and 400
fpm). Notice also that any increase or decrease in airspeed results in a greater sink rate.

Of more interest is the point on the curve where a straight
line drawn from the point of zero airspeed (lower-left corner)
barely touches (or is tangent to) the curve. Point A represents
the *optimum* glide, a combination of airspeed and sink rate that
allows an airplane to glide as far as possible for each foot of
altitude lost. Although the aircraft has more of a sink rate at

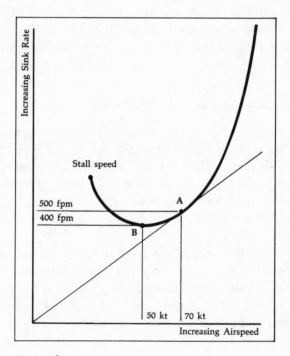

FIGURE 8

point A than at point B, it more than compensates for this by going considerably faster. In other words, a 25-percent increase in sink rate (from 400 to 500 fpm) is more than offset by a 40-percent increase in forward speed (from 50 to 70 knots). Any deviation from point A (either slower or faster than 70 knots) results in a steeper glide angle and less range. This demonstrates the futility of trying to stretch a glide by using an airspeed other than that recommended by the manufacturer.

But there are exceptions. When the airplane is gliding into a headwind, airspeed should be increased slightly. Conversely, gliding with a tailwind suggests reducing airspeed slightly.

Figure 9 shows the same curve of sink rate versus airspeed. As before, the optimum glide speed (point A) is determined by

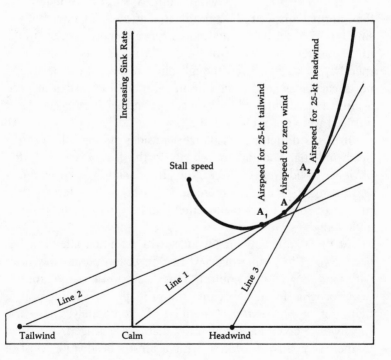

FIGURE 9

line 1. But when there is a wind, this so-called line of tangency must originate elsewhere.

When considering wind (which has a profound effect on gliding range), the bottom, horizontal scale also is used to represent wind speed. As shown, tailwinds are plotted to the left and headwinds to the right.

Assume a 25-knot tailwind. The line of tangency (line 2) is drawn from the 25-knot point on the horizontal scale to where it barely touches the curve. The result is point A_1, which indicates the need to maintain a slower gliding speed. This results in a reduced sink rate, which prolongs ground contact and takes advantage of the tailwind for a longer period of time. Glide range is extended in an optimal fashion.

Line 3 is used to determine the optimum airspeed when gliding into a 25-knot headwind. Point A_2 suggests using a faster than normal airspeed. This results in a greater sink rate. But the sink rate is offset by the additional forward speed, which minimizes the retarding effect of the headwind because less time is spent flying against it. Although glide range with a headwind never can be as great as gliding in calm air, increasing airspeed against a headwind extends range beyond what it would be if airspeed were not increased at all.

If this is difficult to visualize, consider gliding into a direct headwind that is equal in velocity to the true airspeed. Quite obviously, glide range is zero; the aircraft simply settles along a vertical flight path. Any increase in airspeed, therefore, results in at least some forward movement and a quantum increase in glide range.

At this point, you may wonder why so much attention has been devoted to gliding flight when this section presumably deals with long-range cruise control. This discussion lays the groundwork for what follows, because the principles of gliding and of flying for range are *almost* identical. Unfortunately, many use this logic to conclude erroneously that cruise range is extended by increasing airspeed when flying against a headwind. Most of the time, however, the analogy is fallacious. Increasing cruise airspeed against a headwind usually has the opposite effect.

Figure 10 is a curve of power versus airspeed (for a given altitude and airplane) and is similar to the curves used previously to describe gliding flight. Point C on this power curve represents the airspeed at which minimum power is required to maintain altitude. Notice that any increase in airspeed requires additional power (because of increased parasite drag), and any less airspeed also requires more power (because of an increase in induced drag at large angles of attack). Point C , therefore, represents the speed to use when you are flying for endurance and do not necessarily care about forward progress (such as when

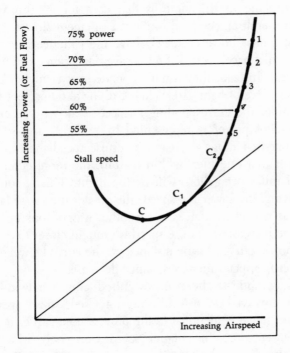

FIGURE 10

in a holding pattern). Power and fuel flow are at a minimum.

The speed to use for maximum range is determined in the same way that optimum glide speed was determined earlier. A line is drawn from the corner of the chart (the point of zero power and airspeed) that barely touches (or is tangent to) the power curve. The result is point C_1. Notice that, although more power and fuel flow are required, there is a proportionately larger increase in airspeed. At point C_1, the airplane is flown more miles per pound of fuel burned than at any other point on the curve. Varying speed faster or slower, therefore, decreases range.

Unfortunately, manufacturers seldom publish speeds for maximum endurance or range. But these performance numbers can be approximated from information that is available.

For practical purposes, maximum-range speed for propeller-driven airplanes is the same as that used for optimum glide. Maximum-endurance speed is about 25 percent slower.

Most pilots, however, rarely have the patience to cruise at such a snail's pace, even if fuel is saved and range extended in the process. Instead, they usually operate much "higher up" on the power curve of figure 10. When cruising at 60-percent power, for example, the corresponding airspeed is at point 4; cruising at 70-percent power is represented by point 2, and so forth. Remember that range decreases as cruise speed increases. Or, the slower that one flies (within reason), the more efficient (in terms of miles per gallon) will be the flight. This is consistent with driving; the lower the speed, the greater the range (as long as the car is kept in high gear). Another way of looking at it is that range increases as cruise speed is brought closer to point C_1 on the power curve. As the distance on the curve between point C_1 and cruise speed increases, range decreases.

Now complicate the issue by introducing a tailwind. The principle involved in determining a revised, lower speed for maximum range is identical to the process used earlier to determine a lower, more efficient glide speed. Conversely, when flying against a headwind, the speed for maximum range increases from point C_1 on the power curve to a new, higher speed represented by point C_2.

"Aha!," you say, "maximum-range speed *does* increase when flying against a headwind. By his own admission, Schiff is all wet."

Not quite. Notice that, although the speed for maximum range does increase against a headwind, the pilot invariably is cruising at some higher speed (65-percent power, for example). To increase power at such a time only causes airspeed to accelerate and move further away from point C_2 on the power curve. Consequently, range suffers. To increase range against a headwind, therefore, airspeed must be reduced and brought closer to point C_2 on the power curve.

As the headwind increases, point C_2 (the speed for maximum range) steadily moves up the power curve and, if strong enough, eventually could reach a point where it is higher than cruise speed. In such a case, acceleration from normal cruise (to the faster point C_2) would be justified. But this would require a hellacious wind.

Consider a Cessna P210N cruising at 65-percent power at 12,000 feet. To justify a power increase to increase range, the headwind component must be at least 100 knots. The same headwind component is required to justify increasing the power of a Beech V35B Bonanza cruising at 65-percent power at 6,000 feet.

In most lightplanes, power can be increased to stretch range only when the headwind component exceeds half the true airspeed. And, even then, the benefit is of dubious value. This is because most engine manufacturers allow leaning to peak exhaust gas temperature (EGT) only when cruising at less than 70- or 75-percent power, a valuable fuel-saving technique (cylinder head temperature permitting). Adding power may require a richer mixture (for cooling purposes), which reduces cruise efficiency further. Judicious leaning, of course, is a necessary ingredient during any attempt to maximize range.

There is one occasion when increasing power can be justified. If a pilot is masochistically cruising at the airspeed for best range (which is about the same as the speed for optimum glide), encountering a headwind component will change the maximum-range speed to some higher value. Acceleration to this speed (for example, point C_2 on the power curve in Figure 10) would optimize range under the new wind condition.

This information ought to destroy the myth. Under most circumstances, range is increased only by reducing cruise speed. This applies to flight with a tailwind, against a headwind, or in calm air. Reducing power, fuel flow, and parasite drag almost always is the key to extended range.

As every pilot ought to know, the indicated airspeed used to fly an optimum glide does not vary with altitude. The same is true of the indicated airspeed used to achieve maximum range. This suggests that flying for maximum range becomes less agonizing as cruise altitude increases.

Assume that the maximum-range speed of a Cessna Skylane is 80 knots indicated. At sea level, this results in a dismally slow true airspeed of 80 knots. But the same indicated airspeed at 10,000 feet on a standard day produces a slightly more tolerable true airspeed of 93 knots. As the airplane approaches its service ceiling, the speeds for maximum range and maximum cruise are approximately equal. Although altitude allows a faster flight while you are attempting to achieve maximum range, range itself is not extended (unless the climb results in latching onto a strong tailwind). An extended climb, of course, has a detrimental effect on range because of the fuel expenditure necessary to reach lofty heights. Climbing, therefore, should be avoided unless advantageous winds aloft can justify the added fuel burn. Under no-wind conditions, maximum range is achieved by flying low and slow (in piston-powered aircraft).

If a pilot does not have the patience to endure a flight at so low an airspeed and elects instead to cruise at a more normal power setting, then flying high has a beneficial effect on range (as long as the climb can be justified and headwinds do not increase with altitude).

Consider a V35B Bonanza cruising at 65-percent power at sea level; fuel flow is 13.3 gallons per hour. Both true and indicated airspeeds are 154 knots, resulting in a specific range of only 11.6 miles per gallon. But at 8,000 feet, for example, true airspeed increases to 163 knots, while fuel flow remains constant. This results in an improved specific range of 12.3 mpg, a 6-percent increase in cruise efficiency. Maximum available power at 12,000 feet yields a specific range of 13.7 mpg, an 18-percent improvement in range.

Range increases with altitude at cruise power settings for the simple reason that indicated airspeed decreases with altitude and becomes closer to the indicated airspeed required for maximum range. In the preceding example, the Bonanza has an indicated airspeed of 154 knots at sea level, 144 knots at 8,000 feet and 131 knots at 12,000 feet. The indicated speed for maximum range is that required for an optimum glide, or 105 knots.

The bottom line is this: Range increases as indicated cruise speed decreases (everything else being equal).

Power management also has an effect on range, a valuable lesson taught by Charles Lindbergh to military pilots during World War II. He discovered during oceanic flying that an engine delivering a given amount of horsepower consumes less fuel when rpm is reduced and manifold pressure is increased. This is because high rpm causes more internal engine friction than does low rpm. Consequently, the engine is less efficient and consumes more fuel per horsepower.

Many pilots are reluctant to operate an engine with a combination of relatively low rpm and high manifold pressure. But this need not be a concern when managing a modern powerplant and taking advantage of the rpm/manifold pressure combinations allowed by the operating handbook.

For example, consider the range of power settings allowed by Avco Lycoming for its 235-hp, O-540-B engine. When developing 60-percent power, the pilot is allowed to use a variety of power settings that vary from 2,575 rpm and 20 inches of manifold pressure (MP) to 2,000 rpm and 22.6 inches MP. At the 2,575-rpm setting, fuel flow is 13.1 gph, but at 2,000 rpm, fuel flow is only 11.6 gph. Without sacrificing power or speed, fuel consumption is decreased by 1.5 gph and cruise range is extended by 13 percent. Also, the pilot's ears are assaulted by less noise.

Other engines, of course, have different fuel consumption characteristics. But the one cited above is not an unusual example.

When striving to extend range, climb and descent techniques can have a significant effect. As soon as practical after takeoff, reduce power so as to be able to lean the mixture to peak EGT. This usually requires a power setting of no more than 75 percent, but check the operating handbook to be certain. Then, cruise-climb the airplane at as small a rate of climb as terrain, operational requirements, cylinder-head temperatures, and patience will allow. By the way, this technique usually does not increase total, en route flight time.

Anyone who has been listening attentively to air traffic control frequencies knows that airline pilots save kerosene by staying high as long as possible and then retarding the thrust levers to idle for a gliding descent. This technique is very efficient because of the fuel consumption characteristics of turbine engines and the exceptionally low drag profile of a jet-powered airplane. But this procedure is not efficient when applied to propeller-driven aircraft. Instead, the descent should begin as far from the destination as possible, while using minimal rates of descent and only slightly less than cruise power. Also, do keep the mixture leaned until nearing traffic-pattern altitude.

In other words, climbs and descents should be as shallow as is practical and possible.

Other tricks of the trade include keeping the leading edges of the wings and the propeller blades clean and smooth, flying with an aft center of gravity (within limits) and reducing actual useful load to a minimum. Each 1-percent decrease in gross weight increases range by approximately the same amount.

In these days of scarcity, it is becoming fashionable and economical to maximize dwindling resources. But when flying with a dwindling fuel reserve, conservation becomes essential.

FLYING IN TURBULENCE

Most of the time, turbulence is only an annoyance. But occasionally it can attack with a vengeance, assaulting the aircraft unmercifully. For those inside, this can lead to fatigue, nausea, and injury. Deterioration of vision also may be experienced, because turbulence excites an airplane's natural vibrations, making it almost impossible for a pilot to read the instruments.

Considering the hazardous potential of turbulence, it is unfortunate that so little advice is available to those who find themselves being flung about the sky like a leaf in the wind. Oh yes, pilots are told to stow loose objects that could become unguided missiles and to tighten their seat belts and shoulder harnesses. They are then cautioned to fly the aircraft at its published maneuvering speed (V_a), advice that could lead to structural failure. This is because V_a most often is *not* the best turbulence penetration speed. This may sound like heresy to those who have been taught that flying at V_a is guaranteed to protect an airplane against damaging structural loads, but it nevertheless is true.

To appreciate why V_a frequently is not the best turbulence penetration speed, it first is necessary to understand what maneuvering speed really is and how it is determined.

Pilots know that stall speed increases in proportion to the square root of the applied load factor. For example, stall speed doubles during a 4-G maneuver (because the square root of four is two) and triples when the load factor is nine.

Most general aviation, normal-category airplanes are certified to withstand 3.8 Gs, a limit load factor that must not be exceeded. (When pinned to the wall, designers concede that even though a load factor of 3.8 Gs is "within limits," numerous exposures to such an extreme can result in airframe fatigue and ultimately, deformation and damage.

One way to prevent exceeding the limit load factor is to make sure that an aircraft stalls first. This is because a stall is a form of aerodynamic relief and prevents additional maneuvering loads from being applied. The airspeed that guarantees a stall at the limit load factor is called maneuvering speed and usually is determined by multiplying the flaps-up, power-off stall speed by the square root of 3.8 Gs, which is 1.95. For example, a Cessna Hawk XP has a "clean" stall speed of 54 knots (the bottom of the green arc on the airspeed indicator) and a published maneuvering speed of 105 knots (determined by multiplying 54 by 1.95). In other words, a Hawk XP being flown at 105 knots would stall at precisely 3.8 Gs.

For those not wanting to suffer through the mathematical derivation of V_a, suffice it to say that there is a theoretical basis for claiming that flight at maneuvering speed prevents an airplane from being overstressed. But this applies only when the control surfaces are rapidly deflected to their limits. In the case of turbulence, however, there is a significant difference between theory and reality.

Although the concept of V_a seems plausible, there are two reasons why it fails as protection against overstressing the airframe. First of all, pilots doing battle with turbulence are usually flying with power. And as every pilot knows, the power-on stall speed of an airplane is significantly lower than its power-off stall speed. Consequently, an airplane being flown with power at its maneuvering speed does not stall at 3.8 Gs. Something more than this limit load factor must be applied before the aircraft will stall and shed the applied Gs. And it is this "something more" in the way of load factor that can be the G that breaks the airplane's back.

A second and perhaps more significant reason not to use V_a when penetrating heavy turbulence is the effect that gusts have on airspeed. Since all turbulence is a form of wind shear (or vorticity), pilots recognize that this often causes airspeed to fluctuate. Gusts that strike from ahead of the aircraft (increasing headwind shear) have the effect of increasing airspeed so that a pilot attempting to maintain V_a most likely will exceed this target speed. How much V_a is exceeded depends, of course, on the intensity of the turbulence and the horizontal component of the gusts.

During studies conducted by Great Britain's Royal Air Force some years ago, it was determined that light turbulence can cause airspeed fluctuations of five to 15 knots. Similarly, moderate turbulence can cause fluctuations of 15 to 25 knots, and severe turbulence can result in airspeed variations of more than 25 knots. In extreme turbulence, *rapid* fluctuations well in excess of 25 knots can be expected.

Consequently, a pilot should penetrate turbulence at least 10 knots below V_a to account for the stall-delaying effects of power. He also should reduce airspeed several knots more to compensate for the effect of horizontal wind shear (depending on gust intensity).

Operating handbooks for many aircraft specify a single maneuvering speed, one that is valid only when the aircraft is at its maximum-allowable gross weight. This speed, however, is not applicable at lighter weights when stall speeds are reduced. For example, the Hawk XP's V_a of 105 knots is valid only for a gross weight of 2,550 pounds (maximum allowable). At 2,150 and 1,750 pounds, maneuvering speed is reduced to 96 and 87 knots, respectively. In other words, maneuvering speed decreases as gross weight decreases because a lightly loaded aircraft is accelerated more easily by gusts than one that is heavily loaded.

Although V_a can be computed for various gross weights (it is proportional to the square root of the *actual* aircraft weight divided by the square root of the maximum-allowable gross weight), it is easier to approximate using a rule of thumb. For the typical lightplane, reduce the published V_a by two knots for each 100 pounds below maximum-allowable gross weight.

All of these factors demonstrate that the safest turbulence penetration speed usually is significantly less than the published maneuvering speed. Reducing airspeed below V_a has other benefits, too. Since the G load produced by a given gust is directly proportional to airspeed, going slower reduces the G load and makes the ride more bearable. Reducing airspeed also decreases the frequency of gust encounters because it takes longer to fly from one gust to the next. In other words, the slower the better.

"Wait a minute," someone will say, "flying too slowly in turbulence increases the risk of an accelerated stall as the aircraft is pounded by G-producing gusts."

Quite true, but the stall induced by a gust usually is very brief. The wings stall and recover almost before the pilot has an opportunity to realize what is happening. A pilot is not likely to jeopardize safety unless he manhandles the controls, is close to the ground, or is flying an airplane with undesirable stall characteristics. Research pilots who intentionally fly through fully developed thunderstorms (in *properly* equipped aircraft) report that flying substantially below V_a is a key to survival.

One can carry a good thing too far, however. Flying too slowly can result in poor control responsiveness and a succession of high-speed stalls. The best target speed in turbulence is well below V_a, well above stall, and largely a matter of experimentation and judgment. (Unless the aircraft has a designated turbulence-penetration speed, V_b, a good speed to use in heavy turbulence is 1.6 or 1.7 times the "clean" stall speed.)

Just as reducing airspeed decreases the G load produced by a given gust, so does increased wing loading have a similar effect. In other words, flying an airplane with a light wing loading through a given gust results in more of a G load than when flying through the same gust in an airplane with a heavy wing loading. This is one reason why the pilot of a Cessna 310R, which has a wing loading of 31 pounds per square foot, may report light turbulence, while a pilot flying through the same turbulence in a Cessna 172, which has a wing loading of only 13 pounds per square foot, may report moderate turbulence. This explains also why a pilot report of turbulence is virtually useless unless aircraft type is mentioned. (The wing loading of a Boeing 747, for example, is so high that the aircraft is very resistant to vertical acceleration. This explains why the aircraft is certified with limit load factors of only −1.0 to +2.5 Gs.)

It is not surprising that heavy wing loading suppresses the G load produced by a given gust. After all, the smaller a wing is in proportion to aircraft weight, the more difficult it is for a gust to displace (accelerate) the aircraft. An aircraft with a relatively large wing wing area is accelerated more easily. Also, heavier aircraft generally provide the most comfortable ride because their inertia makes them less likely to be displaced by gust action; the gusts, however, usually appear to be sharper in these aircraft.

Since most general aviation aircraft are certificated from −1.52 Gs to +3.8 Gs, many conclude that these aircraft can accept more than twice as much positive load as they can negative load. This misconception results from a simple misinterpretation of the numbers. When an aircraft is accelerated to +3.8 Gs, it experiences a net change from its normal, 1-G flight of only 2.8 Gs. On the other hand, a negative load of 1.52 Gs is a change of 2.52 Gs from level flight. In other words, most light aircraft can tolerate about as much of a downward gust (negative acceleration) as they can an upward gust (positive acceleration).

Airplanes are protected from excessive negative Gs in the same way they are protected from excessive positive Gs. The wing stalls before any damage can be done (as long as airspeed is less than V_a). The negative-G stall occurs because a sufficiently powerful downward gust makes the wing "feel" as if it were being flown inverted at too large an angle of attack. The only significant difference between a negative-G stall and a positive-G stall is that everyone on board is momentarily lifted from his seat and pressed against his restraints until the negative load is relieved. (Some aircraft are more docile during a negative-G stall than when stalled conventionally.)

When an aircraft is flown into severe turbulence (or worse), gust loads are punishing and are potentially destructive. Unfortunately, many pilots compound the problem by rapidly jerking and shoving the controls in an effort to maintain a reasonably level attitude. The effect of this, however, is to create *maneuvering* loads that combine with gust loads to make the total G load greater than necessary. Although a pilot understandably is filled with anxiety (and possibly fear) at such a time, he must make every effort not to contribute to the hazard. The controls should be moved deliberately, yet smoothly. There should be no attempt made to maintain altitude (unless the plane is about to strike something more solid than a gust). Nor should the pilot chase airspeed; needle fluctuations can be so erratic that he might pull when he should push and simply compound the problem.

If a pilot elects to escape turbulence by turning, a shallow bank angle should be maintained despite the eagerness to reverse course. The Gs created during any maneuver, including those produced during a steep turn, add to those resulting from turbulence; aircraft have been damaged by pilot-induced loads.

Even jetliner manufacturers recognize that the greatest flight-path deviations caused by turbulence require the most timid control inputs. This is why the Boeing 747 autopilot, for example, has a turbulence mode. When this mode is engaged, the autopilot does no more than maintain attitude. Additionally, flight control input from the autopilot is reduced by 50 percent to prevent overstressing the aircraft.

Since most general aviation autopilots do not have a turbulence mode, they should not be used when the going gets rough because their flight control inputs may be excessive.

Pilots seem obsessed with maintaining a specific altitude. Although this normally is admirable, such a goal should be discarded when the going really gets rough. Attempting to maintain altitude not only can be futile and induce damaging loads, it also can work against the pilot. This is especially true when flying through vigorous convective turbulence.

When an aircraft enters a powerful updraft, a pilot tends to lower the nose (to maintain altitude) and perhaps reduce power. This not only violates the first rule of flying in turbulence (*maintain attitude*), but also is counterproductive. For one thing, an updraft should be used to advantage to gain altitude because just as night follows day, downdrafts ultimately follow updrafts. The altitude gained from an updraft then is available for sacrifice when the downdraft is encountered. Also, lowering the nose increases airspeed (another hazard in turbulence) and reduces time spent in the updraft, time that could be used to gain additional "free" altitude.

When the transition to a downdraft finally occurs, a pilot's instinct is to raise the nose (to maintain altitude). Since this results in airspeed decay, more time than necessary is spent in the downdraft. Instead, maintain target airspeed and traverse the area as quickly as possible so as to minimize the downdraft's detrimental effect. (Fighting a summer downdraft by raising the nose and adding power also may result in an overheated engine.)

By maintaining attitude and going with the currents (instead of against them), the flight is safer, more comfortable, and more efficient. Purists who argue that a specific VFR cruise altitude must be maintained in accordance with the hemispherical rule should recognize that this regulation applies only when maintaining altitude. When climbing and descending, such a rule obviously is inapplicable. If severe turbulence is encountered when flying on instruments, a pilot always has the option of exercising emergency authority and allowing altitude to vary as necessary. But please keep air traffic control informed of such regulatory deviations.

A discussion of flight into turbulence is not complete without mentioning V_{no}, an airplane's maximum structural cruising speed. This speed is known most commonly as the beginning of the yellow arc (or "top of the green") on an airspeed indicator. The precise definition of V_{no} has become mathematically complex over the years, but it is approximately the maximum speed at which an airplane safely can endure a sharp-edged 30-fps vertical gust. In theory, such a gust is the most intense a pilot is likely to encounter in other than severe conditions. But as an aircraft is taken deeper into the yellow caution range, tolerable gust intensity decreases significantly.

Although a normal-category airplane is built to withstand its negative limit load factor at V_{no}, airframe tolerance for these negative Gs fades to zero between V_{no} and the red line (V_{ne}). Consequently, airspeed above V_{no} should be avoided when turbulence is even remotely anticipated; the yellow arc is strictly for smooth-air operations.

Since abiding by limit load factors is so essential to one's health and well-being, it seems odd that pilots are not provided with a means of determining when these outer limits are being approached. The only instrument normally available is the uncalibrated, Mark IV gluteus maximus. A pilot desiring more than seat-of-the-pants accuracy might consider installing a G-meter. Many of these self-contained, inexpensive instruments not only indicate G load, but also record the maximum positive and negative G loads encountered during each flight. A G-meter not only can fill one of those blank spots on the instrument panel, but also is invaluable to a pilot seriously concerned about maintaining the airplane's structural integrity. It is obvious that if a pilot does not know when he is approaching the outer limits, he soon may find himself beyond, where even test pilots fear to tread.

DETERMINING AIRCRAFT PERFORMANCE

The U.S. congressman planned his flight with meticulous care. According to his calculations, he could make the nonstop flight to Albuquerque in his newly acquired aircraft with slightly more than the FAA-required fuel reserve of 30 minutes (for daylight, VFR flights).

While en route, the congressman noted that progress was better than anticipated. This, plus a distant view of the destination, gave him the confidence to overfly an en route airport even though one tank of fuel had been consumed and the gauge for the other indicated almost empty.

As he throttled back for the gradual descent, the engine faltered and then failed completely, necessitating a forced landing on a secondary road. Although the congressman had run out of fuel, the FAA could find no fault with his planning or procedure. The flight should have ended routinely. The pilot was guilty only of having had too much faith in the performance data in the pilot's operating handbook (POH).

The blame for this and other similar accidents may well rest with the FAA. During training, a pilot is taught to rely upon performance charts. He then is given a written examination that requires him to extract data with such accuracy that failing to consider the width of pencil lead can result in a wrong answer.

This is a form of negative training because it encourages a reliance on performance charts and graphs that often cannot be justified because these data occasionally are grossly inaccurate. There are several reasons why performance charts are not as reliable as they appear.

- Performance data are obtained by engineering test pilots trained to extract maximum performance from an aircraft and employ techniques that other pilots may not have the skill or desire to duplicate. To determine landing distance, for example, a test pilot might be required by his employer not to flare prior to touchdown because this consumes additional distance. Instead, he simply allows the runway to interrupt his descent, even though most pilots will not be flying in this fashion (at least not intentionally).
- Test flights are made in brand-new airplanes. A used model, however, usually cannot perform as well because of the performance toll extracted by the likes of wing dents, propeller nicks, added antennas, an out-of-rig condition, or a mid- to high-time engine. Conversely, test aircraft often are tuned to perfection and rigged to more exacting tolerances than those that subsequently roll off the production line.

- Since aircraft cannot be tested under all conditions, mathematical formulas are used to extrapolate performance data. An airplane manufactured at or near sea level, for example, usually is not taken to high density altitudes to determine takeoff performance under these conditions. Instead, the manufacturer of light aircraft usually extrapolates the data obtained at lower density altitudes. The accuracy of these results is the subject of controversy and in many cases has been proven to be excessively and dangerously optimistic.
- Prior to 1979, the FAA did not require pilot operating handbooks for any airplane with a maximum-allowable gross weight of less than 6,000 pounds. Any performance data the manufacturer did provide was strictly voluntary and frequently incorrect or incomplete. Consider, for example, that the published range of an early-model Piper Cherokee 180 assumes that an entire flight is conducted at cruise altitude (without considering the extra fuel required for takeoff and climb) until the tanks run dry. The published range also seems to include the gliding distance following fuel exhaustion. There simply is no way to fly this aircraft as far as the manufacturer claims without a benevolent push.

Pilots, especially those who fly older aircraft, should regard all critical performance data with skepticism until having an opportunity to verify their accuracy. The best way to do this is to compare actual performance with that published in the handbook. There is often a significant difference.

Determining actual performance requires a bit of ingenuity and the desire to really learn how well (or poorly) a specific airplane performs. The results are particularly meaningful because they take into consideration an individual pilot's technique and procedure, which can vary substantially from those used by a test pilot flying a new airplane. Flight testing an airplane also educates a pilot about the true capabilities of the aircraft and eliminates the need to have blind faith in published performance data.

Determining takeoff distance, for example, ordinarily is a difficult and trying process, especially without the sophisticated equipment normally used to make such measurements. But there is a simple procedure that can be used in conjunction with the POH to determine how much in error the takeoff performance charts may or may not be.

The procedure requires flying to an airport with a reasonably high density altitude and a relatively long runway. Prior to take-off from that airport, determine the pressure altitude, outside air temperature, head- or tailwind component, and actual gross weight of the aircraft. Runway slope, which is shown in the FAA's *Airport/Facility Directory*, also should be determined. Then consult the POH to calculate the predicted rolling distance. Remember that this is based on properly inflated tires; underinflation reduces takeoff performance. Next, position an assistant at the predicted lift-off point. (Based on runway light positioning, this point should be easy to find, since the runway lights are usually 200 feet apart.)

Before takeoff, be certain to configure the aircraft and use the takeoff technique specified in the handbook. This usually requires, for example, that the engine develop maximum power prior to brake release. Also be certain to begin the takeoff roll as close to the beginning of the runway as possible. (One manufacturer is known to have minimized takeoff distances by pushing the aircraft into position before engine start so that the main landing-gear tires literally were at the edge of the runway threshold.)

During the takeoff roll, do not try to validate the predicted takeoff distance by rotating prematurely and forcing the aircraft into the air before it is safe to do so. Instead, take off as you normally would. (Unless otherwise specified in the POH, lift off at $1.2 \times$ stall speed.) In the meantime, your assistant will note where actual liftoff occurs with respect to where he is standing. Do not be surprised to learn that the takeoff requires several hundred or even a thousand feet more than was predicted. It may be shocking to learn that your aircraft does not live up to expectations, but it is far better to determine this under controlled conditions that offer a wide margin of safety than when taking off with your family from a genuinely short runway at a high density altitude. On the other hand, you may be pleased to have confirmed that man and machine perform as expected.

Consider also that if an aircraft uses 25 percent more runway than was predicted at 4,000 feet (density altitude), for example, the additional runway required at higher density altitudes could double and even triple.

When actual conditions indicate that a safe departure with a full load is questionable, experienced mountain pilots sometimes use a similar procedure to "test the water." Before fueling the aircraft and loading passengers, such a pilot makes one departure to determine how much runway is actually required at light weight. This distance then is compared to that shown in the POH. Any percentage difference is applied to the distance shown in the POH for takeoff with a heavier load. In other words, if 30 percent more runway is required with a light load, assume that the distance required for a heavy takeoff (as shown in the POH) also must be increased by 30 percent. Such a procedure is not mathematically perfect, but it does provide a close approximation of the distance required. In any event, if such an operation does not appear to be entirely safe, it should be postponed until more favorable conditions exist.

The same procedure also can be used to determine the actual effect of an unimproved surface on takeoff performance. A performance chart might indicate, for example, that takeoff distance should be increased by 10 percent when the runway consists of short grass. But how short is short? And how soggy is the sod? When runways are critically short, such rules of thumb can be woefully inadequate.

The congressman mentioned earlier learned the hard way that range charts should be viewed with skepticism. This is because differences in leaning and piloting techniques have a profound effect on range. So does engine condition, specific fuel consumption, and actual true airspeed, which varies between aircraft of the same make and model.

Rather than rely on range charts, which may or may not be realistic, a pilot might prefer to establish a maximum practical (or personal) range (MPR) and compare this to data shown in the handbook, MPR, however, is expressed in time, not miles. If maximum practical range turns out to be three hours 50 minutes, for example, then a pilot must plan to be on the ground after three hours 50 minutes of flight, irrespective of the distance flown.

(When performance charts cite range in miles, the manufacturer is referring to air miles, *not* ground miles. The air miles, or air distance, for a given flight is found by multiplying average true airspeed by ground distance and dividing the result by average groundspeed.)

The procedure for determining MPR may vary between one aircraft and another, but the following process provides the basic idea. (MPR is particularly useful when flying aircraft with inaccurate fuel gauges.)

Before your next cross-country flight, fill the tanks completely. When you begin the takeoff roll, note the time. Then climb to the altitude most typically used on your cross-country flights. Upon reaching cruise altitude, do not retard the throttle. Instead, maintain climb power until the aircraft has accelerated to cruise speed. Then close the cowl flaps (if applicable), set cruise power, and lean the fuel-air mixture. After completing this step, which marks the end of the climb segment, note the time, and switch to another tank, which may not be possible in some training aircraft.

The cruise segment of this flight should last at least one hour, preferably two. At the beginning of descent, note the time once again and switch back to the tank used for takeoff and climb. Execute a normal descent, land, and note the time. Then top off the tanks.

Assume that the left tank was used for taxi, runup, takeoff, climb, descent, and landing. Assume also that this tank was topped off with 12 gallons and had been used for 30 minutes.

Next, assume that the right tank had been used for two hours of cruise flight and was topped off with 22 gallons. It now is known that the engine consumes 11 gph at the power setting and altitude used for that flight. It might be interesting to compare this rate of consumption with that specified in the handbook.

The next step to finding MPR requires subtracting the climb-and-descent fuel from the total useable fuel. If the tanks hold 60 gallons of useable fuel, there are 48 gallons available for cruise and reserve in this case.

Determine how much reserve fuel is desired. Many pilots consider the FAA's 30-minute requirement inadequate. I agree; I get uncomfortable when planning to land with less than an hour's worth of fuel in the tanks. If an hour of reserve is desired, subtract this amount of cruise fuel (11 gallons) from the remaining 48 gallons. This leaves 37 gallons available for cruise, which—at 11 gallons per hour—equates to three hours 22 minutes of cruise flight. This plus the 30 minutes required for departure and arrival result in an MPR of three hours 52 minutes. Some might prefer to subtract another 15 minutes to account for miscellaneous variables. This leaves three hours 37 minutes and becomes the self-imposed limit for remaining airborne when utilizing the concept of maximum practical range.

Compare MPR to the range published in the POH. There are likely to be significant differences between these practical and theoretical limits.

Although MPR may be disappointingly lower than the published range, it does offer greater assurance of completing a lengthy flight without the risk of fuel exhaustion.

A pilot may want to establish MPRs for various other altitudes (especially those who fly turbocharged aircraft). To do so, simply record the required data during subsequent cross-country flights made at different altitudes and perform the simple calculations afterward. Comparing these various MPRs should prove interesting.

There obviously are many other aspects of aircraft performance that can be determined or verified. A bit of imaginative thinking should enable a pilot to investigate any of these. (An interesting and accurate method of determining the actual true airspeed of an aircraft is discussed in chapter 4). Should you become fascinated with these procedures, you can apply them to learn things about your aircraft that are not published in the handbook.

For example, the glide performance (or glide ratio) of an aircraft can be increased by placing the propeller pitch control (on those aircraft equipped with constant-speed propellers) to the minimum-rpm (or high-pitch) position. But how much does this improve performance on a particular airplane? It also is known that stopping a propeller (when the engine is dead and there is no chance of a restart) reduces propeller drag and increases glide performance even more. But how much more? Is it worth the effort?

The procedure required to answer these questions is relatively simple and serves as another example of how educational performance flight testing can be. The airplane used for the following example of the procedure was a stock 1978 Cessna Skylane.

The first test, a normal glide, was made from 3,000 to 2,000 feet at exactly 70 knots indicated airspeed (the recommended glide speed) in smooth air. It was important that the airplane be in a stabilized glide, with the engine idling, prior to sinking through 3,000 feet. Since vertical-speed indicators are not particularly accurate, it was necessary to record the time required to lose 1,000 feet. This turned out to be one minute 35.9 seconds; the calculated rate of descent, therefore, was 625.7 fpm.

The second test was identical to the first except that propeller pitch was set to minimum rpm. The time required to lose the same 1,000 feet increased to one minute 49.5 seconds, which equals a sink rate of 547.9 fpm.

A third and final test was conducted with the propeller stopped (while above a long runway, just in case). In this configuration, the descent from 3,000 to 2,000 feet took two minutes 1.2 seconds, which yields a sink rate of 495.0 fpm.

The data, along with the average outside air temperature, were recorded on a pad of paper during flight. After landing, the average true airspeed during the 1,000-foot descent was computed to be 74.2 knots, which equals a forward speed of 7,514 fpm. Dividing forward speed (in fpm) by sink rate provides the glide ratio. During a normal glide, therefore, this 182 had a glide ratio of 12.0:1. With the propeller set to high pitch, the glide ratio improved to 13.7:1. That represents a glide performance increase of 14 percent. With the propeller stopped, glide ratio was 15.2:1. This amounts to a whopping 27-percent improvement in glide range and could pay a dividend to someone coping with total power failure at altitude. (Note: A propeller stops only when engine compression exceeds windmilling forces and usually occurs only at a very slow airspeed. For this reason, a propeller should be stopped only at a safe altitude and only when absolutely necessary.)

The point of this is to demonstrate by example that the aircraft we fly are marvelous mentors. With a little imagination, a pilot can obtain a variety of other performance data (such as the best speed for maximum endurance, the minimum-sink speed, climb rates and angles for different airspeeds, and so forth). All that is needed is the desire to learn more about the aircraft we fly.

2

TECHNIQUE AND PROFICIENCY

THE GO–NO GO DECISION

To abort or not to abort a takeoff is a decision that can involve life and death. When confronted with unexpected difficulties during a takeoff, a pilot has only a few precious seconds (or less) to elect the safest course of action.

The aborted takeoff is a procedure not usually given sufficient consideration by many single-engine pilots. Rather, it is a maneuver generally associated with multi-engine operations. Twin-engine pilots, for example, are trained to abort when an engine falters during the takeoff roll.

But there are numerous instances when it similarly would be wise to abort a takeoff in a single-engine airplane. Unfortunately, however, single-engine pilots rarely are given the necessary training and mental preparation. Often, the takeoff is continued when unexpected occurrences dictate otherwise.

This is one reason why one out of five general aviation accidents occurs during the takeoff phase of flight. And these accidents are lethal, too. They are characterized by a fatality rate that is more than double that of approach and landing accidents.

Complacency is one reason for the alarming number of departure accidents. The takeoff seems such a simple procedure that pilots anticipate little or no difficulty. But this confidence may be misguided. It is during the takeoff that a pilot first puts his aircraft to the ultimate test. If a system is not performing satisfactorily or the preflight duties were not carried out diligently, a safe departure may not be possible.

An alert pilot, however, attempts to sense these discrepancies before the aircraft is committed to flight. Frequently, a danger can be detected during the takeoff roll: a vibration, a strange noise, or perhaps unsatisfactory acceleration. These and a host of other conditions may dictate an aborted takeoff.

But will the average pilot take the necessary action at such a time? Probably not. Studies indicate that the takeoff will be continued because of a behavioral phenomenon known as psychological set.

When a pilot applies takeoff power, he subconsciously anticipates that he will take off and depart routinely. In other words, he is programmed to complete the maneuver. Should he sense something amiss during the ground roll, he may be unable to immediately throw his mind into reverse gear. He tends to perceive the situation on the basis of desire or expectancy instead of reality.

Those who do not accept this might attempt to explain in other terms why so many pilots continue with a takeoff when conditions clearly dictate otherwise.

Some years ago, I participated in a study of this problem with a group of private pilots. While taxiing onto the runway with each of them, I sneakily unlatched the right door. Invariably it would pop open at between 20 and 40 knots, resulting in frighteningly loud noises. But, even though there was more than enough runway to safely and comfortably abort the takeoff, the majority of these pilots continued with the departure—examples of how the lack of mental preparation prevents logical action.

There is a simple countermeasure to this behavioral phenomenon. A pilot needs only to have a brief chat with himself while taxiing onto the runway. All he has to do is tell himself that something *could* go wrong during the takeoff and to be prepared for the possibility. In other words, he destroys the psychological set and can't be taken by surprise. When anything out of the ordinary occurs, he simply retards the power, stomps on the binders, and brings his machine to a halt.

If this seems unnecessary, then consider that this is a ritual practiced by airline pilots. As I nudge a jetliner onto a runway, I mentally review the steps necessary to abort a takeoff.

The list of possible reasons to abort is lengthy, but these are the most common:

- Power surges or any indication of an engine abnormality.
- Any unusual noise—such as squealing, grinding, or whistling—that might indicate a mechanical abnormality.
- Any unusual smell.
- Any visible obstructions, such as an oblivious pilot taxiing across the departure end of the active runway.
- Unusual vibrations.
- Abnormally slow acceleration.
- Difficulty with directional control such as might be caused by a dragging brake.

And don't forget to include anything that might be perceived by a pilot's sixth sense. If something, anything, doesn't seem quite right, even this might suggest hauling back on the reins while sufficient runway remains ahead.

The decision to abort must be made quickly; there is usually very little time to debate the subject. An argument can be made in favor of an abort even when investigation reveals later that there was no need to be so discreet. It is a matter of being safe instead of sorry.

The devil's advocate claims, however, that an aborted takeoff is not without risk. A high-speed abort might require more runway than is available. The result could be a pile of bent aluminum without justifiable cause, not to mention possible injury to those inside.

Although the abort procedure seems rather straightforward, it is not always as simple as it first appears. This is because much of the runway has been left behind and there may be precious little ahead. This is a worthy consideration prior to making an intersection departure.

Once the decision is made to abort, retard the throttle(s) immediately. One common mistake is to reduce power gradually or indecisively, an error that shrinks time and distance to the end of the runway. At 50 knots, for example, each second of delay consumes 84 feet of forward progress.

Simultaneous with power reduction, apply maximum braking commensurate with controllability and efficiency. Most pilots wait until the engine is at idle before braking, a habit developed during normal landings where this is the conventional sequence of events. But not so when attempting an emergency stop within a critically limited distance. *Reduce power and apply brakes simultaneously.*

Maximum deceleration is not achieved by jumping on the brake pedals with full force. Excessive brake application locks the wheels and induces skidding, which can cause a 50-percent loss of tire friction. Maximum braking occurs when sufficient brake pressure is applied to almost stop wheel rotation. This is difficult to achieve without practice, and no one wants to do that with an expensive set of rubber paws. The recommended procedure is to apply enough brake pressure to induce skidding and then back off slightly.

This technique cannot be used by airline pilots because they cannot hear the anguish of screeching tires above the assaulting roar of reverse thrust. Instead, they rely on sophisticated antiskid systems that electronically do the same thing.

The pilot simply depresses the toe brakes mightily. If the system detects that a wheel is about to stop rotating, it causes brake pressure to that wheel to be temporarily reduced. Subsequently, brake pressure is modulated to each wheel independently and as necessary. Without such exotic hardware, the pilot of a heavy jet could expect to destroy—with a bang—one or more tires when braking heavily.

Maximum braking effectiveness occurs when as much aircraft weight as possible is placed on those wheels being braked. In general aviation planes, this refers to the main wheels since only these are equipped with brakes. (The nosewheels of some jet aircraft also have brakes.) In other words, the main wheels should have as much aircraft weight as possible placed on them.

During an abort, the wings often are at some positive angle of attack and generate lift. The amount may not be enough to lift the aircraft off the ground, but it does relieve the main gear of some aircraft weight, which decreases braking effectiveness. To maximize deceleration, therefore, it is necessary to destroy as much lift as possible.

One way to do this is to retract the flaps if they were extended for takeoff. But one must be extremely careful not to do this hastily. It is possible to grab the wrong switch in some airplanes, and inadvertently raise the landing gear. Although a wheels-up rollout usually is quite short, it is not recommended. (You can tell when the gear has been retracted because it takes so much power to taxi.)

The importance of shedding lift certainly is appreciated by the designers of jetliners because these aircraft are equipped with spoilers. At or shortly after touchdown, these large, flat, rectangular surfaces are deployed and rise from each wing, destroying instantly most of the residual lift. Abruptly, more than 80 percent of the aircraft weight compresses the landing gear shock struts to enhance braking performance.

When braking heavily, considerable aircraft weight is forced onto the nosewheel. To maximize deceleration, some of this weight can be transferred to the main landing gear by exerting back pressure on the control wheel. The idea is to take as much weight off the nosewheel as is possible without excessively decreasing nosewheel steering capability.

This technique has two additional benefits: It helps to prevent a pilot from "wheelbarrowing" helplessly along an unpredictable arc toward the edge of the runway, and the raised elevator causes a negative aerodynamic load on the tail which has the effect of increasing aircraft weight and, therefore, braking effectiveness. (With respect to this latter benefit, it is possible that the increased tail load—on some aircraft—is only sufficient to offset the slightly increased wing lift caused by this technique.)

One common misconception is that full nose-up back pressure should be applied during an abort. The proponents of this theory claim that raising the nose increases total aircraft drag and aids deceleration. No way! When airspeed is less than that required for flight, the drag created by rolling along the runway in a nose-high attitude doesn't even begin to offset the loss of braking power this creates (by "unloading" the main landing gear wheels).

Aerodynamic braking is a convenient way to save wear and tear on brake linings and tires, but only when sufficient runway length is available.

Once an aborted takeoff has been safely accomplished, it is possible in some aircraft that the brakes will have overheated (depending, of course, on the ground speed at the time the abort was initiated, aircraft gross weight, and the amount of braking force exerted). When returning to the tiedown area, consider this possibility and try to avoid taxi speeds that might call for reliable braking. When the brakes are hot, the necessary stopping power may not be available.

If a pilot is alert, an abort usually can be performed in about the same or less distance than would be required to land under similar conditions. Takeoff planning might include such a consideration.

A fully loaded Cessna 177B Cardinal, for example, requires a takeoff roll of 1,105 feet at a density altitude of 5,000 feet (no wind); a landing under the same conditions (ground roll only) requires 700 feet. The distance necessary to accelerate to rotation speed and then abort immediately is, therefore, approximately 1,800 feet. This does not include any distance that might be consumed during a few valuable seconds of indecision.

It is worth remembering that generally, but not always, it takes more distance to accelerate an aircraft to a given speed than it does to decelerate from that same speed. (This means also that it is often possible to land on a very short strip from which a subsequent, safe departure may be impossible.)

Prior to departing a very short runway, compute the necessary *landing* roll distance under the same conditions and deduct this from the total runway length. A pilot then knows how far the takeoff can proceed and still leave room to abort. According to a popular rule of thumb, if the aircraft cannot accelerate to 70 percent of the necessary liftoff speed by the time only the required landing distance remains, an abort should be considered. This broad generalization, however, is valid mostly when operating from unpaved surfaces at high density altitudes.

Although air carriers generally require a quarter-mile of visibility to make an instrument departure, general aviation pilots operating under Part 91 of the Federal Aviation Regulations (FARs) are not so restricted. They legally can take off in zero-zero conditions.

The hazard of a takeoff under such conditions is that there is no guarantee that the runway is clear of obstacles. Numerous accidents have occurred when a departing aircraft simply rammed into another aircraft (or ground vehicle) taxiing (or being towed) across the active runway. Unless the pilot is mentally prepared for an abort (or a premature liftoff) under these conditions, avoiding the impending disaster may be impossible. It is worth noting that this type of accident occurs most frequently at *controlled* airports.

It is a shame that statistics of the National Transportation Safety Board (NTSB) reflect so many takeoff accidents and fatalities. This is the one phase of flight that affords a pilot all the time that could be needed to plan and prepare. Many of these casualties could have been avoided by being aware of the insidious psychological set.

"To abort or not to abort" can be a difficult question, but is one that every pilot must be prepared to answer without hesitation.

TRIMMING

It was one of those satin-smooth nights over the Mojave Desert when an airplane could be flown as straight and true as the moonbeams that danced on our wings. This was my first ride in a twin-engine airplane, and I sat quietly and somewhat in awe as Joe DeBona guided the new 1955 Cessna 310 along Amber 2 (a low-frequency airway) toward Las Vegas, Nevada.

He must be a perfectionist, I recall thinking. His hands were in constant motion twiddling with knobs, buttons, and levers, tuning the great machine as if it were a Steinway being readied for a concert.

"Hey, Barry. Why don't you take it?" Joe volunteered. "I'm getting tired."

Concealing my excitement, I slid my seat forward, found the rudder pedals with my feet, and wrapped a paw around one side of the wheel. But as Joe relinquished control, the airplane lurched into a forward slip to the left and pitched up sharply.

After long seconds of wrestling with the controls and restoring some semblance of order, I glanced toward the left seat for help and an explanation. But Joe just sat there with a smug expression and a hint of a grin.

Then it dawned on me. All of that tweaking with the controls was intended to throw the Cessna completely out of trim. And with every movement of a tab, Joe had countered with just enough deflection of the primary control surfaces to keep the 310 on an even keel.

Once he knew that I knew why the airplane was misbehaving, he leaned back, lit that rotten old pipe of his, and said, "Okay, kid, trim 'er out." Several minutes later, the 310 was flying only slightly askew. Sensing my frustration at being unable to trim the aircraft perfectly, Joe volunteered some pointers that led me to better appreciate those often misused and misunderstood secondary flight controls known as trim tabs.

Although operating pitch trim is a straightforward procedure, the water gets muddier when pilots are exposed to airplanes that also have roll (aileron) and yaw (rudder) trim. Unfortunately, many never really learn to trim an airplane about all three axes properly. As a result, a flight often involves a continual series of corrections that otherwise might be unnecessary. This leads to increased workload and a premature onset of fatigue, especially during prolonged instrument flight.

Engineers usually design an airplane so that control surfaces and trim tabs are streamlined as much as possible during level flight to maximize cruise performance. But when an airplane is mistrimmed, control surfaces and tabs are unnecessarily deflected, creating trim drag, which has a negative effect on airspeed and fuel economy.

The effect of excess trim drag varies between aircraft. Some mistrimmed aircraft may lose only a few knots of airspeed while others, such as the Piper Saratoga, occasionally mush along with a 10-knot loss.

Airline management and corporate flight departments justifiably are concerned about the potential cost of mistrimming. Although one might think that pilots who fly for a living should be able to trim an aircraft perfectly, several studies indicate otherwise. So some technological assistance has been made available. Inertial navigation systems (INS) can be modified to incorporate an along-track-acceleration mode. After the aircraft has been stabilized in level flight, the pilot makes minor adjustments to the rudder and aileron trim systems. The effect of moving each is to either decrease or increase drag and is shown on the INS display in terms of acceleration or deceleration in milli-Gs (52 mGs equals a one-knot-per-second acceleration). By taking his time, a pilot can optimize rudder and aileron deflection and achieve a worthwhile airspeed gain.

Pilots of aircraft that lack such exotic hardware also can optimize performance and eliminate some of the en route workload, but they must rely on more traditional methods. The devices and indications most often relied upon to trim an airplane, however, frequently are misused. An airplane may or may not be in trim even when the slip-skid ball is centered, the attitude indicator shows that the wings are level, the control wheel is centered, and the trim indices are zeroed. This is because slip-skid balls and attitude indicators often lack the necessary precision or are installed improperly. (A Cheyenne II that I recently flew had three slip-skid balls; all three disagreed.) Also, control-wheel and trim-indicator positions depend on aircraft loading and rigging. It is a rare machine indeed that is not slipping serenely through the sky when all of these devices indicate that the aircraft is in perfect trim. (Excess trim requirements may be the result of an out-of-rig condition, something that often can be corrected by an airframe mechanic.)

The technique of trimming is relatively simple, but only when a pilot knows what to look for. Simply stated, an airplane is in trim only when the need to apply control forces has been eliminated, the wings are perfectly level, and the aircraft has no tendency to yaw—conditions best achieved by looking out the window and applying a fine touch to the controls.

The task of optimizing trim, however, begins on the ground. Given the option, spanwise fuel load should be symmetrical so that aileron trim (read: drag) will not be required in flight. Similarly, consider seating your passengers and distributing the cargo in the aircraft so as to maintain lateral balance.

Once the aircraft is leveled at altitude, do not be in a rush to trim it. Allow cruise conditions to stabilize because trimming an airplane at one airspeed usually means that an out-of-trim condition will exist at another. When flying multiengine aircraft, use available instruments to be sure all engines are developing equal power.

Next, zero the rudder and aileron trim tabs even if this means temporarily worsening the control inputs required to keep on an even keel. If applicable, turn off the yaw damper.

Now select a distant point on the horizon and apply whatever rudder pressure is needed to keep that point dead ahead. Do not allow it to move even a fraction of a degree. Although some pilots prefer to use a gyroscopic heading indicator to maintain heading, the left-right movement of the nose relative to a point on the horizon is much easier to detect than a movement of the indicator.

Simultaneously apply the control wheel (aileron) pressure necessary to maintain a wings-level attitude. But do not just stare straight ahead. Look at the wings to be certain each wing tip has precisely the same position with respect to the port and starboard horizons. (When trying to visually establish and maintain a perfect wings-level attitude, consider moving your head toward the center of the cockpit to eliminate the viewing error caused by parallax.)

If the wings are level and if the heading remains constant, crank in whatever rudder trim is necessary to relieve the pressure being applied to the pedal while manually holding the wings level. After the proper amount of rudder trim has been applied, use aileron trim to relieve roll pressure being applied to the wheel. In theory, the airplane now is in perfect trim despite possible instrument indications to the contrary. A pilot should, however, note positions of the slip-skid ball, attitude indicator, control wheel, and trim indices for future reference. He also should disconnect the autopilot and yaw damper every hour or so to see if additional fine tuning is required.

If an unbalanced fuel load requires additional corrections, just adding aileron trim may not be sufficient. Deflected ailerons may create enough adverse yaw to require retrimming the rudder. This additional trim increases drag, suggesting that fuel imbalance be avoided as much as is practical.

The technique described applies equally well to a twin-engine airplane being flown on one engine. The only significant difference is that the twin should be trimmed to maintain a five-degree bank (as shown on the attitude indicator) toward the operative engine to optimize engine-out performance.

Since many aircraft do not have cockpit-controlled yaw or roll trim systems, their pilots must resort to using ground-adjustable tabs—small pieces of sheet metal riveted to the trailing edges of ailerons and rudders. Some aircraft do not have even these primitive devices for trimming roll. However, an owner usually can have one inexpensively installed on an aileron after first obtaining permission from the FAA, a usually effortless procedure (especially when an approved modification kit is used).

Trimming an airplane with ground-adjustable tabs is largely a trial-and-error technique that is simplified by using the procedure described previously. After determining which way the rudder needs to be deflected, simply bend the tab about an eighth of an inch in the opposite direction. Do not bend the tab using only the fingers because this may result in a warped tab or a loosened rivet. Instead, lay a stiff straightedge against the tab and bend it uniformly. During subsequent flights, determine if more or less rudder trim is required and make the adjustments.

Once the need for additional rudder trim has been eliminated, then—and only then—go about the task of adjusting the aileron tab, if necessary. The sequence of events is important if the procedure is to be executed with a minimum of fuss and bother. Applying corrections randomly usually compounds the problem.

Although pitch trimming is second nature to most pilots, there are a few points worth considering. Some pilots, for example, use nose-up trim to relieve the considerable control-wheel back pressure often required when practicing steep turns. In my opinion, this is a bad habit. This is because zeroing out the elevator pressure makes it easier to overstress an airplane or cause an accelerated stall, since a pilot cannot feel how much control force actually is being applied. Also, a rapid rollout from such a turn (necessitated perhaps by a traffic conflict) may result in a surprisingly strong pitch-up that could require a hefty push on the control wheel to arrest.

The FAA has developed a maneuver known as the elevator trim stall to demonstrate the dangers associated with a mistrim that results from a rapid change in flight conditions. The maneuver is entered by establishing an airplane in landing configuration (gear and flaps down) while descending in a normal glide. Considerable nose-up trim obviously must be applied to maintain this profile without having to hold back pressure on the control wheel. After the aircraft is stabilized and properly trimmed, the pilot is instructed to advance the throttle(s) smoothly and fully, simulating a go-around and not to push forward on the control wheel until the stall is imminent, which usually is quite soon.

One trim feature that has become popular is the electric elevator trim. It also is called a beep trim because it is operated by "beeping" a small thumb switch on the control wheel. Unfortunately, many pilots misuse this aid by beeping in *excessive* nose-up trim during a landing flare. Although this technique relieves a pilot of having to exercise his forearm at least once during each flight, it can have grave consequences.

A few years ago, the pilot of a light twin was about to touch down following a prolonged flare. He apparently realized that he was running out of runway and jammed the throttles home. The nose rose so sharply that the pilot was unable to correct the situation in time to avert the departure stall; all aboard were killed. It was discovered during the post-crash investigation that the elevator trim was in the *full* nose-up position.

Another potential problem is runaway elevator trim. This occurs when an electrical short keeps the trim motor operating even after the trim switch on the control wheel has been released. Pilots aware of this possibility should perform a preflight test to guarantee that the trim system can be overridden manually and deactivated (while the thumb switch is depressed) by using the primary power-on/power-off switch or circuit breaker.

A final note with respect to all cockpit-controlled trim tabs is to pay particular attention to them during the preflight. A tab that is loose because it is not attached securely or is operated by either slack or frayed cables has the potential to destroy an aircraft. This is because such a tab can cause its primary control surface to flutter divergently and uncontrollably, a case of the tail really wagging the dog.

Most pilots understand a trim tab is deflected in one direction to cause a primary control surface to deflect in the opposite direction (Figure 11). It can be said that the tab acts as a form of boost or power assist because it makes the primary control lighter to the touch and easier to operate. But a slight price is paid for this convenience.

Figure 12a shows the tail of an airplane with a considerable amount of nose-up trim applied. Notice that the tab is aligned more with the relative wind than is the elevator. Since the tab normally contributes to the surface area of an elevator, it is obvious that deflecting the tab away from the relative wind reduces elevator effectiveness.

This piece of knowledge can be especially useful to a pilot about to land with a nosewheel that cannot be extended, for example. Since he desires to keep the nose off the ground as

Figure 11

long as possible after touching down on the mains, he could simultaneously apply nose-*down* trim and full nose-up elevator. Figure 12b shows that this causes the tab to deflect more into the relative wind, which increases elevator area and effectiveness. The pilot will be deboosting the elevator (making it harder to use), but he can delay the nose from digging in.

This discussion of boosting (conventional tab usage) and deboosting (opposite tab usage) leads conveniently to the subject of stabilators. During the preflight inspection of a stabilator (or all-flying tail, as it is sometimes called), raise the trailing edge as you would an elevator. Something strange happens; the trim tab rises with respect to the stabilator (Figure 13). Lower the stabilator and the tab deflects downward. This seems odd because, when a conventional elevator is moved, the position of the tab remains fixed.

The tab on a stabilator serves two purposes. In addition to being a trim tab, which operates conventionally when adjusted from the cockpit, it also is a leading balance tab and is used to deboost a stabilator (making it harder to use). If a stabilator were not deboosted this way, control pressures would be too light, making it easy to overcontrol the stabilator and inadvertently overstress the airplane. Leading balance tabs also are known as anti-servo tabs.

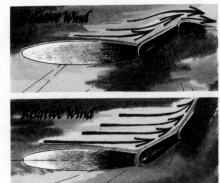

FIGURE 12a

FIGURE 12b

FIGURE 13

Occasionally designers want control forces to be light. This was the case with several World War II aircraft. To guarantee that fighter pilots could roll their aircraft effortlessly, designers provided these aircraft with lagging balance tabs (Figure 14), features also found on some sophisticated lightplanes and business jets. As these ailerons are deflected, the tabs automatically deflect in the opposite direction. It is just as if the pilot were adding aileron trim every time he moved the stick (or wheel) left or right. Lagging balance tabs commonly are referred to as servo tabs, even though this technically is incorrect.

A true servo tab (Figure 15) is used almost exclusively on large aircraft. With such a configuration, the primary control cables from the cockpit are connected to the tab; there is no direct connection between the cockpit controls and the primary control surface. When the control wheel is pulled aft, the servo tab on the elevator moves down, and vice versa. This aerodynamically forces the elevator to rise, which causes the nose to pitch up.

FIGURE 14

FIGURE 15

Common to older Cessna Skylanes and all Cessna 180s and 185s is an adjustable horizontal stabilizer that is used in lieu of an elevator trim tab. When nose-up trim is applied, the leading edge of the stabilizer moves down and vice versa. Such a system may be the most efficient because it creates minimal trim drag; whenever the aircraft is in trim, the elevator is streamlined with the stabilizer. (Late-model Skylanes have fixed stabilizers and conventional elevator tab systems because Cessna feels this is more suitable for autopilot adaptation.)

Although all four-place Mooneys also have adjustable horizontal stabilizers, these aircraft incorporate a unique design feature: The vertical stabilizer is attached to and moves with the horizontal stabilizer. Consequently, when nose-down trim is applied during cruise flight, for example, the leading edge of the horizontal stabilizer moves up in the normal manner. This causes the vertical stabilizer to sweep aft, which theoretically reduces fin drag. Conversely, when nose-up trim is applied during an approach to landing, the leading edge of the horizontal stabilizer moves down conventionally. This makes the vertical fin sweep forward into a more vertical posture, which theoretically increases rudder effectiveness during slow flight.

Trim systems and tabs may not be the most exotic features of an airplane, but they are essential elements of the flight control system. And although they may be small and inconspicuous, like so many other aspects of life, it's the little things that count.

──────────────── Coping with Wind Shear

There is nothing new about wind shear. It has existed in the atmosphere ever since air began to circulate. It was not perceived as a hazard, however, until flight data recorders in jetliners led accident investigators to discover that wind shear could substantially affect aircraft performance.

Prior to the flight data recorder, there was no way to prove the effect of wind shear in fatal accidents. Accidents caused by this phenomenon were blamed on pilots who were said to have "lost control." Even today, many wind-shear-induced, general aviation accidents are blamed on pilot error. It is difficult to estimate how many lightplane accidents have resulted from wind-shear encounters, but there have been many more than is generally appreciated.

A wind shear is a change in wind velocity (direction and/or speed) that occurs over such a short distance that it is impossible for an aircraft to accelerate or decelerate to its original airspeed within the time and distance required to fly through the shear event.

It is popularly held that light aircraft are not affected as much by wind shear as are airliners. Presumably, this is because heavier aircraft have more inertia and cannot easily recapture lost airspeed. This is true to a certain extent, but airliners are vulnerable to more than just inertia. A transport-category aircraft usually penetrates a shear line with greater airspeed than does a lightplane. Consequently, these faster aircraft have less time within which to accelerate and recapture airspeed being lost during a wind-shear encounter.

In this regard, slower aircraft are less vulnerable to wind shear. But since lightplanes often have less reserve performance with which to combat a shear, they also are vulnerable. This is particularly true when operating at relatively heavy gross weights and high density altitudes.

There are two basic types of wind shear—horizontal and

vertical—and they are most dangerous when encountered by an aircraft in an approach or departure configuration at less than 1,000 feet above ground level (agl). The horizontal shear is a rapid change in either the head- or tailwind component and has the primary effect of either increasing or decreasing airspeed.

For example, a pilot flying into a rapidly increasing headwind or experiencing a rapidly decreasing tailwind will notice an increase in airspeed, a tendency for the nose to rise, and a substantial improvement in climb performance (albeit temporarily). A performance-decreasing shear, on the other hand, occurs when a pilot encounters a rapidly decreasing headwind or a rapidly increasing tailwind. The result of this type of shear is reduced airspeed, a noticeable nose-down pitching moment, and decreased climb performance.

In the extreme, it is possible to encounter horizontal, low-level wind shears that approach a 30-knot change in wind per 100 feet of altitude. There are few aircraft that—when in an approach or departure configuration—could survive a performance-decreasing shear of this magnitude.

Vertical shears are commonly referred to as up- and downdrafts. An updraft, or common convection current, is a performance-increasing type of vertical shear; flying into a thermal obviously improves climb performance or airspeed, depending on how the pilot elects to handle the situation. Downdrafts, on the other hand, detract from performance. The common downdraft, however, normally is not a serious threat.

When a column of rain falls from a cumulus cloud, it cools the surrounding air and increases its density. If sufficiently dense, this column of cool air may become an intense, severely localized downdraft.

Dr. T. Theodore Fujita, a research meteorologist from the University of Chicago, has studied downdrafts extensively. He classifies severe downdrafts in two categories: downbursts and microbursts. According to Fujita's theory, downbursts affect a surface area of approximately 15 miles in diameter. Microbursts are smaller, affecting surface areas one mile or less in diameter.

To qualify as a downburst or microburst, Fujita says, vertical velocity must be 720 fpm or greater at 300 feet agl. Some microbursts are known to have vertical velocities in excess of 1,800 fpm at only 200 feet agl.

The terms *downburst* and *microburst* are entering common usage. Some experts are critical of Fujita's terminology and say that downbursts and microbursts are nothing more than the usual downdrafts that accompany changing wind patterns.

Can such a downdraft force an aircraft into the ground? You bet it can. Proof of such a downdraft reaching the ground is revealed in a dramatic photograph that shows several acres of wheat compressed by the force of a microburst. In another photograph, branches in a pine forest are shown broken in a clear radial pattern. (The center of the pattern marks the center of the downdraft.)

Upon entering a low-level microburst, an aircraft begins to sink with startling suddenness. Since the relative wind comes from above, longitudinal stability forces the aircraft to assume an almost equally abrupt nose-up attitude. Unless an aircraft can outclimb the microburst or fly quickly through it, the aircraft may crash in a tail-low attitude.

Although the most severe microbursts are produced by thunderstorm activity, vigorous ones can be produced by lesser clouds. Devastating vertical shears have been encountered when flying through rainshowers emanating from cumulus and towering cumulus clouds. Virga, which is rain that evaporates before reaching the ground, usually originates from high-based clouds over arid regions. It is a seemingly peaceful, innocuous phenomenon, but it can produce sufficiently powerful downdrafts to force departing and arriving aircraft to crash.

Several years ago, a Boeing 727 departing Denver's Stapleton Airport was forced onto an open field by the effects of virga. Virga is most threatening when surface winds are light, the surface temperature exceeds 75°F, and the spread between temperature and dew point exceeds 35°F.

Microbursts alone are bad enough, but a recent study funded by the National Aeronautics and Space Administration (NASA) indicates that the effect of heavy rain on lift and drag might add to the effect of a wind-shear encounter. This is because a buildup of rain on an airfoil can result in a 30-percent loss of lift and as much as a 20-percent increase in drag. Additionally, the impact of heavy rain causes an aircraft to lose some momentum. (The weight of rainwater on an aircraft can increase gross weight up to 2 percent and is not considered significant.)

There are many causes of horizontal and vertical wind shear. These include: gradient winds; terrain irregularities (when combined with strong surface winds); temperature inversions; low-level jet streams; mountain waves (at airports downwind of the wave source); strong convection activity; and sea-breeze fronts (at airports near bays, large lakes, and oceans). Although any of these conditions can be cause for concern, investigations show that most wind-shear-related accidents occur in the vicinity of cold and warm fronts, thunderstorms, and other rain-producing clouds that have not necessarily grown to thunderstorm intensity.

Pilots learn early in their weather studies that frontal passage is often accompanied by a shift in wind velocity. This usually is perceived only as a surface event. Such a shift, however, occurs along the entire frontal surface, which separates warm and cold air, and poses a low-level wind shear threat to arriving or departing aircraft whenever the frontal surface is less than 1,000 feet agl. In the case of a cold front, a wind-shear hazard can exist for up to one hour after the front passes an airport. When penetrating the surface of a cold front, a pilot can expect a sharp change in wind direction with little or no change in wind speed. The greater the temperature difference across the front, the greater the potential for a hazardous shear. In general, be on the alert when the temperature difference across a front exceeds 10°F and the front is moving at 30 knots or more.

In the case of a warm front, the most critical period is the six hours *prior* to the time the front passes the airport. A typical warm front produces a shear characterized by a significant change in wind speed with little or no change in direction. Even though cold fronts are more dynamic than warm fronts, the latter appear to produce more dangerous wind shears than do cold fronts.

Although many fronts (both warm and cold) are dry and have little or no associated weather, this does not necessarily reduce the potential for a wind-shear encounter. A frontal-related shear can occur as easily during visual conditions as it can during instrument conditions.

Since microbursts most often are produced by heavy, localized rainshowers, these hazards (with the exception of virga) are almost always associated with thunderstorms or convective clouds. As a result, such showers may or may not be accompanied by lightning. In either event, the activity responsible for microbursts usually is easy to see and avoid.

One word of caution regarding thunderstorms. Although microbursts are found beneath the chimneys of these meteorological behemoths, such a storm cell generally has a gust front that typically precedes the cell by five to 15 miles, or as much as 30 miles in some cases.

A thunderstorm's gust front (Figure 16) is similar to an intense, miniaturized cold front. It can produce wind shears with intensities of up to 90 knots. When a thunderstorm moves across a desert, it is possible to see the gust front because of the dust and sand kicked up far ahead of the cell. In other regions, however, the gust front may not be visible, which points out how foolhardy it can be to race a thunderstorm to an airport—that gust front may beat you there, even though the cell itself lags far behind. It is wiser to either wait until the cell has passed or find another haven in which to roost. Some of general aviation's most tragic thunderstorm-related accidents have occurred in clear air several miles ahead of an advancing cell.

There has been considerable publicity in recent years about methods of coping with wind shear. The trouble is that the advice applies almost exclusively to jet-powered airplanes. Pilots

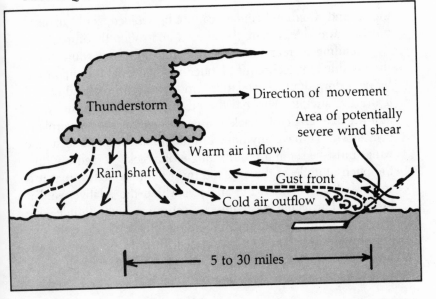

Figure 16

of these aircraft are advised to fire-wall the thrust levers and trade airspeed for altitude until the onset of the stickshaker, a stall-warning device that operates only a few knots above stall. Although there is some controversy regarding this technique, it works reasonably well because jet aircraft have tolerably good climb performance at stickshaker speed.

The same procedure is not nearly as effective in piston-powered airplanes. One reason is that these aircraft do not perform well near stall because of the rapid drag rise associated with flying behind the power curve. Trading airspeed for altitude usually does not work well because propeller-driven airplanes decelerate so rapidly when the nose is pulled up.

When a low-level shear is encountered in a lightplane, the best procedure is to use all available power, retract the gear and flaps (if practical), and establish a speed as close to V_x (best angle-of-climb speed) as possible. Do not allow the speed to bleed farther even if this means having to accept a sink rate near the ground. If ground contact cannot be avoided, some airspeed must be available to flare the aircraft and soften the impact.

Handling a microburst requires the same procedure but a slightly different technique. Notice in Figure 17 that upon entering a downdraft, the relative wind comes from ahead of and *above* the aircraft. This has the effect of establishing the wings at a negative angle of attack and is one reason why the airplane goes down. To have any hope of outclimbing a microburst, the wings must be set at a positive angle of attack. To achieve this, the pitch attitude of the airplane must be increased so that it is somewhat steeper than the angle at which the relative wind is blowing. This generally requires a very nose-high attitude, one that may seem radical and uncomfortable. It is, nevertheless, the only possible way to coax needed lift from the wings. Failure to assume such a nose-high attitude probably will allow the

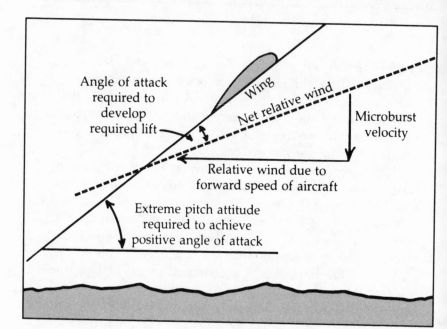

FIGURE 17

microburst to have its way. Should the aircraft make it to the other side of the microburst, however, be prepared to lower the nose quickly to avoid stalling.

A pilot has two weapons with which to combat wind shear: avoidance and excess performance. Since many light aircraft do not have excess power, pilots must make every effort to prevent an encounter with low-level wind shear. Avoidance is best practiced by remaining clear of the conditions most likely to generate wind shear. A pilot also must take aggressive action whenever wind-shear clues begin to appear.

In Figure 18, for example, an aircraft on final approach enters a rainshower. Simultaneously, airspeed begins to increase because of an increasing headwind. This is the pilot's first indication that the aircraft is entering a microburst. Unless he executes a maximum-effort missed approach, he soon may pass into the downdraft portion of the microburst, where the head-

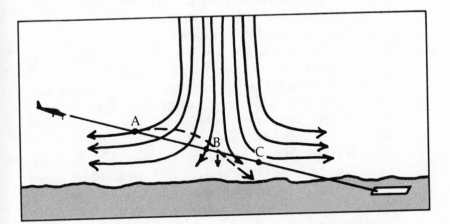

FIGURE 18   A pilot approaching the airport enters the microburst at point A and experiences a rapidly increasing headwind. Airspeed increases and the aircraft rises above the glideslope. The pilot reduces power to recapture the glideslope and finds (point B) that the headwind has disappeared and the aircraft has entered an intense downdraft. A rapidly increasing tailwind follows (point C), adding to the improbability that the aircraft can remain airborne.

wind shears into a tailwind. This combination of sinking air and loss of airspeed due to wind shear is what occurred when a Boeing 727 crashed on Rockaway Boulevard instead of landing on JFK's Runway 22L in 1975.

Whenever there is an indication of a strong wind shear or microburst, initiate a climb and get the aircraft out of the condition as rapidly as possible. Pilots generally tend to be hesitant about taking such immediate action upon encountering a wind shear because they may not appreciate how desperate the situation can become. But unless a pilot acts quickly, the situation may erode to a point where no amount of effort can resolve the problem.

If wind shear conditions are indicated or reported, the pilot should delay departure or arrival until the condition passes. Wind shear and microbursts usually are very dynamic and tend to move quickly.

If a pilot only suspects the possibility of wind shear and opts to make the approach anyway, he can take a few steps to reduce the risk. These consist of increasing the approach speed by up to 20 knots, using the smallest flap setting consistent with safety, and establishing a stabilized approach (constant power setting, airspeed, attitude, and sink rate) prior to descending below 1,000 feet agl. While on the approach, compare aircraft performance with tower-reported winds. If it appears that the winds during the approach are substantially different than those on the surface, or if the approach becomes destabilized due to changing atmospheric conditions, consider an immediate pullup. (Many airports have a low-level wind-shear alert system—LLWAS—a network of anemometers established at the center and periphery of an airport that can warn controllers and pilots of potentially hazardous wind shear. If wind speeds and directions vary significantly among the anemometers, controllers are supposed to warn arriving pilots of the possibility of wind shear.) Successful extrication from a low-level shear depends not only on the availability of reserve power, altitude, and performance, but on the ability of the pilot to perceive the hazard and take the necessary action.

In extreme cases, however, no amount of skill and performance may be sufficient to assure survival.

Consider the case of a rainshower and a relatively weak microburst over the departure end of a runway. Although an aircraft can accelerate well into the headwind, it soon can enter a downdraft and experience a headwind-to-tailwind shear. Such a situation, even when caused by something as seemingly innocent as virga, can prevent the successful departure of practically *any* aircraft. When the possibility of a departure shear exists, the pilot would be wise to park the airplane until conditions improve.

In the final analysis, the safest way to cope with wind shear is to avoid it. This requires learning which conditions are most likely to spawn a shear and then regarding them as if they were official aircraft limitations, which—in a sense—they are.

───────────────────────────── **GOING AROUND**

From the tower controller's point of view, it had seemed as though I had lost my senses. He had observed the yellow-and-blue Cessna 140 execute a go-around, reject a landing, and finally recover from a horrendous bounce. Immediately following this display, he had seen me climb out of the taildragger and release my student to make her first solo flight.

Outraged by my apparent lack of professionalism, the controller reported his observations to the local FAA district office. He also prepared to summon the emergency vehicles, just in case.

The FAA inspector in the familiar gray Ford drove toward me just in time for both of us to witness my student's first solo landing. It was a greaser.

I explained later that it was my practice to determine that a student about to solo was capable of dealing with unexpected contingencies. The go-around, the rejected landing, and, yes, even the bounce were maneuvers I had induced to test my student's preparedness.

Unfortunately, a surprisingly large percentage of certified pilots are not as prepared to shift mental gears as was the student in this example. Psychologists attribute this to what is called the landing expectancy, or set, an anticipatory belief (or desire) that conditions are not as threatening as they are. The more experience a pilot has, the more likely he is to be a victim of landing expectancy. This is because years of successful approaches and landings reinforce confidence in the ability to overcome adversity.

As a result, pilots may continue an approach or landing when conditions dictate that the attempt be aborted. FAA records support this claim. Innumerable accidents have occurred because a pilot was unprepared to abandon an unsatisfactory approach or landing while there was sufficient time, speed, distance, or altitude to do so.

Fortunately, there is a countermeasure for battling the complacency induced by landing expectancy. During every approach, a pilot should ask, "Am I as prepared to reject this approach or landing as I am to continue?" The simple act of reminding oneself of the option usually is all that is necessary to prepare for the possibility.

At least one major airline goes one step further. It instructs its pilots to execute a pullup if the airplane is not in the landing configuration (gear and flaps extended) at 500 feet agl with engine power, airspeed, and sink rate stabilized. If all these conditions are not met, or if any surprises of a hazardous nature develop during the approach, a miss is mandatory. This philosophy is known as being aggressively safe. Positive action is taken to neutralize a threat or to prevent a doubt from deepening or lingering during *any* phase of flight.

One of several tools available to the aggressively safe pilot is the go-around, a maneuver used in VFR (visual flight rules) conditions whenever it appears inadvisable to continue an approach. (The IFR, or instrument flight rules, equivalent is called a missed approach and is discussed in chapter 6.) This relatively simple procedure is not used as frequently as it should be because a pilot often is "programmed" to land; he is not mentally prepared to reverse his course of action. He may get to a point where a potential hazard no longer can be ignored, but then it may be too late. Numerous accidents result from not taking positive action *soon enough.*

The go-around is simple in concept, but many execute it improperly. The most common error is the failure to apply maximum-allowable power. Some pilots are timid about shoving the throttle(s) to the fire wall. Since the aircraft at that time is in a high-drag (flaps and gear extended), low-airspeed configuration, it may continue to settle at an alarming, irrecoverable rate.

One reason for this reluctance to apply full throttle may be that pilots trained in turbosupercharged aircraft are told to avoid rapid throttle movements. Another reason may be that pilots are trained in lightly loaded aircraft at relatively low density altitudes. During practice go-arounds, the pilot notes subconsciously that the aircraft performs quiet well and that perhaps that much power really is not needed.

But then he takes a summer flight to a high-elevation airport with a full load. Under these conditions, the aircraft may have no go-around capability in the landing configuration.

One way to establish an airplane's pullup performance is to practice the maneuver, before it really is needed, at various altitudes and a relatively heavy weight. At an 8,000-foot density altitude (DA), for example, establish the aircraft in landing configuration at the normal approach speed and sink rate. Upon reaching some target altitude, such as a 7,000-foot DA, execute a simulated, full-power go-around. Unless the engine is turbocharged, performance is likely to be marginal.

Every airplane has a go-around ceiling, a critical *density* altitude above which a positive climb rate cannot be established in the landing configuration. Unfortunately, this kind of performance data is not published in pilot operating handbooks. Consequently, pilots rarely consider such a "limitation." Many learn the hard way that a go-around is impossible when above the critical density altitude.

Experienced mountain pilots often execute a simple performance test before committing to a landing. While on the downwind leg of the traffic pattern, the airplane is established in the landing configuration at its normal approach speed. Full power is applied, and a climb is attempted. This technique reveals just how much go-around performance is available under a given set of circumstances.

While the throttle is fire-walled, the pilot also can lean the mixture for maximum power, in case a genuine go-around becomes necessary. Some pullup attempts fail only because the mixture is adjusted improperly.

If the simulated pullup at pattern altitude is marginal or impossible, consider executing the approach with less than maximum flap deflection. The second half of flap extension provides most of the drag and usually contributes very little stall-speed reduction.

Typical, for example, is the Cessna 182. At a gross weight of 2,800 pounds, deflecting the flaps 20 degrees reduces stall speed from 56 to 50 knots, a six-knot reduction. But extending the flaps fully, to 40 degrees, reduces stall speed only two knots more, to 48 knots. With respect to stall speed, therefore, an approach can be executed at half-flap or full-flap deflection at essentially the same airspeed without compromising safety. The advantage, of course, is that initial climb performance (should it be needed) is considerably better with half flaps than with the barn doors fully open.

When nearing the airport boundary and preparing to commit to a landing, extend the flaps completely to attain maximum stall protection and drag. Inexperienced pilots, however, probably should not delay flap extension until so close to the ground. This is because of the powerful pitch changes that sometimes occur during flap extension. But if a pilot is prepared for the trim change and the probable need to add power, there is nothing particularly difficult about this procedure.

Pilots should be capable of countering the effects of flap extension at only a hundred or so feet above the ground. When pullup performance is *known* to be satisfactory, however, a stabilized approach is recommended during the last 500 feet of descent.

There are numerous reasons for executing a go-around, including such surprises as an aircraft taxiing unexpectedly onto the runway or an indication of a landing-gear malfunction. But one of the most insidious causes is wind shear.

The airspeed-robbing effects of wind shear are well known and were discussed earlier in this chapter. To review, a sudden headwind loss results in an almost corresponding airspeed loss; a sudden increase in the headwind component causes an almost corresponding airspeed gain. The logical conclusion then is that a loss of headwind is responsible for undershooting the runway because of the sudden loss of some lift and the accompanying tendency of the airplane to pitch downward.

Surprisingly, the opposite also can occur. Noticing an airspeed loss and a deepening sink rate, the pilot adds considerable power and raises the nose in an effort to regain a position on the visual (or electronic) glideslope. Unless the pilot judiciously retards the throttle and lowers the nose at precisely the right time, he is likely to climb *above* the glideslope, resulting in an *overshoot*. Conversely, and for similar reasons, an increase in the headwind component can result in an undershoot.

The important point to remember is that any low-altitude wind shear can produce disastrous effects. When such a condition interferes with a stabilized approach near the ground, the wisest course of action is to climb to a safe altitude and wait for the condition to subside. Wind shear is a very dynamic phenomenon and characteristically tends to move on. An approach that is hazardous one moment might be perfectly safe 10 to 20 minutes later.

Approaches made through strong thermals, downdrafts, and turbulence also can be difficult to negotiate. If such problems are encountered and conditions tend to become unmanageable, consider the attempt a trial run, an effort to test the water. Go around and try again. As they say in basketball, "No harm— no foul." But to press on when conditions suggest otherwise might result in penalties more severe than having to sit on the bench.

Preparing for the possibility of a go-around suggests early completion of the before-landing checklist. This includes selecting the fullest fuel tank (or *both* tanks in Cessna singles), adjusting the mixture properly, and, when applicable, lowering the landing gear, turning on the auxiliary fuel pump, and adjusting the propeller pitch control to maximum rpm (low pitch).

When a go-around is warranted, do not hesitate. Use *all* allowable power, and rotate the nose to achieve the maximum possible climb rate. Do not forget to open the cowl flaps (if available), because these usually are closed during descent.

If performance is anemic and the flaps are extended fully, retract them halfway (or to the position recommended by the aircraft manufacturer). This can be a critical move because raising flaps, even partially, decreases the wing's effective angle of attack and dumps a measurable amount of lift. To avoid settling, the nose must be raised *just enough* to reenlarge the angle of attack and maintain lift. But be careful about raising the nose too much. Proficiency in this critical maneuver can be achieved by practicing go-arounds at altitude.

If the airplane has retractable landing gear, do not raise it until a positive climb rate has been established at a safe airspeed. This delays the temporary drag *increase* that often accompanies gear retraction. And if the go-around is begun from a very low altitude, there is the possibility of settling temporarily onto the ground. It is infinitely more comfortable to touch with rubber than with metal.

Once the airplane is stabilized at its best-rate-of-climb airspeed at a comfortable altitude, retract the flaps fully. Consider, however, that this speed usually decreases with altitude and gross weight.

The salient point is that a go-around rarely is difficult or problematical when initiated soon enough. Failing to recognize the need and delaying initiation of the maneuver usually are most responsible for this kind of accident.

Being aggressively safe is an attitude, a conscious awareness of all the available options and the willingness to employ them. It means not being intimidated into doing something that poses a threat to safety. It means going around when landing conditions are not satisfactory. It means you are in command.

PREVENTING WHEELBARROW LANDINGS

There are more than 2,000 landing accidents in the U.S. every year. These are of four basic types. The first is the overrun, which most often is the result of excessive approach speed and altitude, too short a runway, a slick surface, brake-system failure, a downwind or downhill landing, wind shear, optical illusions, indecision, or the compulsive determination to land, even when conditions are unsuitable.

The second type of landing accident, the underrun, usually is caused by wind shear, downdrafts near the approach end of the runway, power failure, optical illusions, or inadequate airspeed and altitude on final approach.

The majority of over- and underruns could have been avoided by the timely recognition that all was not as it should have been, followed immediately by a go-around (when operating VFR) or a missed approach (when operating IFR).

Gear-up accidents comprise the third type of landing accident. They are caused by system failure, distraction, and forgetfulness.

The fourth type of landing accident occurs when a pilot loses control, such as when he is unable to cope with a crosswind or when he allows the aircraft to ground loop.

Ground loop?! The mere mention of the word conjures up the mental image of a taildragger pirouetting out of control. Few pilots envision a tricycle-gear airplane misbehaving in such a way because of the misconception that such aircraft are immune to ground looping. Unfortunately, the accident records prove otherwise. Ground-looping accidents in tri-gear airplanes are not rarities. Although some aircraft are more prone than others, virtually every type—including large multiengine aircraft—can be made to ground loop when sufficiently mishandled.

A ground loop in a tri-gear aircraft almost always is the result of wheelbarrowing—a situation where the main tires lift off the runway and force the nosewheel to support more than its share of aircraft weight. The resultant instability is similar to that of a wheelbarrow rolling on its nosewheel while being supported and pushed from behind. Anyone who has ever used a wheelbarrow knows how little side force is required for the wheelbarrow to begin heading off in one direction or the other.

An airplane most frequently behaves like a wheelbarrow during an attempt to land on a short field with an excess of airspeed or groundspeed (such as when landing downwind). As the aircraft crosses the boundary, the pilot reduces the sink rate and begins to flare for landing. But since speed is excessive, the flare consumes considerable distance and seems to take forever. The remaining runway length shrinks rapidly, and the pilot begins to sense that he had better get the aircraft on the ground before running out of runway. So instead of biting the bullet and pulling up, he impatiently and erringly pushes forward on the control wheel and forces the aircraft to land either nosewheel first or in a three-point attitude. The pilot exerts additional forward pressure on the wheel to prevent the aircraft from becoming airborne due to its excessive airspeed.

With the nosewheel supporting most of the weight and the lowered elevator holding the tail high, the main-gear tires barely touch the runway, if at all.

The first indications of a problem are loss of braking effectiveness and pronounced skipping of the main-gear tires. When these occur, the risk of an overrun can be almost as great as if the airplane had been held in the flare to dissipate excess airspeed.

Although wheelbarrowing can lead to an overrun, the greatest potential for hazard is the subsequent loss of directional control.

The tricycle-gear airplane is directionally stable when on the ground because the main-gear tires, which are behind the aircraft's center of gravity, offer substantial resistance to sideways movement. This is demonstrated easily by pushing against the fuselage of a parked airplane at some point above the main landing gear. The aluminum surface probably will give before the airplane can be moved. It is this sideways resistance to yaw that makes the airplane directionally stable on the ground.

Now assume that an imaginary crane has been used to hoist the tail of the same aircraft so that the main tires no longer touch the ground. It then would be possible to yaw the aircraft by pushing against the fuselage with only the force of a fingertip. With the main tires so lightly loaded (or completely unloaded), the aircraft becomes at least as directionally unstable as a taildragger with a swiveling tailwheel.

If an airplane is allowed to wheelbarrow with the main tires barely touching the surface, it cannot tolerate any side forces. Consequently, a crosswind, the use of nosewheel steering, or bumping into a clump of dirt is all that might be necessary to cause the aircraft to shoot off the runway and ground loop like a wheelbarrow out of control. Once the ground loop begins, the pilot might not have the skill or the presence of mind to regain control before something breaks.

A ground loop is rarely fatal and seldom injurious to those inside. It can, however, bruise a pilot's ego and create an expensive embarrassment. Depending on the severity of the maneuver, a pilot might have to replace a damaged nosewheel strut, a collapsed landing-gear leg, bent engine mounts, a buckled fire wall, an out-of-balance crankshaft, or a twisted propeller. If centrifugal force is sufficient to roll the aircraft onto its outboard wing tip, throw in a new wing.

Structural damage can result from wheelbarrowing that does not lead to a ground loop. If the main-gear tires are lightly loaded (barely touching the runway), a sufficient side force, generated by any strong tendency of the aircraft to yaw, can damage or fail a main-landing-gear assembly because of excessive side loading.

Although wheelbarrowing can occur in any type of tri-gear airplane—including jet transports—some aircraft have more of a tendency to wheelbarrow than others. Those with stabilators instead of elevators, for example, are the easiest to wheelbarrow. This is because stabilators usually are more effective than elevators and, therefore, are more capable of lifting the tail during a ground roll at high airspeed.

Everything else being equal, aircraft with fully swiveling nosewheels have less of a tendency to ground loop than those with steerable nosewheels. Both types, however, have similar propensities toward wheelbarrowing.

Wheelbarrowing is most likely when landing with flaps extended fully and a relatively forward center of gravity. With flaps down, the wing's center of lift moves aft. This, combined with a forward center of gravity, makes it easier for the horizontal tail surfaces to lift the main tires off the runway. The tendency to wheelbarrow also is increased by heavy braking, which creates a nose-down pitching moment and relieves the load on the main-gear tires.

Wheelbarrowing is most hazardous when operating on an irregular or slick surface in the presence of a crosswind or strong gusts.

Considering how easy it is to avoid wheelbarrowing, it is surprising that it is a cause of landing accidents in the first place. If touchdown occurs without an excess of airspeed in a nose-high attitude and with the control wheel held well aft of neutral, wheelbarrowing is almost impossible. It does occur most frequently when a pilot bungles the approach by coming in too hot or too high. Instead of executing a go-around, he prematurely forces the aircraft onto the ground and hopes to salvage a poor approach with what could turn out to be an even worse landing. If an improperly flown approach precludes the possibility of a normal landing, another attempt should be considered mandatory. It is almost axiomatic that a safe landing generally is the result of an accurate, stabilized approach. If airport conditions make a normal landing seem unlikely, consider landing elsewhere.

If heavy braking is required after landing, simultaneously bring the control wheel aft and hold it there until braking no longer is required. This not only prevents wheelbarrowing, but increases braking effectiveness. By unloading the nosewheel, most of the aircraft weight is transferred to the main wheels where it belongs. This helps the deceleration process, because braking is improved by adding weight to those wheels equipped with brakes. (This advice does not necessarily apply when operating one of those few aircraft equipped with nosewheel brakes.)

If an aircraft begins to wheelbarrow, the pilot can recover by simultaneously easing back on the control wheel, releasing the brakes, and retracting the flaps. As soon as the recovery is complete, apply brakes as necessary while holding the control wheel aft.

Some sources recommend recovery by executing a rejected landing (a go-around) following touchdown. It is wise not to attempt this unless performance, remaining runway length, and obstacle clearance provide a safe margin. And since wheelbarrowing often is a result of not having enough runway left upon which to make a normal landing, the wisdom of attempting a rejected landing has dubious merit. Besides, if a crunch is inevitable, it usually is much safer to accept a landing accident at relatively low speed than an impact that occurs while attempting to take off or climb at relatively high speed.

Also, adding power while wheelbarrowing might compound

the problem—especially if the control wheel is not brought aft simultaneously. This is because the added propwash increases tail effectiveness and lifting power (except in T-tail aircraft), which can exacerbate wheelbarrowing.

After the throttle(s) is retarded, an aborted takeoff becomes a landing roll. Some have learned the hard way not to shove the control wheel forward during an abort because this can lead to wheelbarrowing.

It may come as a surprise, but wheelbarrowing can and does occur during takeoff. This is particularly hazardous because the aircraft is accelerating, and the potential for injury is greater than when a loss of control occurs while decelerating. And, yes, ground loops can occur during a mishandled takeoff run.

The cause of wheelbarrowing during takeoff is the same as when landing: Too much forward pressure is applied to the control wheel, and the main tires slowly unload as the wing develops lift (especially with flaps partially extended). The phenomenon might begin to occur at less of an airspeed during takeoff than landing due to the increased lifting power of the horizontal tail surfaces and inboard wing panels caused by propwash.

One may wonder why a pilot would apply nose-down elevator during takeoff. There are several reasons—not all of which are without some logic.

Many pilots, for instance, apply substantial forward pressure on the wheel when taking off from a slick runway under the influence of a strong crosswind. The reasoning behind this technique claims that the increased weight on the nosewheel improves tire traction and enhances nosewheel steering during such adverse conditions.

Unfortunately, this has led to some serious wheelbarrowing and loss of directional control (including runway excursions in airplanes both large and small). Contributing to the wheelbarrow tendency is the aileron correction normally applied during a crosswind takeoff. With a left crosswind, for instance, the control wheel is turned left during the takeoff roll. This increases the lift on the right wing and partially unloads the right main tire, which could cause a premature onset of wheelbarrowing on that side.

Holding forward pressure on the control wheel seldom is justifiable. A proficient pilot should be capable of keeping the aircraft pointed along the runway centerline by the proper application of aileron, rudder, and nosewheel steering. If directional control cannot be maintained in this manner, the takeoff should be aborted before the option no longer is available.

Some pilots hold the control wheel forward during takeoff simply to build airspeed above and beyond that required for normal rotation. They believe that additional speed equates to added safety. This philosophy is popular with many multiengine pilots who prefer to exceed minimum-controllable airspeed (on one engine) by a large margin prior to committing themselves to flight.

Although there is some merit to this, it does not outweigh the hazards that can ensue. And just because a pilot has been employing such a procedure successfully does not mean that he necessarily will continue to survive it. A slight variation in conditions may be all that is necessary to induce wheelbarrowing and a loss of control. There are techniques recommended by the manufacturer of each aircraft, and these should be regarded seriously before ignoring them in favor of others that have not been proven safer.

Wheelbarrowing and its potential consequences also occur during conventional touch-and-go landings. During the approach (especially when the flaps are fully deployed), considerably more nose-up trim is used than will be required for the subsequent takeoff. After touchdown, in their zeal to prevent the nose from rising prematurely after power is applied, some pilots are overly aggressive about applying nose-down elevator pressure. They literally shove the control wheel against the forward stops. This, of course, can be a perfect setup for wheelbarrowing.

There is no need to apply such a strong nose-down pitching moment, especially if the tail surfaces are in the path of prop-wash. Even if wheelbarrowing does not occur, such misuse of the elevator can overstress the nosegear strut or cause a weak tire to fail.

During a touch-and-go landing, apply only whatever forward control pressure is required to maintain the desired attitude. (As the trim is repositioned, forward pressure on the control wheel can be relaxed.) Overcontrolling can result in too much of a good thing.

There may come a time—such as when confronted with an inescapable and potentially disastrous overrun—when it might be desirable to intentionally ground loop. This is because such an emergency maneuver might offer less potential for injury than plunging headlong into an obstacle or falling into a ravine at the end of the runway. Numerous fatal overruns occur every year (some are the result of forced landings) that could have been avoided by the timely execution of at least a ground-loop entry.

To attempt an intentional ground loop, close the throttle(s) and apply full nose-down elevator. To take advantage of the weathervaning effect of whatever crosswind might be present, apply maximum upwind rudder and brake (left rudder and left brake in a left crosswind, for instance). Simultaneously apply full opposite aileron. The adverse yaw effect created by the deflected ailerons helps to yaw the aircraft into the wind, while the opposite-direction rolling movement assists centrifugal force in tipping the aircraft onto its outboard wing tip.

All of this might result in bending some metal, but lives might be saved in the process.

Unintentional wheelbarrowing and ground looping in tricycle-gear aircraft almost always can be avoided through the proper use of the flight controls. Regard the main-gear tires as the primary weight supporters and the nosewheel as only a steering device. Operating an aircraft in this manner can go a long way toward preventing it from throwing you for a loop.

CRASH LANDINGS

One of aviation's popular adages defines a good landing as one from which a pilot can walk away. This simplistic attitude originated when engines were no more reliable than a politician's promise and emergency landings occurred with predictable regularity. Today, however, engines usually drone on without interruption, and the adage has become anachronistic. More often than not, it is used to console someone who has made an embarrassingly poor landing.

Unfortunately, emergency landings still occur for mechanical or pilot-induced reasons. According to the NTSB, one of every four general aviation accidents is associated with an emergency landing.

Emergency landings fall into two basic categories. One is the precautionary landing. It is considered less hazardous because a pilot has elected to land (on or off an airport) instead of continuing into what are perceived to be worsening conditions. Power is available, and this allows some choice of landing sites.

The other is the forced landing—more ominous because a pilot is compelled to land (usually without power), and the available landing sites are more limited.

When engine power no longer is available, a pilot will attempt to glide to a dirt road, a farmer's field, or even an airport. But because of fate or poor planning, the landing often must be made on more hostile terrain. A pilot then is faced with an emergency landing of the worst kind. Airframe damage is probable and the threat to life, substantial.

Crash landing is a grim prospect, but pilots should take some comfort in knowing that such an emergency usually is survivable. By being forearmed with the proper attitude and the understanding of some of the basic principles involved, a pilot usually can expect to make a landing from which he and his passengers can walk away.

When any in-flight emergency occurs, a pilot has two immediate obligations: maintain control of the aircraft and attend to the cause of the emergency, in that order. If the problem cannot be corrected and the emergency dictates an untimely descent, the pilot must immediately shift mental gears and deal with the crisis. Although this sounds logical, it is not unusual for a pilot confronted with a genuine emergency to initially reject reality; he is reluctant to accept the emergency. He becomes mentally paralyzed and subconsciously desires to alter the facts. This interferes with his ability to adapt to the circumstances and leads to wasted time and possibly to errors that further compound the emergency.

Consider the victim of an engine failure on takeoff who, in his zeal to protect the aluminum, turns back to the departure runway from too low an altitude or attempts illogically to stretch a glide, so as to avoid landing on rugged terrain. Such maneuvering often leads to graver consequences, such as a stall/spin accident.

It has been demonstrated that a pilot who accepts an emergency and takes command of both the airplane and his emotions has a much-improved prospect for survival, no matter how dire the circumstances appear. This admittedly is easier said than done.

Anyone who drives an automobile is reminded frequently that speed kills. In reality, speed alone does not kill: It is the extremely rapid dissipation of speed that does, especially when one is driving or flying headlong into an immovable object. In other words, the potentially destructive forces present during a crash landing are determined by the groundspeed at touchdown *and* the distance used while coming to a halt.

The extent to which excessive speed contributes to injury often is not appreciated fully. This is because the potential for disaster increases with the square of the impact speed. A crash at 71 knots, for example, is twice as dangerous as one at 50 knots; it is three times safer to crash at 50 than at 87 knots.

This indicates that touchdown should be made into the wind

(if possible) and at as low an airspeed as will still allow adequate control of the airplane.

The second factor in the emergency landing equation—stopping distance—also plays a key role. Survival depends on the obvious need to use as much distance as possible for deceleration. Although a few thousand feet of tarmac would satisfy this requirement nicely, such a luxury may not be available. Nor is it a necessity. In theory, very little stopping distance is required if groundspeed can be dissipated uniformly. This is because modern general aviation cockpit frames are designed to withstand up to nine Gs of forward deceleration.

For example, if an airplane touches down at 50 knots and decelerates uniformly at nine Gs, the required stopping distance is a remarkable 12.3 feet. Doubling groundspeed to 100 knots, however, quadruples the distance to 49.2 feet. These distances, however, have little practical value, because it is virtually impossible for a pilot to control deceleration so precisely. There simply are too many variables that influence stopping distance. And, although the cockpit structure might be able to withstand such a shock, those rattling around inside probably cannot.

When confronted with having to land and decelerate within a very short distance, a pilot obviously cannot rely on the wheel brakes. He must be willing to sacrifice some or all of the airplane's dispensable structures and use them as shock absorbers. The techniques to use vary with the terrain, and this makes it extremely difficult to offer specific advice. One of the best known involves aiming the nose of an airplane between two trees during runout. This may shear the wings from the fuselage, but a considerable amount of destructive energy and speed will be dissipated in the process. Landing distance is reduced substantially before the airplane reaches something else (such as a cliff) that poses an even greater threat. (Several years ago, a student pilot applied this technique quite successfully. The only problem was that the two trees he headed for were the only obstacles on an otherwise flat, 80-acre field.)

There are, of course, numerous other options, such as intentional ground looping; landing with the wheels up (when possible) to reduce rolling distance; landing with the wheels down to allow the gear to be broken off by rocks (which act as shock absorbers that help to dissipate forward speed); and aiming for soft spots (such as brush, bushes, or small trees) that offer reasonably good cushioning and braking effects.

The point is that a pilot must use his wits and be prepared to sacrifice dispensable airplane structure to absorb speed and destructive energy, while keeping the cabin intact. Only in extreme circumstances should the nose of the airplane be allowed to hit a solid object.

It was mentioned earlier that touchdown should be made as slowly as possible, but not so slowly as to sacrifice controllability. Insufficient airspeed invites a stall, an excessive sink rate, and an impact with the ground in a nose-low attitude, factors that can reduce to nil the probability of survival. Touchdown requires a minimal sink rate to reduce the possibility of creating vertical Gs. Although the rigid bottom construction (especially of low-wing airplanes) might sustain such a shock, the frail, human vertebrae may not. The backbone is very intolerant of such abuse. When landing on soft terrain such as a dry, sandy beach, an excessive sink rate may also cause the nose to dig in and cause extreme forward deceleration.

(Simulated forced landings occasionally lead to actual emergency landings at a high sink rate when the engine fails to respond immediately to throttle movement. Automatically raising the nose without waiting for power to develop can result in a hair-raising rate of descent. During any go-around or missed approach, maintain a safe attitude and airspeed until power really is available.)

An emergency landing on rugged terrain also should be made with the wings parallel to the ground and the aircraft in a somewhat nose-high attitude. Every effort must be made to prevent the nose from burrowing into the ground or hitting a solid object. In addition to excessive deceleration, a nose-low attitude can cause the airplane to tumble.

There is evidence that indicates that low-wing airplanes are the more crashworthy. This is because they usually have more structure (in the form of wing spars) beneath the cockpit to absorb destructive forces and are less likely to nose over. High-wing airplanes generally are more top-heavy because of the high-wing structure and fuel in the wing tanks. Consequently, they are more prone to flipping and cartwheeling.

Almost as important as the touchdown technique is the need to prepare the cockpit and those aboard for the crisis. If there are any empty rearward-facing seats, have passengers sit in these, because they generally offer the most protection during a crash landing. Be certain that everyone cinches his lap belt and shoulder harness as snugly as possible and that he knows how to unlatch them after the airplane comes to rest. If any clothing or pillows are available, place these between the control wheels and those seated up front. Pilots often are killed or seriously injured by control wheels puncturing their chest cavities during otherwise survivable landings. If practical, and time permits, also cover other sharp objects in the cockpit with clothing. Those persons in front might consider sliding their seats as far aft as possible to reduce the risk of having their heads flung into the panel during post-touchdown deceleration.

A controversial subject involves the cockpit (or cabin) door. Some maintain that it should be kept closed until after the landing to help preserve the integrity of the cabin structure, thereby offering more protection for those inside. Others, myself included, prefer unlatching the door prior to touchdown, as long as this does not interfere with airplane controllability. An unlatched door better ensures the ability to evacuate after the airplane comes to rest. A fuselage deformed during a crash landing could jam a closed door and prevent it from being opened without a crowbar.

Other prelanding duties might include transmitting an

emergency message to a nearby facility, tuning the transponder to the emergency squawk (7700), turning on the emergency locater transmitter (if possible), and making handy any available emergency equipment (such as a fire extinguisher) that might be needed immediately after landing. Also turn off the electric master switch prior to touchdown to reduce the likelihood of a post-crash fire. Do not do this, however, until you are assured that electrical power no longer is needed to operate vital aircraft systems (such as flaps and landing gear).

Although the magnetos and fuel valve(s) also should be turned off prior to impact (to cool the engine and further reduce the fire hazard), do not be in a hurry to do this if some engine power is available. Even a modicum of power can vary the descent path enough to allow a wider choice of landing sites.

If possible, choose a landing area that allows an uphill, upwind touchdown and has an approach path relatively free of obstacles. It often is better to accept landing on rugged terrain than to risk flying into an obstruction. Once a landing area has been chosen, avoid vacillating and selecting another unless you are certain that the alternate is within glide range, can be reached without excessive maneuvering at low altitude, and offers a safer haven. It usually is preferable to accept a controlled landing on inhospitable terrain than to risk crashing uncontrollably in a stall while trying to stretch a glide to a more inviting, yet excessively distant, piece of ground.

The nature of terrain can play a key role in determining the application of other useful techniques. Although it would be presumptuous to attempt to provide advice for all possibilities, the following guidelines may be helpful.

- If the landing site is extremely confined, it might be advisable to force the airplane to contact the ground prematurely with some excessive airspeed rather than to risk floating and delaying touchdown. Deceleration is much better on the ground than in the air, and this can reduce substantially the speed at which obstacles at the far end of the "runway" may be met.

- A landing on the shallow edge of a body of water generally is more survivable than a landing on adjacent, rugged ground.
- If landing on a beach, do so on the moist, hard-packed sand below the high-tide mark. At high tide, land in the water immediately below the high-tide mark to avoid the risk of nosing over in the higher, drier, softer sand.
- Unless wind is a strong overriding factor, it usually is best to land in a swift-moving stream or river in the direction of the current. This reduces groundspeed (or water speed) and the potential for damage and injury. If the river is extremely shallow, however, and the belly of the airplane will touch down on what amounts to a bed of rocks, land upwind.
- When landing on a large expanse of water or snow or in such limited visibility that depth perception may be a problem, do so without a significant flare. Otherwise, you risk stalling high above the ground and a potentially lethal pitching down of the nose.
- Mountainous terrain offers extreme challenges to someone so unfortunate as to have to attempt a forced landing there. At such a time, it often is useful to maintain some additional airspeed with which to alter the glide path of the airplane so as to match that of the upslope gradient upon which the landing might be made. Avoid touching down on terrain that has a severe lateral twist because this could snap roll the airplane into an adjacent gulley.
- Landing in a forest is not an attractive prospect, either. Successful tree landings require gliding into the higher branches at slightly above stall speed and in a nose-high attitude. The goal is to have both wings and the belly make simultaneous contact with the crowns. Avoid widely spaced, tall trees, because the aircraft is likely to drop from an uncomfortable height after forward speed dissipates. (A free-fall from 75 feet

can result in an impact velocity of 4,000 fpm.) Short, closely spaced trees with dense crowns offer the best hope.

- Perhaps the most ominous predicament is the powerless glide at night to terrain smothered in zero-zero fog. There is little to do except fly the aircraft upwind in a wings-level attitude while maintaining the minimum airspeed and sink rate consistent with controllability. Some airplanes do this best with a slight deflection of flap, but avoid a full-flap descent. Although this allows a slightly slower forward speed, the accompanying high sink rate is unacceptable.

Someone with a bizarre sense of humor once remarked that a pilot in such a dilemma should turn on the landing lights before landing. "If he doesn't like what he sees, turn 'em off."

It can be sobering and uncomfortable to review the procedures that might be employed if and when fate's finger points your way toward a crash landing. Perhaps the most valuable lesson to be extracted from all of this is that those who plan their flights with respect to the terrain and modify their routes accordingly probably have the least to fear.

TO SPIN OR NOT TO SPIN

The Los Angeles *Times* recently carried an article that was highly critical of current pilot certification requirements. The one-sided story essentially contained the sentiments of Tony LeVier, former Lockheed chief test pilot, who believes that although "pilots are taught to avoid emergencies, they are not required to learn how to stabilize an aircraft that is out of control."

LeVier also was quoted as saying that "there are people flying commercial airliners who have never been upside down in an airplane. But an airplane flies in three axes (sic), and God help these pilots who get into a stall or a spin."

LeVier obviously favors spin training for general aviation pilots, a topic of controversy that has been dormant in recent years.

Although most aircraft are capable of spinning, only flight instructor applicants are required to have spin training. This is because spins were deleted from pilot certification requirements in 1949. Since an airplane cannot spin unless first stalled, it was believed that the stall/spin accident rate could be reduced by shifting the training emphasis to the prevention of and recovery from power-on and power-off stalls. The elimination of spin training was intended also to be an incentive for manufacturers to develop spin-resistant aircraft, according to Civil Air Regulation (CAR) Amendment 20-3, which was adopted by the Civil Aeronautics Administration (CAA) on June 15, 1949 (the date spins were deleted from pilot certification requirements).

The emphasis on stall training seems to have had a beneficial effect. During the four-year period preceding the deletion of spin training, stall/spin accidents accounted for almost half of all fatal accidents. In recent years, they account for one-fourth.

Spin-training proponents point out, however, that there are still 140 spin accidents every year. They also claim that spin accidents have an 80-percent fatality rate, which is greater than for any other type of accident, including midair collisions.

Knowing how to recover from spins would not necessarily prevent these accidents, because fewer than 5 percent of all spin accidents begin high enough to allow sufficient altitude for spin recovery. Those fortunate enough to survive a spin accident usually do not even realize they have spun, and recall only a mushing yaw prior to impact. One can only speculate about the accidents that were averted and never became statistics because the pilots did have the altitude and proficiency needed to effect a timely recovery.

In the early 1980s, there was a proposal to reintroduce spin training. The General Aviation Manufacturers Association (GAMA), representing the airframe manufacturers, opposed this proposal in favor of the development of non-spinnable designs. Although there has been some encouraging research in this area, the goal remains elusive. In reality, the development of high-performance aircraft has resulted in spin characteristics less favorable than those associated with predecessor aircraft. (It has been suggested that GAMA's reluctance to support spin training was due to the negative impact this ultimately might have had on aircraft sales.)

At least one manufacturer favors spin training. Schweizer Aircraft says, in the *Schweizer Soaring School Manual*, "Since all aircraft can be spun, it is important that students be taught to spin and recover before solo."

William K. Kershner, author of several popular flight training manuals, has taught all of his students to spin because he believes that this best demonstrates the conditions that lead to inadvertent spins. He also believes that such training builds a student's confidence and reduces his anxiety.

Although Kershner advocates spin training (he has done 6,000 spins, 4,000 with students), he fears that most "flight instructors aren't ready. If there was an edict that spin training would begin at noon tomorrow, the accident rate would become impressive indeed." Kershner admires "the courage of a flight instructor who has been signed off with perhaps a half-turn spin in each direction—and no aerobatic training—who is out there with students who could get him into situations for which he has neither the knowledge nor the skill to recover."

Some instructors confess privately that they have *never* spun an airplane despite the spin endorsements etched in their logbooks.

Jack J. Eggspuehler, president of the National Association of Flight Instructors, believes that the current generation of instructors attempting to teach spins would be "like the blind leading the blind." He shudders at the thought of "how many instructors and students would have to be picked up in the fields if spin training were to be reintroduced."

Unlike Kershner, Eggspuehler generally opposes spin training and believes, like the FAA, that if "we maintain an adequate margin above stall, we certainly will avoid the spin." He says that it is contradictory to tell students to avoid deep stalls and spins and then go out and show them how to perform these maneuvers.

There is no doubt that stall avoidance precludes the possibility of spinning. Those who favor spin training concede that if pilots could avoid the inadvertent stall, spin training would be unnecessary. According to accident statistics, however, current training standards appear far from meeting that goal. Stall/spin accidents continue to occur.

Some fear that a reintroduction of spin training would encourage pilots, either unwittingly or otherwise, to spin unsuitable aircraft. This alone could result in an alarming increase in the stall/spin and structural-failure accident rates. This is because many pilots may not understand the reasons certain airplanes are not approved for spins.

To begin with, Normal category airplanes are not certified for spinning, and anyone who does so intentionally is flirting with aerodynamic disaster. Anyone spinning an aircraft placarded against spins should assume that the aircraft will become uncontrollable.

Those opposed to spin training point out that it does little good for a pilot to know how to recover from a spin in one type of aircraft if the procedure is not effective in another.

The truth is that a Normal category airplane may or may not be recoverable. Such aircraft do undergo spin testing prior to certification, but the factory test pilot needs to demonstrate only a one-turn spin in each direction and recover within one additional turn. Beyond this, no one knows how the aircraft might behave; it is unexplored territory. The aircraft might be docile and responsive, or it might be uncontrollable. Nor do we know how difficult it might have been for the test pilot to conform to the one-turn spin requirement. Consequently, the FAA regards such tests only as an investigation of aircraft behavior during a delayed stall recovery.

Aircraft approved for spinning include all aerobatic aircraft and those in the Utility category that meet the Aerobatic category spin requirements. These requirements are substantially more rigorous than those required for Normal category aircraft.

Pilots who spin approved aircraft are not altogether home free. Unless the aircraft is loaded within the weight and balance limits specified in the pilot's operating handbook (POH), there is no assurance of satisfactory spin recovery. This is particularly true when the aft center-of-gravity limit is exceeded. At such a time, an airplane has less yaw stability, has less of a nose-down pitching moment, is capable of entering a deeper stall, and is more susceptible to the effects of centrifugal force while spinning. These factors may combine to flatten the spin, making recovery difficult if not impossible. Recovery from a conventional spin also might be difficult because of the limited rudder and elevator power available with an excessively aft center of gravity.

There are some aircraft that are difficult to spin intentionally. Paradoxically, some of these are most prone to spinning *unintentionally* and the most difficult in which to effect recovery.

A spin is a complicated maneuver involving simultaneous roll, pitch, and yaw rates, with large side-slip angles, during which an airplane (or glider) descends rapidly (5,000 to 10,000 feet per minute is typical) in a helical movement about its vertical axis at a stalling angle of attack of as much as 90 degrees; rotation rates of up to 300 degrees per second are not uncommon.

A spin begins when one or both wings stall and the aircraft "departs," which is the uncommanded motion that takes place between a stall and a recognizable spin. Departure is the beginning of the incipient phase, that portion of the maneuver that lasts until the spin becomes relatively stable. This incipient phase usually takes about two rotations. The second, or steady, phase is recognizable by a relatively constant and slow airspeed accompanied by a nearly constant altitude loss per turn and a nearly constant rotation rate; roll, pitch, and yaw acceleration is virtually nil. The steady phase lasts until the third, or recovery, phase is begun. Recovery begins when rotation stops and airspeed increases or when the maneuver is interrupted by a less desirable event.

As mentioned, a spin can develop only when one or both wings stall. Assume that during a conventional, wings-level stall, the airplane begins to roll left. As the left wing descends, its angle of attack becomes larger. This is because the relative wind "comes up" to meet the wing at a larger angle. Ordinarily, an increase in angle of attack increases lift and helps to restore a wings-level attitude, a form of lateral stability. But since the wing is stalled, the larger angle of attack results in a deeper stall, less lift, and more drag for that wing. In other words, the more the wing drops, the more it wants to drop, a definite form of instability.

Conversely, the right wing is rising and its angle of attack becomes smaller. Such a decrease in angle of attack usually decreases lift to assist in restoring a wings-level attitude. Not so in this case. Since the right wing also was stalled, a decrease in angle of attack causes the wing to develop more lift (and less drag) than when the wing was stalled. In other words, the right wing, which is rising, wants to rise farther.

Now we have an aircraft that has begun to roll and has become so laterally unstable that the roll rate continues to increase. Consider the effect of the added drag created by the descending left wing and the reduced drag on the rising right wing. This difference in drag creates a yaw to the left. (Other factors, which include weathervaning and a difference between the alignment of the lift vectors of each wing, also contribute to the leftward yaw).

In the case described, yaw is a result of roll. Similar dynamics occur when roll is a result of yaw that occurs (intentionally or otherwise) during a stall. It matters not which comes first—the roll or the yaw—because once the process of spin entry begins, it continues automatically, which helps to explain why spinning is called autorotation. The spin motions continue to accelerate until aerodynamic, gyroscopic, and inertial forces and moments reach a state of equilibrium.

But what is a pilot most likely to do when the aircraft begins to roll inadvertently during a stall? Based on currently taught methods of stall recovery, he will apply coordinated aileron and rudder opposite to the direction of roll. (If he reverts to habitual aileron-and-rudder usage, he probably will apply more aileron than rudder.)

Now consider the consequence of such aileron input. If the left wing is falling and the control wheel is moved right, the left aileron will deflect downward and increase the angle of attack of the left wing even farther, which can drive the wing into a deeper stall. Additionally, the adverse yaw effect resulting from such a control input strengthens the yaw that drives the aircraft into the spin.

Is the procedure recommended for stall recovery a form of negative training that increases the likelihood of an inadvertent spin? Many instructors think so and propose reexamining the practice of aileron usage during stall recovery. They believe that pilots should be taught to use aggressive rudder input to counter undesirable rolling or yawing during stall recovery. If the nose is held in place and prevented from yawing, the aircraft cannot spin.

It would be convenient if a universal spin-recovery procedure were suitable for all aircraft. There is no such animal. The best procedure available for a particular aircraft is in the POH. One recovery procedure, the NASA standard, is the one most often recommended and is given here to provide general guidance:

- Recovery should be effected with the flaps retracted. The wake turbulence from extended flaps can erode elevator and rudder effectiveness. Also, spin recovery ends with a high-speed dive that may damage extended flaps.
- Close the throttle(s). Engine power produces a nose-up

pitching moment that makes it more difficult to apply nose-down elevator, a step explained later. In extreme cases, power produces such a strong pitch-up moment that the aircraft can be driven into a flat spin from which recovery may be impossible. Also, power produces excess airspeed during the dive following spin recovery.

An exception concerns spinning in multiengine aircraft. Power from the inboard engine can be used along with rudder (explained later) to arrest spin rotation. A pilot probably is better off not using power at all for this purpose because, during the confusion, he might inadvertently increase power from the wrong engine, which will tighten the spin's grip. Besides, most spins in multiengine aircraft occur in the direction of the dead engine as a result of stalling with asymmetric power.

- The ailerons should be neutralized. Applying aileron opposite to spin rotation might be tempting but can increase the rotation rate because of adverse yaw. (This method is used by aerobatic pilots to transition into a flat spin. In this regime of flight, rotation rate increases, the nose rises, the wings level somewhat, and the angles of attack of both wings increase to between 45 and 90 degrees. At this point, rotation consists mostly of yaw, and the rudder and elevator become partially or completely ineffective.)

- Apply full rudder opposite to the direction of spin rotation. This may not be immediately effective in arresting rotation because the horizontal stabilizer/elevator combination may partially blanket the rudder (except in T-tail aircraft). If in doubt about which rudder pedal to push (yes, a spin can be that bewildering), refer to the turn needle or turn coordinator indicator (not the slip-skid ball) and push opposite to the direction of indicated yaw. Lacking any of these clues, try pushing on the pedal offering the greatest resistance.

- As rotation begins to slow (or shortly after applying rudder), briskly neutralize the elevator to unstall the wings. Do not apply nose-down elevator prior to applying rudder because this can increase the rotation rate. Also, excessive and prolonged forward pressure while still autorotating can tuck the aircraft into an inverted spin. This can be so disorienting that a pilot may not be able to recover at all. At such a time, a pilot might be best advised merely to release all flight controls and allow the airplane to recover by itself. This is not as farfetched as it might seem. Most aircraft will recover from a spin as soon as the pilot relinquishes control (or lack of it).

Interestingly, spin disorientation is most common in closed-cockpit airplanes. When spinning an open-cockpit airplane, a pilot usually can see the horizon. But when spinning a closed-cockpit airplane, the horizon cannot be seen as easily. This condition not only contributes to spin disorientation, but also makes the nose-down attitude seem steeper than it is in reality.

- When rotation stops, neutralize the rudder. It is imperative that rudder neutralization not be delayed. If antispin rudder pressure is held after rotation stops and while the wings are still stalled, the aircraft simply may begin spinning in the opposite direction.

- As airspeed builds, recover conventionally from the resultant and probably steep dive. The amount of back pressure on the wheel must be sufficient to prevent excessive airspeed, yet not so much as to risk excessive Gs or an accelerated stall.

Although this recovery procedure works well in most light singles, additional procedures have been developed for aircraft with unusual design characteristics or mass distribution. Aircraft that have their mass concentrated in the fuselage (such as jet fighters) seem to recover best when ailerons are applied *in the direction of spin rotation*. Airplanes with substantial outboard mass (engines and large fuel tanks, for example) often respond best by applying nose-down elevator to arrest rotation. This is why the POH must take priority in determining the best way to recover from a spin in a given airplane.

Although the controversy regarding spin training may never be completely resolved, pilots have the luxury of settling the issue for themselves. Those pilots opposed need take no action; those in favor have the option of seeking out a qualified instructor and a suitable airplane. Learning firsthand the causes of spin entry and developing the proficiency needed to both avoid and recover from a spin can bring their own rewards.

DESERT FLYING

Historically, man has avoided the desert, a sun-seared, windswept, forbidding wasteland. There have been exceptions, of course, such as Bedouins, aborigines, and other desert dwellers who long ago adapted to the perils and discomfort of desert life. But those from moister climates have chosen to stay away—until recent times.

Airways and highways have made accessible the desert and its breathtaking geological formations, spectacular sunsets, and countless other displays of nature's splendor. Resorts such as Palm Springs and Las Vegas thrive in areas that once were considered uninhabitable. Recreational areas and national parks beckon visitors in ever-growing numbers. Even that stretch of scorched isolation known as Death Valley in California has become alluring to pilots wanting to escape the beaten path.

Those planning to fly the desert, however, should be aware of unique problems. Even when the destination is elsewhere, it's difficult to fly in the southwestern U.S. without crossing a part of the North American Desert. Of the world's 13 major deserts, it is the fifth largest and occupies more than a half-million square miles.

The word *desert* comes from Latin, means "abandoned," and is not a totally inaccurate description of much of the southwestern U.S. The desert contains numerous pockets of population, but these are fairly widespread, as are desert airports. Because of this and the hostility of the desert toward careless pilots. flight planning should be conducted with exceptional care.

Airways, for example, often are established without regard to the landscape. Blindly obeying needle deflections can lead a pilot over some of America's most rugged and inhospitable terrain. It often is wiser to follow major highways and railroad tracks. This may add distance to a flight, but is navigationally more reliable. Also, a long and lonely highway can be a welcome sight should an emergency landing become necessary.

Additionally, desert navaids often are few and far between. Because of this and the nature of the desert's often mountainous terrain, there are many areas where radio signals cannot be received. To place all your navigational eggs in this basket is risky. Stick to well-traveled ground routes.

While cowboy movies have led us to believe that the West consists of wide-open spaces, such is not the case for general aviation pilots. The military has absconded with large chunks of desert airspace, leaving behind a proliferation of restricted areas. These areas must be respected because within them lurk all manner of undetectable health hazards, such as ground-to-air artillery and missile activity.

Just because a restricted area is printed on the chart, however, does not mean that a pilot can't fly through it. If detouring is undesirable, check with a nearby Flight Service Station (FSS) or military facility to determine if the area is being used, or is "hot." When it is not in use, or is "cold," permission may be given to penetrate the area without restriction.

During the summer, it usually is preferable to fly the desert in the early morning or late afternoon. This is when thermal activity is either nil or relatively mild. During the midday hours, the desert floor can spawn teeth-rattling turbulence that rises to 15,000 feet or more.

Although turbulence penetration techniques were discussed in chapter 1, this is an opportune time to review the basic principles.

First, airspeed should be reduced in heavy turbulence to minimize the possibility of structural damage to the aircraft.

When in a strong updraft, do not lower the nose to maintain altitude: This could result in dangerously excessive penetration speeds. An updraft is beneficial; it gives something for nothing—altitude. So take advantage of the updraft and accept the gift graciously. This extra altitude may soon be needed because, just as night follows day, downdrafts follow updrafts.

When the updraft weakens and the pilot finds himself sinking helplessly in a downdraft, he should—again—not try to maintain altitude. The result of a climb attitude is an airspeed loss that could place the aircraft in jeopardy of stalling. Also, the application of climb power when flying slowly in the hot desert air can result in excessive oil and cylinder-head temperatures.

Trying to outclimb a strong downdraft is usually an exercise in futility because these downdrafts frequently have sink rates considerably in excess of an airplane's ability to climb. Also, the airspeed loss resulting from an attempted climb only delays passage through the downdraft and prolongs the agony.

When caught in a strong "sinker," resist habit. Accept the altitude loss and either maintain airspeed or lower the nose slightly to increase airspeed. This prevents engine overheating and enables passage through the downdraft in minimal time.

During the summer it is wise to fly reasonably high, not only to escape low-level turbulence, but also to keep the cabin cool and comfortable. Since it is not uncommon for desert surface temperatures to exceed 120°F (in the shade), it might be necessary to fly at least 14,000 feet agl to maintain a cabin temperature at 70°F—which is another argument for avoiding a midday flight. Parenthetically, the highest temperature ever recorded in the United States was 134°F (Furnace Creek in Death Valley, 1913).

Since there is so little moisture in the desert air to retain heat, surface temperatures can drop 60 degrees between midday and midnight. Also, do not venture into the night-clad desert without an IFR ticket in your hip pocket. After sunset, the desert floor can be the blackest black you'll ever experience, with ground lights few and far between. Combine this with a high overcast and it can be impossible to tell where the ground ends and the sky begins. Even experienced pilots avoid flying the night desert unless the moon is available to light the way and ease the strain of a VFR flight.

During their first desert flights, Easterners often are confused when trying to correlate terrain features with the symbols on their charts. Rivers and lakes never seem to appear as advertised. This is because newcomers expect to see water. Since a desert—by definition—receives less than 10 inches of rain annually, most desert lakes and rivers are dry nine to 10 months of the year; others are perennially arid.

A topographical chart is a pilot's most reliable navaid, especially if he can translate contour lines on the map to the terrain below, an essential skill when airways and highways are unavailable. Striking out across the desert without having something to follow requires either the instincts of a camel or some skillful dead-reckoning and an abundance of fuel.

A side note about dry lakes. Some can be used as emergency landing sites, but others may be too soft, too rough, or occasionally too wet. If the surface has a dark or brown complexion, the lake probably is wet. The safest place to land is near the edge of the lake. It's drier there, and adjacent terrain features (sagebrush, cacti) provide peripheral reference for judging height above the ground.

Rogers Dry Lake in southern California may qualify as the world's longest runway. Adjacent to Edwards Air Force Base, it is 12 miles long and is used regularly by NASA's experimental aircraft.

Desert weather is generally severely clear, but when a relatively moist, unstable air mass visits the summer desert, the result is a widespread forest of mushrooming, violent thunderstorms. Although summer storms can reach massive proportions, they generally are widespread and circumnavigable. Extreme caution, however, is required when threading through the desert under these conditions.

Early morning flying precludes a pilot from having to do battle with cumulonimbus clouds because these usually do not develop fully until shortly before noon. Once full-grown, desert thunderstorms can remain vigorous until well after midnight.

Fortunately, tornadoes are a rare desert occurrence, but the desert does have "twisters." Although dust devils are considerably smaller and less violent than tornadoes, they must be regarded with caution.

A tornado is born in the belly of a thunderstorm and grows downward. Dust devils, on the other hand, are not related to thunderstorm activity. They are caused by intense surface heating and grow from the ground upward.

Dust devils have the appearance of small tornadoes but are usually only 50 to 100 feet tall. It is not unusual to see a half dozen or more dancing across the desert, and during the summer they are so common as to seem a part of the landscape. On rare occasions, a desert twister matures into a full-blown sand pillar that can extend up to 1,000 feet agl (or higher) and must be avoided.

Since dust devils usually are small and hug the ground, they are a problem during arrivals and departures. Flight through a desert twister can place an airplane instantly out of control, but the difficulty usually is over before a pilot realizes what has happened—unless the encounter occurs during takeoff or landing. This can be disastrous and explains why some desert fliers prefer to land on unpaved runways where twisters can be seen more easily. When dust devils play tag on the runway, delay takeoff or landing until their frivolity takes them elsewhere.

Dust devils should be avoided while taxiing, too. Should one head your way, taxi in another direction, *pronto!* If an encounter is unavoidable, head the aircraft directly toward the twister and take it head on. Never allow one to overtake you from behind, since this can lift the tail of the aircraft and flip it on its back. This is rare, but it happens.

Another desert phenomenon is the sandstorm, a widespread affair that occurs when blustery surface winds lift enough sand to darken the skies. A sandstorm can extend for thousands of square miles and generate dense clouds of sand to heights of 10,000 feet or more. This type of storm obviously should be avoided because of turbulence, substantially reduced visibility, and the damage that sandblasting can do to an airplane and its engine.

Desert flying requires an intimate familiarity with the erosion of aircraft performance that results from increasing density altitude. Mountain fliers are aware of this problem because of the elevations at which they operate, but desert visitors frequently overlook the need to compute and compensate for density altitude because of the comparatively low elevations usually involved. But this oversight can be dangerous in the simmering heat of the summer desert.

Consider departing Las Vegas, Nevada, for example. The elevation of McCarran International Airport is only 2,200 feet msl (above sea level), but when the mercury hits 120 degrees F, the density altitude exceeds 6,400 feet. This doubles takeoff roll and decreases climb rate by almost 50 percent. (Consider also that the temperature immediately above the runway, which is not in the shade, is much higher than the reported temperature, which is measured in the shade.)

Some desert airports are above 5,000 feet msl. Combine this with 120 degrees of sizzling Fahrenheit and density altitude soars to 11,000 feet.

Figure 19 shows the relationship between density altitude, pressure altitude, and ambient temperature. But for those who prefer rules of thumb, there is a mental exercise that can be used to determine density altitude without computers or charts.

It is first necessary to determine the standard temperature for the elevation under consideration. As an example, consider an airport with a pressure altitude of 4,000 feet msl and an outside air temperature (OAT) of 105°F. The standard temperature at sea level is 59°F, and since the standard temperature decreases

Standard Temp.	Temp. Elevat.	80° F	90° F	100° F	110° F	120° F	130° F
59° F	Sea Level	1,200'	1,900'	2,500'	3,200'	3,800'	4,400'
52° F	2,000'	3,800'	4,400'	5,000'	5,600'	6,200'	6,800'
45° F	4,000'	6,300'	6,900'	7,500'	8,100'	8,700'	9,400'
38° F	6,000'	8,600'	9,200'	9,800'	10,400'	11,000'	11,600'
31° F	8,000'	11,100'	11,700'	12,300'	12,800'	13,300'	13,800'

FIGURE 19

3½°F (or 2°C) per 1,000 feet, the standard temperature at 4,000 feet must be 59°F − (4 × 3½°F), or 59°F − 14°F, or 45°F.

Now compare the standard temperature at 4,000 feet (45°F) with the actual temperature (105°F). The difference between them is 60°F.

Now the rule: For each 10°F that actual temperature exceeds standard temperature, add 600 feet to the elevation. In this case, actual temperature exceeds standard temperature by 60°F, which means that 3,600 feet (6 × 600) must be added to the field elevation (4,000 feet) to arrive at a density altitude of 7,600 feet.

This rule of thumb is reasonably accurate and produces a result rarely more than 200 feet in error. But once density altitude is determined, it is absolutely meaningless unless used to derive realistic performance data from the pilot's operating handbook for the aircraft being flown.

If a novice desert flier were to consult a grizzled veteran about desert operations, he would most likely be given the following tips about landing in the desert:

- Be careful about sloped runways. The desert is chock-full of them. A runway with an uphill gradient gives a pilot on approach the illusion of being too high, and the result is a tendency to undershoot. Conversely, a downhill gradient gives the pilot the illusion of being too low, and there's a resultant tendency to overshoot.
- On a hot day, strong thermals encountered during the approach can lead to an overshoot.
- But, on the other hand, an airplane tends to settle more rapidly in hot, thin air.
- As density altitude increases, true airspeed, and therefore, groundspeed, increases for any given indicated airspeed. So be careful about higher touchdown speeds.
- Use the same indicated airspeeds for takeoff and landing procedures as you would at lower density altitudes.
- Crystal-clear desert air makes objects seem closer than they really are and can lead to premature descents.
- On windy days, be careful about sudden wind shifts, a desert trademark.
- When the air is hot and dry, resist using carburetor heat, especially during touchdown and rollout. It is unnecessary and allows damaging, sand-filled air to enter the engine without being filtered.
- Don't refuel after landing; wait until you are ready to leave and know what the temperature will be and how it will affect performance. Then refuel and load accordingly.
- Secure the aircraft firmly, even during very short visits; the desert is notorious for sudden increases in surface wind.
- When using a portable tiedown kit, beware of screw-in de-

vices that are incapable of getting a firm grip in the soft desert soil (sand).

- When surface temperatures exceed 100°F, the temperature in the cockpit of an aircraft exposed to the sun can exceed 180° F. Park in the shade whenever possible.
- If parking in the shade is not possible, hide plastic computers and plotters from the direct rays of the sun; otherwise, these items may warp permanently.

Regarding departures, the desert pro might offer this advice:

- Consider a morning departure. Temperatures are lower, and density altitude is less of a problem.
- Prior to boarding, open all cockpit doors and windows and allow the cockpit to cool; otherwise, controls, switches, and seatbelt buckles may be so hot that operating them without gloves may be painful.
- When departing from an airport that does not have paved surfaces, avoid extending the flaps of a low-wing airplane until immediately before takeoff; extended flaps are easily damaged by pebbles picked up by the prop while the aircraft is taxiing and during engine runup.
- If the runup cannot be made on a clean, paved surface, perform it while in motion to prevent prop damage. (Use the brakes to keep the aircraft in check, however.)
- Unless conditions require it, avoid performing a functional check of the carburetor heat. This is to prevent ingestion of unfiltered air into the engine.
- Avoid prolonged runups that can overheat an engine.
- Be skillful at soft- and short-field takeoffs; these are frequent desert requirements.
- On hot days, it may be necessary to climb at higher-than-normal airspeeds to keep cylinder-head and oil temperatures within limits.
- If thermals are available, take advantage of them to gain altitude; avoid downdrafts (if possible) because of the deleterious effects they have on aircraft performance.

- If avionics fail to operate properly, the problem may be caused by transistors that have become too hot while parked in the sun; give them a chance to cool off.

Two of the most frequently neglected desert necessities are a survival kit and an adequate supply of drinking water. This point cannot be overemphasized, and sometimes it is necessary to resort to shock to drive home the point.

A most gruesome and painful death is caused by dehydration. Without water, a person stranded in the summer desert has a life expectancy of two days. But before being relieved of his misery, he resorts to drinking anything available—no matter how nauseating—including engine oil, fuel, and urine. Those with the intelligence to acknowledge the possibility—however slight—of a desert emergency can survive if prepared. A supplemental water supply and a filed flight plan are a desert pilot's best insurance.

The survival kit should contain at least a solar still, chapstick, a signal mirror, emergency rations, a first-aid kit, whistles, hats, sunglasses, sunburn lotion, salt tablets, clothing to protect against cold nights, matches, a knife, nylon rope, a flashlight, a survival manual, water, water, and more water.

Although this discussion emphasizes the problems unique to summer flying, pilots should realize that the desert tames considerably during the rest of the year. Spring and autumn are delightful seasons in which to enjoy and explore the magnificent desert. It is nature's kaleidoscope of wonders to see and things to do.

ADF SIMPLIFIED

If the automatic direction finder (ADF) were human, it would deserve considerable compassion. Poor bird dog, the ignored orphan of avionics, the forgotten stepchild of navigation. It is used more to entertain passengers with news and music than the purpose for which it was designed.

Pilots shy from ADF tracking because of the frequent mental computations usually required. They are discouraged by the way textbooks and instructors elaborate on the mathematical relationship between relative bearings, magnetic bearings, and magnetic headings. Besides, it's much easier to chase VOR (Very high frequency Omnidirectional Range) needles when cross-track winds are strong. Or is it?

Believe it or not, ADF navigation does not have to be a mind-boggling affair. By eliminating most of the arithmetic usually required, ADF usage can be pleasant and relaxing. But reducing ADF to such simplicity requires setting aside textbook navigation.

Assume, for example, that a pilot is about to fly 100 nautical miles to the remote town of Chutzpah. There are no FAA-approved navaids near the destination, but the town does boast an AM-band commercial broadcast station. After takeoff, the pilot tunes his ADF receiver to this station and turns the aircraft until the ADF needle points to the top of the dial; Chutzpah is now straight ahead.

What the pilot does not realize, however, is that a 30-knot, cross-track wind is drifting the aircraft to the right of course. As a result, the ADF needle moves gradually, yet persistently, to the left. Is this pilot concerned? Not at all. He simply turns toward the needle until it once again points straight ahead, repeating this corrective action as often as necessary. Eventually, he arrives directly over the station.

This is not ADF *tracking* because a specific course is not being maintained. The actual flight path consists of a curved line caused by wind drift. The pilot is using a technique known as homing.

Critics point to the inefficiency of homing because flying a curved track consumes more time and distance than the direct route. Agreed. But what they do not realize is that in most cases the additional time and distance are negligible.

Assume, for example, that the airplane in question cruises at 150 knots. With the assistance of an electronic computer, it can be shown that the pilot was subjected to a maximum cross-track deviation of 7.57 miles. This bulge in the track caused the total distance flown to increase by only 2.09 miles, resulting in a 102.09-mile flight that required 41.4 minutes. Flying the direct route would have taken 40.8 minutes. At a cost of only six-tenths of a minute (36 seconds), the pilot spared himself the mental gymnastics associated with ADF tracking.

When the crosswind component is less than 30 knots, the additional time required to "bird dog" a station is even less consequential. (And rarely do crosswind components exceed 30 knots.) Homing (instead of tracking) under the influence of a 20-knot crosswind, for example, adds only 18 seconds to the en route time. Also, homing frequently requires less total time and distance than the dog-legged routes usually associated with VOR navigation.

Purists argue, however, that homing with a crosswind guarantees being blown off course. True, but what's wrong with straying a few miles off the beaten path during a VFR flight. Besides, when the airplane is more than halfway to the station, homing automatically corrects for its own error, and guides the aircraft directly to the beacon. A pilot is no more likely to get lost when homing on a nondirectional radio beacon (NDB) than when tracking a VOR radial without using checkpoints to determine his en route progress.

There is a handy modification of the homing technique that can be used to offset what some consider to be undesirable, cross-track drifting. And it is as easy as child's play.

Assume that prior to departure for Chutzpah, the pilot knew that he would encounter a strong, left crosswind. He could home in on the broadcast station. Instead, he arbitrarily selects a crab angle of, say, 10 degrees.

After takeoff, he turns toward the destination until the ADF pointer shows the station to be 10 degrees right, which indicates that the aircraft is being crabbed 10 degrees left. For the duration of the flight, the pilot simply maintains whatever heading is necessary to keep the ADF needle pointed 10 degrees right.

Regardless of the actual wind velocity, the aircraft will pass almost directly over the station. If this sounds too good to be true, don't fight it. Accept this tip graciously and realize that ADF navigation doesn't have to be a continual exercise juggling numbers on a compass rose.

The logic of this simplified technique is shown in Figure 20. The dotted line would have been the pilot's track had he not applied the arbitrary crab angle and merely homed in on the station. The dashed line represents the track actually maintained because of the crab angle. In this case, 10 degrees of correction was not quite enough. Otherwise, the actual flight path would have coincided with the direct route. But the pilot did compensate for enough of the wind to prevent most of the drift.

Someone is bound to say, "That sounds great, but what if the pilot crabs too much or compensates for a wind that doesn't really exist?" Good question.

Figure 21 shows what happens when crabbing into a non-existent wind. Initially, the aircraft heads 10 degrees left of course. But as the flight progresses, the ADF needle begins to move clockwise. As this occurs, the pilot turns right to maintain a

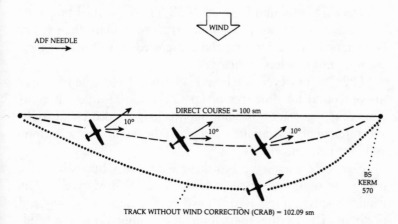

FIGURE 20

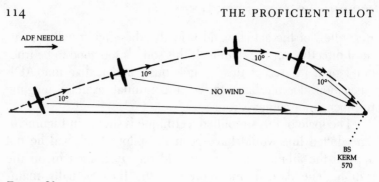

FIGURE 21

constant indication of 10 degrees right. He winds up flying a curved track, but still arrives over his destination.

Assume that a pilot is homing to a station and notices that the ADF needle has strayed from the desired position. He should not simply roll into a turn until the needle is once again in place. Because the ADF needle deflects while banking, it is not fully reliable during turns. Instead, the pilot should first note how many degrees of turn are required to reposition the needle and then execute this amount of turn with reference to the heading indicator. The ADF needle will settle into place shortly after the wings are leveled.

Tracking outbound from an NDB (or commercial broadcast station) for more than a few miles is more difficult than either homing or inbound tracking and is a procedure with which most pilots do not develop proficiency.

There is, however, a relatively effortless technique for tracking outbound for distances of up to about 100 miles. It combines dead reckoning with drift information provided by an ADF, and is reasonably accurate, even when the winds aloft are strong and of unknown velocity.

Figure 22 shows the broadcast station at Chutzpah that a pilot will use to find his new destination, West Maryville. The wind velocity, which is unknown to the pilot, is strong and northerly. He overflies the station and assumes a no-wind heading of 270 degrees. This obviously results in a southerly drift,

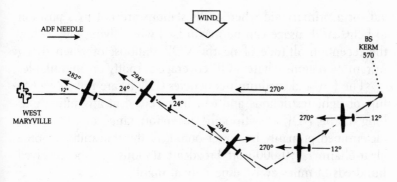

FIGURE 22

as indicated by the ADF pointer in position 1. The pilot, however, is undaunted by this and maintains a heading of 270 degrees for what he estimates to be one-third of the time required for the flight.

At approximately the one-third point of his journey (position 2), the pilot glances at the ADF and notes that he has drifted 12 degrees south of course. (The ADF needle points 12 degrees to the right of the tail.) He then doubles the drift angle and adds the result (24 degrees) to the magnetic heading of 270 degrees to arrive at a new magnetic heading of 294 degrees. This will cause the aircraft to intercept the direct route at approximately the two-thirds point.

The pilot will know that he has intercepted the desired course when, while on a heading of 294 degrees, the ADF needle indicates that the angle of the station "off the tail" is equal to the heading correction of 24 degrees right. At this point, the pilot assumes the original no-wind heading of 270 degrees plus the now-known drift angle of 12 degrees to arrive at a new heading of 282 degrees, which is used for the duration of the flight. Unless the wind changes dramatically, this technique will bring a pilot very close to his destination.

This presentation of simplified ADF obviously is not an argument against the use of VOR as the primary navaid. Rather it is intended to encourage the use of ADF as a supplementary aid, or a primary aid when VOR stations are not in a position to help. ADF usage can be maximized when flying low, below the reception altitude of nearby VOR stations, or when flying in remote regions where VOR coverage is spotty or unavailable.

The low and medium frequencies (L/MF) are not subject to line-of-sight restrictions and can be received at any altitude as long as the ADF is within the reception range of the station (determined primarily by power output of the transmitter). Some clear-channel, 50,000-watt broadcast stations can be received hundreds of miles away, especially at night.

Since distant L/MF signals can be received while parked on an airport situated in a valley, for example, ADF can be used as a quick-and-dirty flight planner. Simply tune to an en route station and begin a taxiing turn until the ADF needle points straight ahead. Look out the front window to find a landmark toward which the aircraft can be headed after takeoff. It's a nifty way to become established on course.

Also while on the ground, look at the compass. This is the no-wind heading to use once the initial landmark has been reached. By then you can probably pick up a VOR signal. If not, simply home in on the L/MF station previously tuned at the departure airport.

Quite obviously, these techniques are not compatible with IFR operations; they are strictly VFR procedures.

Relative to IFR, however, the ADF can play an invaluable role when you are being radar vectored for an instrument landing system (ILS) approach. By tuning in the outer compass locator (LOM), a low-powered radiobeacon co-located with an outer marker, and observing the *behavior* of the ADF needle, approach planning can be enhanced considerably.

Figure 23 shows an aircraft being vectored for an ILS approach. When flying downwind (position 1), a pilot with ADF awareness can sense (by needle movement) that he has quite a way to go before passing abeam the outer marker; he can keep the airplane clean and the airspeed relatively fast. The pilot should plan to reduce airspeed just prior to passing abeam the outer

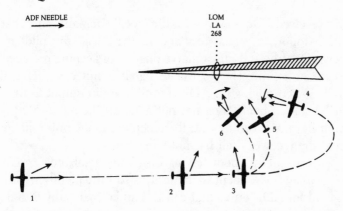

FIGURE 23

compass locator at position 2, and prepare for a turn toward final approach (position 3) shortly thereafter. Premature or late speed reductions can be avoided by carefully observing the ADF needle and by keeping track of aircraft position relative to the outer compass locator.

After the pilot has been turned toward final approach and instructed to intercept the localizer, the ADF can and should be used to verify that intercept will occur prior to reaching the LOM.

While maintaining the last assigned heading, the pilot at position 4 should observe the ADF needle moving slowly left. If the needle remains motionless, then the aircraft (position 5) will intercept the localizer at the locator. Or, if the needle moves slowly clockwise (toward the localizer), intercept will occur inside the locator (position 6). The latter two situations indicate that the assigned heading is incorrect for an intercept outside the locator, and a revised heading should be requested from the radar controller. Carefully watching the ADF needle may provide the only clue to an improper vector or the presence of a strong crosswind about which the controller may not be aware.

Using ADF is not always a bed of roses. The system does not have a fail flag to warn when the desired signal no longer is being received. On many sets, the needle remains in a fixed position following signal loss and may mislead the pilot into believing that he is doing a marvelous job of keeping the needle in place at a time when a usable signal is not even being received. When relying on ADF, monitor audio output to insure that the station being used has not gone off the air, or that the aircraft has not flown beyond the reception range of the station, or that the receiver itself has not failed.

Be very careful about relying on commercial broadcast stations because these identify themselves so infrequently. Also be on guard for ADF errors that can be caused by nearby thunderstorms, mineral deposits, twilight effects, and the refraction that occurs when L/MF signals cross a shoreline. Be alert also for frequency interference caused by simultaneously receiving two stations on the same frequency. This is best detected by an audible whistle or hum and is most likely to occur at night. When the airplane is flying in rain or snow, precipitation static can affect ADF indications and reception quality. Static can be suppressed by static dischargers (sometimes called wick dischargers) on the trailing edges of wings and tail surfaces. Reducing airspeed also may help.

3

POWERFUL TOPICS

Propellers

Those who learned to fly in the air corps during World War I often were introduced to a flying machine by a grizzled instructor who stood at the nose and said, "Gentlemen, this is a propeller."

After issuing a stern warning about walking into the swirling path of a propeller, he promptly ushered his fledglings rearward. He had little else to say about this propulsive device, because it was so simple, little more than a pair of whirling paddles.

Early propellers also were inefficient, converting only a relatively small percentage of engine horsepower into thrust. This is because pioneer designers believed, erroneously, that thrust was produced only by the backside of the propeller. They paid little attention to the face. These designs literally were air screws, a term still endeared to the British.

Designers soon recognized that efficiency could be improved if propeller blades were regarded as revolving wings. Attention shifted to the front of the blade. Camber, or curvature, was added, and performance gains were considerable. As the modern propeller revolves, it creates lift the way a wing does; but

119

since the "lift" of a propeller acts horizontally, it propels the airplane forward.

Figure 24 shows a representative cross section of a typical propeller during the downswing of its rotation. The pitch of the blade is the angle between the chord of the airfoil and the plane of rotation. When this angle is small, the propeller is said to be taking a small bite (of air). As it increases, the blade takes progressively larger bites. The British refer to these conditions as fine (low) and coarse (high) pitch.

But propeller design is not so simple that a pair of miniature wings can be bolted to the engine crankshaft. This is because the rotational airspeed of a propeller varies from relatively slow

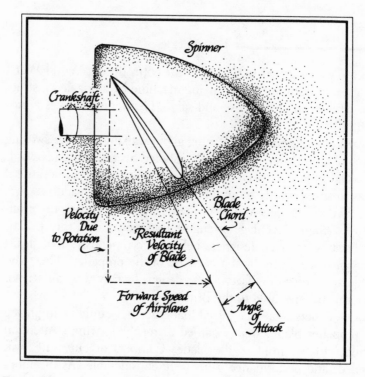

FIGURE 24

near the hub to a high speed at the tip. For example, each tip
of the 84-inch-diameter propeller of a Cessna 185 has a rotational airspeed of 619 knots when spinning at 2,850 rpm. At the
same time, those sections of the propeller located 14 and 28
inches from the hub have airspeeds of only 206 and 412 knots.

As Figure 25 demonstrates, conditions become more complex when the airplane is in flight at some arbitrary airspeed
(140 knots, in this case). The first propeller cross section is 14
inches from the hub and has a relatively slow rotational airspeed, 206 knots. This is combined with the forward speed, 140
knots, to obtain the actual relative wind encountered by this
section of the blade. The result is a 249-knot relative wind that
angles 34 degrees to the propeller's plane of rotation. For this
section of the propeller to generate lift, the blade angle must be
at least 34 degrees.

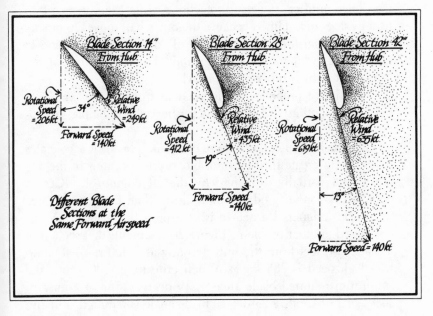

FIGURE 25

At 28 inches from the hub, the relative wind is faster, 435 knots, and requires a minimum propeller bite of 19 degrees. At the tip of the prop, the velocity of the relative wind is at a maximum, 635 knots, and requires a minimum blade angle of only 13 degrees.

In reality, each propeller section should have an angle of attack of about five degrees to generate lift efficiently. In other words, the blade sections shown in this figure should have pitch angles of 39, 24, and 18 degrees, respectively.

Notice that the pitch angle of a propeller blade must decrease steadily as distance from the hub increases, which is why propellers have twisted blades.

Since the outer half of a propeller blade travels faster than the inner half, it is not surprising that it produces most of the thrust. That portion of blade near the hub is primarily a structural necessity, contributing little to propulsion.

Pilots often ask why the inner portion of a propeller blade may have anti-ice or deice protection, while the outer portion usually does not. This is because the outer half moves so rapidly that centrifugal force and the heat of compression combine to obviate the need for icing protection. This is not true of the inner half, which moves more slowly.

Whether a propeller is mounted in front of the engine (a tractor installation) or behind it (a pusher), the principles of propulsion are identical.

The pusher generally is more efficient. The air it accelerates rearward (to create thrust) is not blocked by portions of the airframe and partially explains why the aft engine of a Cessna 336/337 Skymaster produces more thrust than the forward one.

Once designers learned to twist a propeller blade, they encountered another problem. Figure 26 represents that section of a blade two feet from the hub spinning at 2,300 rpm. Its rotational airspeed is 285 knots. When cruising at 100 knots, the minimum required blade angle is 19 degrees. But at a forward speed of 130 knots, a 25-degree blade angle is required. Finally,

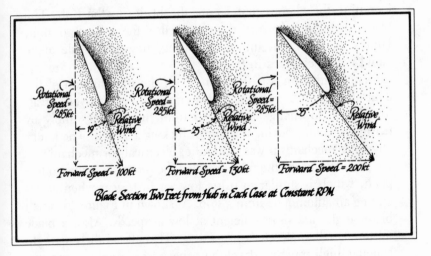

Rotational Speed = 285kt   *Relative Wind*   19°   *Forward Speed = 100kt*

Rotational Speed = 285kt   *Relative Wind*   25°   *Forward Speed = 150kt*

Rotational Speed = 285kt   35°   *Relative Wind*   *Forward Speed = 200kt*

Blade Section Two Feet from Hub in Each Case at Constant RPM

FIGURE 26

a 200-knot forward speed necessitates an angle of 35 degrees. In other words, blade angle should vary with airspeed to optimize performance. A fixed-pitch propeller is only a compromise. For maximum efficiency, a propeller needs a small pitch angle for takeoff, a medium pitch for moderate speeds (climb), and a relatively large angle for cruise.

In the beginning, only fixed-pitch props were available. A pilot could choose between a climb prop with medium pitch or a cruise prop with large pitch. The climb model enhances aerobatic and climb performance at the sacrifice of some cruise speed. Or a cross-country pilot could install a cruise prop at the loss of some climb performance. Early racing airplanes had propellers with extraordinarily large angles. These machines were incredibly fast, but takeoff and climb required the patience of Job.

Depending on his daily needs, a pilot of the helmet-and-goggle era could spend considerable time changing propellers.

Progress surged when manufacturers offered the adjustable-pitch propeller. This enabled a pilot to change blade pitch by loosening the clamps that secure the blades to the hub. The blades then could be turned and locked in the desired position. Unless the pilot was unusually daring, however, blade angle could not be changed in flight.

This limitation was overcome with the introduction of the controllable-pitch propeller. Answering a pilot's prayers, it allowed him to change prop pitch from the cockpit simply by twisting a knob, moving a lever, or flicking a switch. The pitch-changing mechanism was hydraulic, electrical, or mechanical.

Prior to takeoff, the pilot adjusted the propeller blades to low pitch, which is similar to using low, or first, gear when accelerating an automobile from a stop. As shown in Figure 26, small blade angles are most efficient at low airspeeds. Also, a blade set to a small angle creates less drag. This allows the engine to generate high rpm and develop its maximum-rated horsepower. (The typical fixed-pitch propeller has a larger blade angle and does not enable the engine to develop full power during take-off.)

During climbout, the pilot who used a controllable-pitch prop increased the blade angle slightly (shifted to second gear) to achieve optimum climb performance. In cruise, he "shifted" once more. This propeller was a blessing. The airplane could be flown efficiently in every phase of flight by adjusting blade pitch to suit the airplane's gait.

But there remained another problem, an annoyance to those who also operate airplanes that have fixed-pitch propellers.

Assume that such an airplane is stabilized in cruise. The tach needle is steady at 2,300 rpm. Without adjusting power, the pilot raises the nose and the airspeed wanes. Simultaneously, propeller rpm decreases because of increased aerodynamic loading. Similarly, an airspeed increase causes rpm to increase because aerodynamic loading is reduced.

To maintain a constant rpm with a fixed-pitch propeller when airspeed changes, the pilot must adjust the throttle. If flying an airplane with a controllable-pitch prop, the pilot has a choice. He can change throttle position or propeller pitch. Decreasing the blade angle increases rpm, while increasing blade angle decreases rpm.

One way to eliminate this inconvenience was to invent something that automatically changed propeller pitch to compensate for airspeed variations. Enter the constant-speed propeller. This incorporates a governor that maintains whatever rpm is selected by the pilot irrespective of airspeed changes.

Assume, for example, that an airplane is cruising at a given airspeed and rpm. The pilot lowers the nose and the airspeed builds. Normally, this would be accompanied by a simultaneous rpm gain, but not so with a constant-speed propeller governor. In reality, an *imperceptible* rpm increase does occur; but, at the same time, centrifugal force acting on flyweights in the governor also increases. The flyweights move outward and cause a high-pressure oil line to open. Oil pressure from the engine then forces blade pitch to increase and enables the propeller to maintain the original rpm.

Parenthetically, this explains why engine oil pressure changes are indicated on the oil pressure gauge when cycling a constant-speed propeller during runup.

Similarly, the constant-speed governor prevents rpm from decreasing when airspeed decays. If rpm *begins* to decrease, reduced centrifugal force causes the flyweights to move inward. This opens a drain valve, allowing oil in the prop hub to drain and return to the engine. As this occurs, blade pitch decreases to maintain the rpm originally selected with the propeller pitch control in the cockpit.

Adjusting the throttle (within limits) also has no effect on rpm. When power is reduced, the constant-speed propeller moves automatically into a lower pitch to maintain the preselected rpm. Conversely, an increase in power causes pitch to increase. The tach needle never budges.

It is obvious that the tachometer alone cannot be used as a measure of engine power when the airplane is equipped with a constant-speed propeller, because throttle changes have no effect on rpm. Powerplant engineers had to provide something else to assist the pilot in determining power settings—the manifold pressure gauge, which is discussed in detail later in this chapter.

The lift generated by a given wing at a specific angle of attack is related directly to airspeed and wing area. Similarly, propeller thrust is related to rotational velocity (rpm) and blade area. Unfortunately, there are limits to both.

As an example, consider the 84-inch prop mentioned earlier. At 2,850 rpm (redline), the tip of each blade has a rotational velocity of 619 knots. At sea level on a standard day, this equates to 94 percent of the speed of sound (Mach .94). If this propeller were to rotate much faster, the tips would break the sound barrier (660 knots) and produce intense noise, excessive drag, and possible vibration. Also, propulsive energy would be wasted forming shock waves.

Nor could diameter be increased, because this, too, would result in excessive propeller tip speeds.

One way to increase blade area (and thrust) is to widen the chord, resulting in a stubbier, paddle-like blade. Unfortunately, such a propeller may have an unacceptably low aspect ratio (the ratio of span, or blade length, to chord). Like a similarly shaped wing, low-aspect-ratio blades waste horsepower and thrust by generating excessive tip vortices and induced drag. The designer's goal is to provide propellers (and wings) with *high* aspect ratios. Long and narrow is more efficient than short and stubby.

How then can additional blade area be added without excessive tip speeds or an unsatisfactory aspect ratio? Simple: Add extra blades. Three-bladed props, for example, not only provide the additional blade area necessary to accommodate more powerful engines, but offer other advantages as well. First of all, they result in smoother flight, because three pulses of air per revolution strike the airframe instead of two. Also, adding so much area allows propeller diameter to be reduced. This results in lower tip speeds, which reduce noise. (Prop noise is directly related to tip speed and usually is louder than the engine itself.)

Reducing propeller diameter also increases ground clearance. Obvious disadvantages are increased weight, cost, and maintenance.

(Incredibly, there have been a number of experimental one-bladed props. A counterweight provided suitable balance; but, since all thrust was generated on one side of the disc, engine crankshaft and bearings were strained severely.)

As engines became more powerful, the additional and necessary blade area was increased by utilizing four- and five-bladed propellers. Some airplanes have even been equipped with a pair of contrarotating propellers mounted on a single crankshaft. Such a configuration is a delight to fly, because it eliminates the asymmetric effects of a single propeller, such as p-factor, torque, gyroscopic effect, and the energy wasted in developing a swirling slipstream.

A relatively recent development is the Q-tip propeller, containing blades that are bent 90 degrees aft at the tips. Although they seldom are of value to an airplane already equipped with an optimum propeller, Q-tips are advantageous in some special cases.

Consider, for example, an airplane being modified with a more powerful engine. This obviously requires a propeller with additional blade area. But as discussed earlier, simply increasing prop diameter produces excessive noise not only for those on the ground, but also for those inside the aircraft. This is especially true with respect to conventional twins, because increasing blade length brings the tips closer to the cabin (and the ground).

Widening blade chord also may be unsatisfactory, because the efficiency loss of a low-aspect-ratio propeller partially offsets the advantage of installing a larger engine in the first place.

A Q-tip propeller can resolve this dilemma. The inch-long, bent portions of the tips behave much like the winglets seen on the wingtips of some airplanes. The effect in either case is to reduce tip vortex strength and induced drag. Less power is required to overcome these aerodynamic handicaps, allowing the propeller to convert more horsepower into thrust.

The Q-tip is a quieter propeller in that the original noise level is preserved; the additional blade length or rpm normally required to accommodate a more powerful engine would be noisier.

A fringe benefit of Q-tips is that weaker tip vortices reduce the tendency of the propeller to pick up damaging pebbles when operating on unimproved surfaces. A disadvantage is that damaged Q-tips frequently cannot be repaired as easily as conventional tips, if at all.

For a time, experts considered propellers to have reached their practical limits. But contrary to predictions of obsolescence, propellers are making a comeback.

The Hamilton Standard Division of United Technologies, for example, has developed prop fan technology that promises to revolutionize short- to medium-range air transportation. Although technically propellers, these propulsive devices look more like eight- and ten-blade, desk-top fans. They are designed to convert turbine power into shaft horsepower at speeds up to Mach .85, the cruise speed of modern jetliners. By providing a high degree of propulsive efficiency, these swept-blade fans reduce fuel consumption significantly and are quieter than conventional turbofan engines.

Future general aviation propellers probably will incorporate some of this technology. They also will be stronger and lighter than aluminum models. Using composite materials, manufacturers already are developing propellers constructed with carbon-fiber spars, foam filling, and a glass epoxy shell covered by a tough polyurethane coating. Another benefit is that incidental damage to composite blades, which normally would cause metal blades to be scrapped, can be repaired.

Like Mark Twain's reaction to erroneous reports of his death, the predicted demise of the propeller has been greatly exaggerated.

POWER MANAGEMENT

Flying an airplane depends on understanding numerous important relationships. Lift and drag, roll and yaw, weather and water vapor are but a few examples. The relationship between engine manifold pressure and propeller rpm is equally significant but is not well understood, especially by pilots making the transition for the first time to complex airplanes.

First, what is a manifold? It is no more than a system of ducts and plumbing that guides a fluid (such as air) from one place to another. Figure 27 shows an induction manifold, which directs air from outside the aircraft to the engine cylinders for combustion. (An exhaust manifold guides the refuse of combustion from the cylinders to outside the aircraft.)

The figure also shows a throttle valve (or butterfly valve, as it is sometimes called), which is used to control the amount of

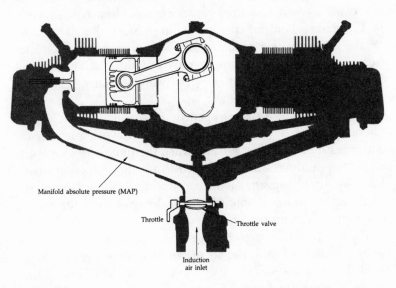

Manifold absolute pressure (MAP)

Throttle

Throttle valve

Induction
air inlet

FIGURE 27

air allowed to enter the cylinders. This valve is an integral part of the carburetor or fuel-injector servo. The amount of air passing the throttle valve is important because it determines how much fuel can be burned and, therefore, how much power can be developed.

Technically, fuel flow and engine power depend on the weight of air entering the cylinder. One way to measure engine power, therefore, is to measure the density of air downstream of the throttle valve, something more difficult in practice than in principle. Much simpler and almost as effective is measuring the pressure of the air (or fuel/air mixture) as it enters the cylinders. This is called manifold pressure or, to be accurate, manifold absolute pressure (MAP), which is measured in inches of mercury by an instrument similar to a crude altimeter.

Notice in the figure that the throttle valve is closed. Very little air (and fuel) is being processed by the engine, which is idling. In the meantime, the pistons—acting like large vacuum pumps—attempt to suck in much more air than the throttle allows. As a result, manifold pressure is quite low (typically nine to 11 inches when the engine is idling). Since the air pressure on the upstream side of the throttle is approximately 30 inches (sea level barometric pressure), only one-third of atmospheric pressure can get to the engine. No wonder that a "throttled" engine develops so little power.

As the throttle valve is opened, increasingly more atmospheric pressure is allowed to enter the low-pressure region downstream of the valve. Finally, when the throttle is wide open, all atmospheric pressure is allowed to fill the induction manifold. Manifold pressure increases to almost 30 inches (at sea level and assuming a nonturbocharged engine) and the engine develops maximum power.

In reality, MAP rarely equals atmospheric pressure because some pressure is lost as the air makes its way through the manifold. Losses of one to two inches are typical. MAP and atmospheric pressure are equal in nonturbocharged engines only when the engine is not running.

(Mooney, for example, has devised an interesting method of recovering some induction loss. When the aircraft is at an altitude where the air is relatively clean, the pilot pulls a knob that allows ambient air to bypass the air filter and go straight to the throttle valve. This, plus the effect of ram-air pressure entering the bypass, increases manifold pressure by at least an inch.)

As an airplane climbs into steadily decreasing atmospheric pressure, maximum-available manifold pressure (in nonturbocharged engines) also decreases because there is less air available to enter the induction manifold. The table in Figure 28 shows the maximum power and typical manifold pressure available up to 25,000 feet.

Although manifold pressure is the primary indication of the weight of air entering the cylinders and often is regarded as a power gauge, it alone does not measure power output. Power is the rate at which work is performed. So if the engine is not moving something, it is not developing power. Manifold pressure can be compared to the legs of a bicyclist. No matter how much muscle is applied, power is not developed unless those legs are used to turn the wheels. Loosely stated, manifold pressure is a form of muscle—energy—a force that can be harnessed to perform a task.

An aircraft engine performs work by turning a propeller. To determine power output, therefore, it is necessary to know how much muscle (manifold pressure) is being applied and how much work (rpm) is being done with that muscle. Consequently, it is the combination of MAP and rpm that determines power output. This is why the pilot's operating handbook for a given airplane specifies that rated engine power is available only when the throttle is wide open (an implied condition for normally aspirated engines), standard conditions exist at sea level, and the propeller is turning at the maximum-allowable (redline) rpm.

It is impossible, however, for the fixed-pitch propeller of a lightplane to achieve redline rpm when the aircraft is motionless on the ground. For example, the engine of a Cessna 152 develops only 2,280 rpm during a full-throttle, static runup, even

FULL THROTTLE HORSEPOWER AND MAINFOLD PRESSURE AT ALTITUDE (for naturally aspirated engines)		
Altitude (feet)	Percent of Sea-level Horsepower	Manifold Pressure (typical, inches of mercury)
Sea Level	100.0	28.7
1,000	96.8	27.7
2,000	93.6	26.6
3,000	90.5	25.6
4,000	87.5	24.6
5,000	84.6	23.7
6,000	81.7	22.8
7,000	78.9	21.9
8,000	76.2	21.0
9,000	73.5	20.2
10,000	70.8	19.4
11,000	68.3	18.6
12,000	65.8	17.8
13,000	63.4	17.1
14,000	61.0	16.4
15,000	58.7	15.7
16,000	56.5	15.0
17,000	54.3	14.4
18,000	52.1	13.7
19,000	50.0	13.1
20,000	48.0	12.6
21,000	46.0	12.0
22,000	44.0	11.4
23,000	42.2	10.9
24,000	40.3	10.4
25,000	38.5	9.9

FIGURE 28

though its redline rpm is 2,550. Nor can the 152's engine develop rated horsepower during the takeoff roll, and this partially explains why aircraft fitted with fixed-pitch propellers have relatively lethargic takeoff performance.

Figure 29 helps to demonstrate why a fixed-pitch propeller is rpm-limited at low airspeeds. The propeller shown in the figure has a 20-degree pitch angle (as measured at a point three-fourths of the way from the center of the propeller hub to the tip). At full throttle and with no forward speed, the propeller

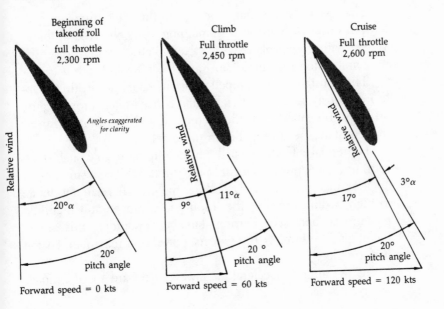

FIGURE 29

can achieve only 2,300 rpm. The large, 20-degree "angle of bite" combines with the relative wind (caused by propeller rotation) to produce a 20-degree angle of attack This angle is quite large and since the blade section is rotating at 364 knots, the resultant drag is quite high. The propeller is said to be heavily loaded (with drag) and the engine simply does not have sufficient power to turn the propeller faster.

When the aircraft is at 60 knots, however, the propeller blade encounters a relative wind that is a result of its rotation (380 knots) and its forward speed (60 knots). As can be seen, the angle of attack now is only 11 degrees. Since this smaller angle of attack results in less drag, engine and propeller rpm increase to 2,450. Finally, at a forward speed of 120 knots, the propeller blade's angle of attack is only three degrees. At such a small angle of attack, the propeller is unloaded (with respect to drag), and its rpm increases to 2,600.

The lesson here is that—for a given throttle setting—propeller rpm varies with airspeed, something easily observed in flight. When flying any airplane with a fixed-pitch propeller, lower the nose and watch rpm increase. Raise the nose and rpm wanes.

The constant-speed propeller (discussed earlier in this chapter) obviously is more efficient than a fixed-pitch prop. Figure 30 helps to explain both the theoretical and operational aspects of a constant-speed propeller in more detail.

During takeoff, the propeller blades are set to low pitch (high rpm) using a control adjacent to the throttle. Since a small pitch angle results in relatively little drag, the propeller can accelerate to high (redline) rpm as the throttle is advanced and manifold pressure is increased. During standard conditions, this allows the engine to develop 100-percent power and maximize takeoff performance.

As the aircraft accelerates, however, forward speed unloads

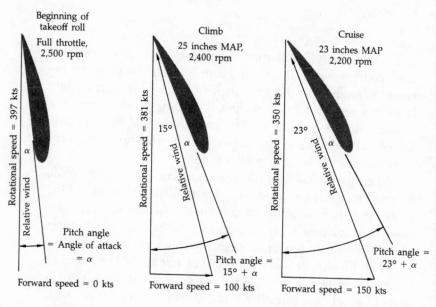

FIGURE 30

the propeller, which tends to exceed redline rpm. The propeller governor senses this overspeeding tendency and increases the blade angles ever so slightly. The added drag on the blades prevents overspeeding and allows the propeller to maintain redline, which, in this case, is 2,500 rpm.

Once the aircraft is climbing at a safe altitude, the pilot can reduce power to that recommended for climb, such as 25 inches MAP and 2,400 rpm, for example. It is important that the pilot make such a power reduction by first reducing manifold pressure and then by reducing rpm.

Reducing rpm first can place excessive strain on the engine. When the propeller control is used to reduce rpm from, say 2,500 to 2,400, the propeller governor simply increases blade angle. This creates the additional drag necessary to decelerate the propeller. Now take this situation to its extreme. Imagine that a pilot attempted to stop the propeller with the throttle wide open. (Although not possible, this helps to illustrate the point.) The tremendous load (added drag) that has been placed on such a propeller would attempt to stop the engine at a time when it—the engine—is trying to do just the opposite. It is obvious that something (such as a crankshaft or a piston rod) is likely to snap in the process.

Although reducing rpm before reducing manifold pressure during a normal power reduction does not impose such a severe strain on the engine, it nevertheless does increase internal engine stresses.

For the same reason, power increases should be made by first increasing rpm and then increasing manifold pressure.

(When the rpm of a normally aspirated engine is increased, manifold pressure drops slightly. This is because the added rpm causes the pumping rate of the pistons to increase, thereby causing a slight pressure reduction in the intake manifold downstream of the throttle valve. Conversely, decreasing rpm reduces this pumping action and causes manifold pressure to increase slightly.)

As the aircraft climbs, manifold pressure decreases because

of the reduction in atmospheric pressure. If operating at less than full throttle, the throttle can be opened farther to compensate for this power loss. Eventually, however, the manifold pressure recommended for climb requires a wide-open throttle. Above this altitude, the manifold pressure and power output of a non-turbocharged engine decrease as shown in Figure 28.

Upon reaching cruise altitude, and after accelerating to the appropriate speed, the throttle and propeller control—in that order—are used to establish the recommended cruise power.

There are two rules of thumb pilots use to set cruise power on a normally aspirated engine. The first suggests using 23 inches MAP and 2,300 rpm, a procedure popularly called "23 square." Although such a power setting can be used in most cases, it is the sign of a pilot too lazy to use available power charts. There are various recommended power settings, and a pilot should use the one appropriate to his mission if he wants to get the most out of his aircraft.

The second rule claims that manifold pressure should not exceed rpm (in hundreds). When using 2,400 rpm, for example, manifold pressure should not exceed 24 inches. While such a conservative technique might have been appropriate when engines were less than reliable, it has no place in the operation of modern powerplants. As a matter of fact, this rule is violated during every takeoff from a low-elevation airport where manifold pressure is close to 30 inches and rpm is as much as "five" less than 30 (even less for geared engines). So much for that rule of thumb.

A pilot can opt to use any combination of MAP and rpm specified in the power charts for his engine. When operating a Avco Lycoming O-540-B, 235-hp engine at 65-percent power, for example, he can use extremes of 2,575 rpm and 21 inches MAP, or 1,875 rpm and 25.2 inches MAP, or any of several in-between combinations. Using reduced rpm and high manifold pressure within approved limits usually is the most advantageous. For one thing, low propeller rpm reduces noise. For another, fuel savings can be significant. When operating the O-540-B at 2,575 rpm and 21 inches MAP at sea level, for example, fuel consumption is 13.8 gph. But when pulling the same power with 1,875 rpm and 25.2 inches MAP, fuel consumption is only 12.1 gph. This represents a 13-percent fuel-flow reduction without affecting power output. (Slow-turning engines are most efficient because they generate less internal friction.)

As a general rule, manifold pressure in cruise flight can exceed rpm (in hundreds) by "four," but this should be confirmed with appropriate power charts.

For those accustomed to fixed-pitch propellers, the constant-speed propeller is a joy to operate. It is similar to making the transition from a car with a single-gear transmission to one with multiple gears. In a way, the contant-speed propeller and automotive transmissions are analogous; each is used to convert engine muscle into locomotion.

The constant-speed propeller not only is more efficient than a fixed-pitch propeller, it also is easier to use. Once the desired rpm is established in cruise flight, for example, it does not have to be adjusted in any way for the duration of cruise flight. Should airspeed vary for any reason, the propeller governor automatically adjusts the pitch of the blades to maintain the selected rpm. Blade angle is increased to prevent an rpm increase and vice versa. Propeller rpm does not vary with minor throttle adjustments, either. If manifold pressure is reduced, the governor decreases blade pitch to maintain a constant rpm; conversely, a power increase causes blade pitch to increase.

Descending with a constant-speed propeller generally requires little attention. Just leave the propeller set to cruise rpm and it takes care of itself. One word of caution, however: Descending rapidly with cruise rpm and very low manifold pressure can cause piston rings to flutter, which eventually can cause them to break. If very-low-power descents are necessary, prevent the possibility of ring flutter by adjusting propeller rpm to the lowest possible cruise setting. Prior to reapplying power, however, increase propeller rpm to its cruise or climb setting, whichever is appropriate.

There is no need to adjust propeller rpm on an approach, either. But prior to descending through approximately 500 feet agl, increase propeller rpm to the maximum in preparation for a possible go-around. In this way, maximum power will be available as soon as the throttle is put to the fire wall.

Constant-speed propellers are so much more efficient than fixed-pitch models that it causes one to wonder why all aircraft are not equipped with them. The answer consists of two words: weight and price, factors that generally make constant-speed propellers impractical for most aircraft with less than 180-hp engines.

TURBOCHARGING

Like man, the normally aspirated (free-breathing) engine is designed to develop maximum power at sea level. At altitude, it runs short of breath, and this has a deleterious effect on aircraft performance.

Consider the Piper Lance as but one example of this inescapable fact of life. This hefty retractable can take off at maximum-allowable gross weight in less than a thousand feet, cruise at 165 knots, and climb 1,000 fpm while hauling up to 1,644 pounds of useful load. The trouble is, it can achieve these feats only at sea level; as altitude increases, performance wanes.

The only way to combat this common problem without installing a more powerful engine is to equip the engine with a turbocharger. The result is a shot of high-altitude adrenaline. Service ceiling of the Lance, for example, is more than doubled, from 14,500 to 30,000 feet, and the time required to climb from sea level to 12,000 feet is slashed from 22 to 12 minutes. Maximum cruise speed increases steadily from 165 knots at sea level to 191 knots at 22,000 feet. Takeoff performance at high-elevation airports is similarly impressive.

Figure 31 is a simplified view of a typical turbocharger installation. A turbine wheel is placed in the path of escaping exhaust, which causes the turbine to rotate like a high-speed windmill at up to 100,000 rpm.

The turbine wheel is connected to a compressor impeller by a short, rigid shaft. When the turbine is powered by exhaust, the impeller rotates at the same rpm and compresses induction (inlet) air prior to it being ingested by the engine. In short, induction air density and manifold pressure are increased, which allows the engine to develop much more power than it could without a turbocharger. The engine performs as if it were being operated at a lower altitude where the air is naturally denser and has more pressure.

Some find it difficult to comprehend this principle. They feel as though they're getting something for nothing. Not really. The hot, high-velocity exhaust gases that exit the normally aspirated engine represent a tremendous waste of energy. The tur-

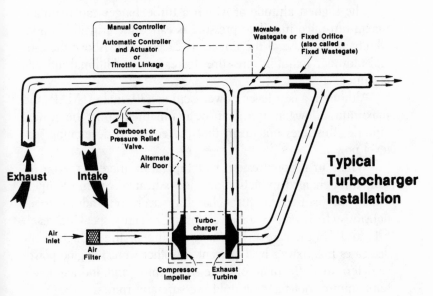

FIGURE 31

bocharger simply extracts some of this energy to drive a compressor. Measurements show that after the exhaust leaves the turbine, its velocity *and* temperature are reduced considerably.

The first such units were superchargers, mechanically driven devices used to increase the power of diesel engines before Wilbur and Orville had ever heard of Kitty Hawk. The earliest aviation application occurred in 1918 when General Electric attached an exhaust-driven turbocharger to a Liberty engine, which then produced more horsepower at the top of Pike's Peak than at sea level and resulted in a 1920 altitude record of 33,000 feet. The first production airplane to be equipped with "blowers" was the Boeing B-17 in 1939.

When a turbocharger is used to maintain up to (but not more than) 30 inches MAP at altitude, the engine is said to be normalized. In other words, the engine never produces more than 30 inches MAP, irrespective of altitude. Almost all retrofit turbocharger installations normalize the engine.

The highest altitude at which a turbocharger can maintain maximum-rated manifold pressure is called the critical altitude, which, in the case of the Lance, is 22,000 feet. Above the critical altitude, manifold pressure decreases as additional altitude is gained.

Although a sea-level power setting (30 inches MAP and maximum-allowable rpm) can be maintained up to the critical altitude, this does not mean that the engine is developing sea-level power.

When air is compressed, its temperature increases. As a result, turbocharged induction air also is heated. Such a temperature rise (caused by turbocharging) decreases induction air density, which causes a power loss. Generally speaking, each 6°F to 10°F increase in the temperature of the induction air decreases horsepower by 1 percent. In other words, engine power is determined by manifold pressure, rpm, and induction air temperature, not just manifold pressure and rpm.

At the critical altitude of the Lance (22,000 feet), for example, the air temperature at the compressor outlet is hot, about 220°F. Because of this, it is estimated that the Lance's engine develops only 81-percent power even though sea-level manifold pressure is being produced. Without a turbocharger, however, only 44-percent power would be available at this altitude.

Although all turbochargers are similar in principle and operation, there are various methods of controlling them. Most turbocharger systems incorporate a wastegate, or valve, in the exhaust manifold that is used to divert engine exhaust into the turbocharger's turbine. When the wastegate is fully open, the exhaust simply flows overboard conventionally. But as the wastegate is closed, the exhaust takes a new path of least resistance (see Figure 31), and flows into the turbine.

The earliest method of turbocharger control consisted of a manually controlled wastegate. With the engine throttle opened fully, the pilot detects the normal decrease in manifold pressure that occurs with an increase in altitude. To recapture this lost power, he begins to close the wastegate (either electrically or mechanically), to divert exhaust into the turbine. As altitude continues to increase, he gradually closes the wastegate further to divert more and more exhaust into the turbine to maintain a constant manifold pressure.

Finally, at the turbocharger's critical altitude, the wastegate is fully closed and almost all exhaust passes through the turbine. This is the altitude at which an aircraft with a normalized engine achieves its maximum cruise airspeed. Above the critical altitude, manifold pressure and airspeed decline.

With a manual system, caution must be taken not to close the wastegate too much at too low an altitude. Otherwise, excessive manifold pressure will occur and engine damage may result. Some installations are equipped with an overboost, or pressure-relief, valve to vent excessive manifold pressure and protect the engine.

Although a manual wastegate control is relatively simple, it is not popular. This is because a pilot must continually adjust the wastegate during changes in altitude to maintain a given manifold pressure. A welcome improvement was the automatic pressure controller, which consists of an electronically-signaled actuator that opens or closes the wastegate as necessary to maintain the desired manifold pressure.

With the throttle open in a climb, for example, the automatic controller gradually closes the wastegate to maintain 30 inches MAP. During descent, the controller similarly causes the wastegate to open so as to prevent manifold pressure from increasing. In other words, the automatic pressure controller maintains whatever manifold pressure is selected with the throttle, irrespective of any subsequent altitude changes.

Such an automatic pressure controller is used on the Aerostar 601P, the Bellanca Turbo Viking, and other airplanes.

Pressure controllers also are used in conjunction with turbochargers used to ground boost an engine. These controllers automatically adjust wastegate position to maintain any desired manifold pressure up to the red-line limit, which—in general aviation aircraft—can be as high as 40 inches.

The notion of ground-boosted engines causes many pilots to wonder how these engines can take so much manifold pressure without causing engine damage. After all, we are warned to avoid overboosting a free-breathing engine by reducing manifold pressure before rpm (when making a power reduction) and increasing rpm before increasing manifold pressure (when adding power).

The explanation is simple. Ground-boosted engines have reduced compression ratios to provide wider detonation margins. A reduction in compression ratio requires additional manifold pressure to compensate for the loss of power this would otherwise create. For this reason, engines with high compression ratios ordinarily are not ground-boosted.

Aircraft equipped with automatic pressure controllers and ground-boosted engines include the Beech B36TC Bonanza and the Cessna 421 Golden Eagle.

When climbing an aircraft equipped with a pressure controller (in conjunction with either normalized or ground-boosted engines), the wastegate is gradually and automatically closed to maintain whatever manifold pressure is selected with the throttle. As altitude increases the turbocharger must work progressively harder to maintain manifold pressure. Consequently, induction air temperature increases steadily throughout the climb. As a result, the horsepower output of the engine usually decreases with altitude even though manifold pressure and rpm remain constant.

The only way for the engine to produce constant horsepower during climb, therefore, is for the pilot to constantly and gradually add manifold pressure to compensate for the power loss caused by increasing induction temperature.

This problem is solved by the automatic density controller. Instead of maintaining a constant manifold pressure during climb (as does the pressure controller), the density controller automatically positions the wastegate so as to maintain constant air density to the engine, which results in a near-constant horsepower output during climb.

Assume that a pilot initiates a climb using 80-percent power at 5,000 feet (32 inches MAP and 2,500 rpm, for example). As altitude increases, the density controller senses a decrease in air density (horsepower) caused by warmer compressor outlet temperatures. It gradually closes the wastegate to increase the manifold pressure to that required to maintain constant air density to the engine. At 10,000 feet, this could be 33 inches, for example. Density controllers are expensive and are found on the Piper Aztec, Navajo, and Chieftain.

Two other types of turbocharger controllers should be discussed because of their simplicity and popularity.

The first incorporates a "slaved," or coupled, wastegate (developed by Avco Lycoming for the Rockwell 112TC and the Enstrom Helicopter). The wastegate is mechanically linked to the throttle in such a way that, as the throttle is advanced, the wastegate begins to close. During the takeoff roll, the pilot must advance the throttle only as far as necessary to obtain maximum allowable, ground-boosted, takeoff power. Full throttle application would completely close the wastegate. While a pressure-relief valve is provided to prevent damaging overboost, this protective device could fail; never rely on it.

The simplest system (developed by Teledyne Continental) is found, for example, on the Piper PA-34 Seneca II and the PA-28RT Turbo Arrow III. It is unique because it does not incorporate an adjustable wastegate. Instead, the exhaust manifold is partially blocked with a fixed-position orifice, which also is called a fixed wastegate and is shown in Figure 31. Some of the exhaust leaving the engine takes the path of least resistance and flows directly to the turbocharger. The rest of the exhaust, however, flows through the fixed wastegate.

This system is operated similarly to one with a slaved wastegate. As soon as the throttle is opened, even slightly, the turbocharger begins to do its stuff. Takeoff power is achieved with less than a wide-open throttle. During a climb with either the slaved wastegate or fixed wastegate system, the pilot must incrementally advance the throttle to maintain a given manifold pressure. However, since the fixed-orifice system always allows some exhaust to bypass the turbo, it has a relatively low critical altitude, on the order of 12,000 to 15,000 feet.

It is interesting to note that in the case of the Turbo Arrow III, for example, 40 inches of manifold pressure is required to obtain the same 200 hp that a similar engine without turbocharging obtains with only 30 inches of manifold pressure. The additional ten inches is needed to compensate for warmer induction temperatures, reduced compression ratio, exhaust back pressure, and induction interference losses (which include a partially closed, "blocking" throttle valve).

As mentioned earlier, one drawback to turbocharging is the heat created when air is compressed. The increased temperature of the induction air is much more substantial than many realize. When a Cessna T210 Centurion is climbing with maximum-allowable power at 15,000 feet, for instance, the air being pumped into the engine is really hot—more than 200°F. At 25,000 feet, where the T210's turbocharger works harder to maintain a given manifold pressure, the compressor-discharge temperature increases to more than 250°F. Such heat can reduce engine power by almost 20 percent, even though engine rpm and manifold pressure have the same values as at sea level. In a manner of speaking, the heat generated by turbocharging is like operating an engine with the carburetor heat turned on.

It is obvious, therefore, that a turbocharged engine generally runs hottest at high altitude. Unfortunately, this makes it all the more difficult to cool the engine. This may seem incongruous, because the standard temperature at 25,000 feet is −30°F. Although this ambient air is quite cold, it has very little density (which is why a turbocharger is needed in the first place) and cannot carry away heat as well as the denser air found at lower altitudes. The poor cooling property of thin air plus the effect of high induction temperatures are the reasons why turbocharged engines have such high operating temperatures at altitude.

High induction temperatures naturally result in high cylinder-head temperatures (CHT). But since the metallic mass of an engine essentially is a heat sink, the temperature of the entire engine tends to increase as well. Often this is reflected in relatively warm oil temperatures.

Heat is one nemesis of a piston engine. Its cumulative effects can lead to piston, ring, and cylinder-head failure, as well as placing thermal stress on other operating components. (For instance, excessive CHT can lead to detonation, which can cause catastrophic engine failure.) Heat also is a primary reason why a turbocharged engine has a lower TBO (time between overhauls) than its normally aspirated counterparts. Another reason for its shorter life span is that turbocharged engines generally are operated at higher power settings a greater portion of the time.

Another problem associated with the heat of turbocharging is thermal shock, or shock cooling. This is caused by a rapid rate of engine cooling and can lead to cracked heads, warped valves and cracked cylinder barrels. When descending from an altitude where the engine is heat soaked, the pilot must be careful to keep the rate of cooling in check by making gradual power reductions and not increasing airspeed too much as the aircraft descends into the denser air of lower altitudes. Thermal shock most frequently occurs when attempting to lose altitude rapidly, or when attempting to simultaneously lose altitude and reduce airspeed during a turbulence encounter.

One way to reduce the problems caused by high induction temperatures is to install an intercooler between the compressor outlet of a turbocharger and the induction inlet of the engine. An intercooler is essentially a radiator, or heat exchanger, that allows ambient air to pass in close proximity to the compressed air. The ambient air then absorbs much of the heat of compression and carries it overboard. This results in cooler, denser induction air, thus reducing engine temperatures and increasing horsepower.

A convincing way to demonstrate an intercooler's effectiveness is to blow a hair dryer through an intercooler resting on a table. This air comes out the other side at a noticeably reduced temperature. And this is without the benefit of ambient air being ducted across the intercooler.

The first aviation application of intercooling appears to have been on military aircraft during World War II where it was used to cool the air between two successive superchargers. (This explains how the intercooler got its name.) The intercooler is extraordinarily simple. It has no moving parts or controls and is one of the most reliable, maintenance-free accessories on an airplane. They are standard equipment on such aircraft as the Piper PA-46 Malibu, the Cessna 414, and some models of the Beech Baron. They also are available as retrofit equipment on numerous other turbocharged aircraft.

Even automobile manufacturers have jumped onto the intercooler bandwagon. Porsche, Saab, and Volvo pioneered the popular use of intercoolers to improve the performance, reliability, and longevity of their turbocharged engines.

HOT STARTS

The virtues of a fuel-injected, air-cooled engine are well known. It is more efficient than a carbureted engine because it more evenly distributes the fuel/air mixture to the cylinders. And since it does not have that miniature refrigerator known as the carburetor, it is much less prone to induction icing.

Fuel injection has its disadvantages, too. Not only is it more costly to buy and maintain an aircraft with a fuel-injected engine, it often raises an operational sword of Damocles when a pilot attempts to restart the engine on a hot day (particularly at high elevations).

Although some pilots have mastered the hot-start procedure, others occasionally suffer the consternation and indignity of not being able to restart the engine before the battery dies of exhaustion. In between is the vast and frustrated majority, those who are uncertain about what to expect after engaging the starter. The engine may start and soon die, simply sputter defiantly, or show no signs of life whatsoever.

It is tempting to thumb our noses at someone intimidated by hot starting. After all, the procedure is published not only in the pilot's operating handbook, but also in the engine operating manual. Or is it?

While researching this topic, I discovered a considerable amount of contradictory advice. For example, Teledyne Continental has published at different times two manuals for its popular IO-520 engine. One advises the pilot to turn on the boost pump while cranking the engine during a hot start, but the other implores him not to. To muddy the waters even more, the operating handbook for one airplane in which the IO-520 is installed offers a third—and more recently, a fourth—hot-start procedure. All of this demonstrates that perhaps hot starting is not an exact science.

The question is, whose advice is more reliable, the airframe manufacturer's or the engine manufacturer's? You would expect the engine manufacturer to know more about its engine than anyone else, but not so. Representatives of Avco Lycoming and Teledyne Continental advise pilots to follow the airframe manufacturer's advice. Although each engine manufacturer develops its own hot-start procedures, they point out that these apply primarily to an engine running in a test cell. An engine installed in an aircraft usually is fitted with its own uniquely designed fuel, cooling, and induction systems. These often modify the technique required to restart that engine. Consequently, the airframe manufacturer presumably knows best how to hot start a given installation. This is why the pilot of a Cessna 210, for example, is advised differently than the pilot of a Beechcraft Bonanza equipped with the same engine. (The fuel and induction systems of these airplanes *are* different.)

Unfortunately, the hot-start procedure developed for an engine by an airframe manufacturer usually has not been tested under all conditions, and the procedure may not work at all times.

Many pilots profess to have developed their own restart procedures based on years of experience. Strangely, many of these never seem to work for anyone else. Others claim never to have had hot-start difficulties. The third and perhaps largest group of pilots concede that rekindling a fuel-injected engine often is a matter of luck, black magic, and having a pair of jumper cables.

Although there is one technique that is all but guaranteed to result in a successful restart, it first is important to understand why hot starting can be so agonizingly difficult. In most engine installations, fuel flows from the fuel tank through an electric boost pump (or two) to the engine-driven fuel pump to the metering unit, a sophisticated device that determines how much fuel to pass on to the engine. (In some cases—predominantly Continental engines—excess fuel delivered to the metering unit is returned via a return line to the fuel tank.) The fuel then flows from the metering unit (called an injector servo on Lycoming engines) to a fuel (or flow) divider, most often mounted on top of the engine crankcase. Fuel-nozzle lines spread from the fuel divider to the intake ports of the individual cylinders.

It is the close proximity of these metal fuel-nozzle lines to the hot cylinders that creates a major problem. After the engine is shut down, the fuel lines are heat soaked due to heat conduction, radiation, and lack of airflow through the cowling. If heated sufficiently, the fuel in these lines begins to boil. This results in liquid fuel being displaced by bubbles of fuel vapor, which makes it difficult to restart a fuel-injected engine. Starting requires that an uninterrupted stream of liquid fuel be available to the intake ports. The extent of this percolation, which occasionally can be heard after shutdown as a hissing sound, is determined by engine and ambient temperatures and usually is most serious between 30 and 60 minutes after shutdown.

(In a few of the very large Lycoming engines such as the IGSO-540 used on Beech Queen Airs and some Aero Commanders, fuel is injected into the supercharger impellers instead of directly into the intake ports. Consequently, these engines are not quite as prone to hot-start difficulties.)

If a restart is anticipated within an hour after shutdown, a pilot might prevent the fuel from boiling by parking the aircraft into the wind and opening the cowling (or the oil-access door, if this is not practical). Opening the cowl not only allows trapped heat to radiate and escape into the atmosphere, but this results also in an updraft of outside air from beneath the aircraft that helps to keep the fuel lines relatively cool.

Many pilots are curious about why hot fuel-injected aircraft engines are so hard to start considering that most modern fuel-injected automobile engines demonstrate no similar characteristics. For one thing, the liquid-cooled block of an automobile engine does not get as hot as an air-cooled engine, and heat is more readily trapped in tightly cowled aircraft engine compartments. Therefore, fuel is more easily vaporized in aircraft engines. Secondly, some automotive engines have *direct* fuel injection. The fuel is squirted into the cylinders and not into the intake ports (upstream of the intake valves), which is typical of general aviation engines. Thirdly, automotive engines have much more powerful fuel pumps that help to purge the system of fuel vapor.

Another problem that complicates restarting a fuel-injected aircraft engine is that the pilot must carefully manipulate the throttle (the air control) and fuel system so as to deliver the proper fuel/air mixture to the cylinders. This is less of a factor when operating carbureted engines because the carburetor does this more or less automatically. Producing the proper—and often critical—mixture for a hot fuel-injected engine on a hot day can be particularly difficult because the induction air has much less density. Unless properly managed, this often and easily leads to either an excessively rich mixture or a flooded engine.

After an engine is shut down, its temperatures begin to stabilize. This means that hot parts begin to cool and cool parts, which include the fuel lines, begin to get hot. During this process, the cylinders cool and contract faster than the pistons inside, an effect that is most pronounced about 20 minutes after shutdown. The result is that the cylinder barrels tighten around the pistons and rings, creating a greater hardship on the starter at a time when this accessory already is hot (read: inefficient) because of its close proximity to the engine and, in some cases, the exhaust muffler. Certainly this contributes to hot-start difficulties and explains why the starter often is the most abused component on the airplane.

Pilots never should engage a starter (especially during a hot start) for more than 30 seconds at a time or longer than recommended in the operating handbook, whichever is more restrictive. If cranking periods are excessively long, the starter will overheat and parts inside will weaken or melt. This is one of the primary causes of starter failure. Besides, if an engine does not start in the existing configuration within 30 seconds, chances are it is not going to start at all. Continued and imprudent cranking serves only to wear down the starter and the battery and reduce the number of potential start attempts. Pilots also should protect their starters against damage by allowing them to cool three to five minutes between cranking periods. Unfortunately, impatience frequently causes many of us to disregard this important consideration.

When confronted with having to restart a fuel-injected engine, a pilot should approach the problem with a specific plan of action. This can be either a procedure that has been used successfully with that particular aircraft model or one published in the pilot's operating handbook. A common mistake is to assume that the technique used to hot start one type of aircraft or engine will apply equally well to another. Other pilots begin the restarting process haphazardly and without realizing what they are doing and why. Such an attempt usually leads to failure.

If the appropriate procedure does not work the first time, do not abandon it. After waiting for the starter to cool, Lycoming and Continental service representatives suggest, try again and then a third time, if necessary. If the engine starts, the book can be closed and tucked away. Should the engine refuse to cooperate, however, a frustrated pilot may begin to experiment with different engine-start configurations, a procedure that usually leads to a dead battery.

Since it is so easy to flood a hot fuel-injected engine, Continental and Lycoming experts believe that a pilot unable to restart using recommended procedures probably has flooded the engine. At this point the cylinders and intake ports should be cleared of fuel, using the flooded-start procedure, during which time the engine should start.

This last sentence contains a clue that may completely solve the mystery of hot starting. Since using a flooded-start procedure is a very reliable way of hot starting a flooded engine, why not intentionally flood the engine in the first place? I posed this question to experts from Continental and Lycoming. They conceded that although this is not the purist's way to start an engine, it can save considerable aggravation and be used successfully to hot start any fuel-injected engine. As a matter of fact, many pilots have discovered this technique on their own and have been practicing it satisfactorily for years. The only disadvantage to using a flooded-start procedure is that it might require a few more seconds of cranking than a conventional hot start that proves immediately successful.

To flood an engine, push the throttle to the firewall, place the mixture control in the full-rich position, and turn on the boost pump for about five or six seconds (or until fuel drips out of the overflow). This also should purge the nozzle lines of fuel vapor. After turning off the boost pump, place the mixture control in the idle-cutoff position. This prevents additional fuel from being pumped to the cylinders prior to engine start. On Lycoming engines, leave the throttle wide open, but on Continental engines, retard the throttle to about three-fourths open. The open (or nearly open) throttle provides the air necessary to help lean the extremely rich (flooded) mixture in the cylinders.

Next, turn on the magnetos and engage the starter. As the engine is being cranked, fuel will be pumped out of the cylinders and into the exhaust system. This may pose a fire hazard with some aircraft because of pooling of fuel. But, in most cases, the exhaust stacks of a shutdown engine are not hot enough to ignite fuel, according to the experts. A pilot, however, might hear fuel sizzling and vaporizing in the exhaust manifold.

Since fuel is leaving the cylinders, there will come a time during cranking when the mixture of air and remaining fuel will be perfect for combustion. At this point the engine should start. As soon as it comes to life, immediately retard the throttle to avoid overspeeding the engine. But do not close the throttle; leave it in a fast idle position. Then advance the mixture to the full-rich position to provide a steady supply of fuel to the engine.

Unless the fuel-vapor problem is serious, the engine should continue to run normally. But be ready just in case. If it starts to sputter, this indicates that fuel vapors still are present in the system. In the case of Lycoming engines, turn on the boost pump and hope that this creates enough additional pressure to purge the fuel lines of vapor. In the case of a Continental engine, alternately turn the boost pump (or electrically operated primer) on and off as necessary to keep the engine running.

If all of this fails and the engine dies, try the flooded-start procedure once more. If this procedure fails a second time, consider having lunch and giving the engine at least an hour to cool. Be sure to leave open the cowling and cowl flaps (if available).

The fuel-vapor problem may be so extensive that either the boost pump or the engine-driven pump (or both) is cavitating and unable to develop sufficient fuel pressure, a situation known as vapor lock. If a steady stream of fuel cannot be delivered to the cylinders, the engine simply cannot operate.

In the case of a Continental engine, an interesting technique might prove successful in overcoming vapor lock. First set the mixture control to the idle-cutoff position and then turn on the boost pump for 30 seconds to a minute. Although this seems like an exaggerated attempt to flood the engine, it is not. With the mixture set to idle-cutoff, fuel cannot flow beyond the metering unit. Instead, what little fuel is delivered to the metering unit by the cavitating fuel pump(s) will simply follow the path of least resistance and flow through the return line to the fuel tank. This also is where the bubbles of fuel vapor will go. Cold fuel from the tank then enters the system, displaces the vaporized fuel, and cools the lines sufficiently to allow a normal engine start. However, if the pump(s) is cavitating so badly that even this procedure proves ineffective, it is indeed time for a very long lunch.

If a pilot has a genuinely serious need to take off immediately and cannot afford to wait for the engine to cool, he almost always can make the engine start with the assistance of a powerplant mechanic. The fuel line must be disconnected somewhere between the engine-driven fuel pump and the fuel metering unit (or servo). This eliminates virtually all resistance to fuel flow. With the loose hose pointed safely toward the ground or into a collector can, turn on the boost pump until the hose stops spitting out fuel bubbles and a steady stream of cool fuel emerges. After the line is reconnected, a steady supply of liquid fuel to the metering unit is assured. The engine should start without difficulty unless something is mechanically wrong with it.

Pilots must not perform this procedure without professional assistance. Fuel lines must be connected with a torque wrench. If the nut is wrenched too tightly, the fitting might crack and result in a fuel line leak. Similar results can be expected if the nut is not torqued tightly enough.

A problem with hot starting is that an understanding of the principles involved does not always translate into success. To paraphrase a philosopher, trying to restart a fuel-injected engine is an enigma cloaked by a paradox. But at least the knowledge of what should be done to achieve a successful hot start may help to avoid a hot collar.

ENGINE FIRES

The Beech A35 Bonanza was being flown from San Francisco to Santa Monica, California. While the airplane was at cruise altitude, an engine fire developed as the result of a fuel leak. Recognizing the need to land, the pilot headed for nearby Paso Robles Airport, overflying a number of suitable emergency-landing sites. By the time he was on final approach, the fire had developed into an inferno that was clearly visible to horrified observers on the ground. Panic apparently dictated the tragic events that followed.

As the aircraft shot across the runway threshold with an extraordinary abundance of airspeed, the right-seat passenger opened the door, jumped out in an attempt to escape the flames, and was killed in the process. The Bonanza then landed heavily on its nosewheel and seconds later was seen cartwheeling into a smoldering aluminum ball, claiming the lives of its pilot and the two rear-seat passengers.

Accident investigators concluded later that everyone aboard could have survived the consequences of the engine fire if the pilot had abided by the recommended procedures for such an emergency. They concluded also, however, that most pilots have only a vague idea of how to react to an in-flight engine fire (as determined by an informal survey conducted several months after the accident).

During a recent 31-month period, 47 general aviation accidents were attributed to engine fires. This is 18 such fires per year. Although the chances of experiencing an engine fire are remote, the nature of the emergency demands immediate action and abiding by recommended guidelines. There is precious little time available to consult a handbook or checklist, both of which often offer inadequate guidance anyway.

The seriousness of an engine fire must not be underestimated. Consider, for example, this advice offered by Britain's Royal Air Force to its pilots: "Landing with an aircraft on fire is seldom justified and very dangerous; there is little chance of saving the aircraft after landing, and there is great risk that the fire may increase or cause structural failure at an altitude where it is unsafe to abandon the aircraft."

Unfortunately, the alternative—bailing out—is an option most general aviation pilots do not have, so they must cope with whatever Fate hands them.

Engine fires usually are caused by the mechanical failure of the engine or an engine-driven accessory, defects in the induction or exhaust system, a flooded carburetor (caused by a sticking float valve), or a leak in the fuel, oil, or hydraulic system.

Although the sight of flames or smoke from under the cowling is convincing evidence of a fire, these are not always the first indications. Pilots of single-engine airplanes who have survived engine fires report that the first sign often was the heat generated in the vicinity of the rudder pedals. They literally got a hot foot (or two). Others stated that the first indication was the smell of smoke. One pilot mentioned that he was aroused by the indication of reduced fuel pressure. He thought at first that the fuel pump was failing, but the flames that developed soon thereafter made him realize that the pressure loss was caused by a serious leak.

When a pilot first notices an engine fire, it already may be well developed, leaving no choice other than to shut down the engine as soon as possible. An engine fire must not be allowed to continue unabated.

In theory, the fire wall separating the engine compartment from the cabin of a single-engine airplane is supposed to keep a fire at bay. But it does not always work that way. Although these bulkheads are ground tested by exposure to flame, this does not mean that they can contain a fire while airborne. The variables of airspeed and flame intensity make it impossible to determine how long the integrity of the fire wall can be maintained. In other words, a fire wall is fire-resistant, not fireproof. Sufficiently intense and persistent flames can penetrate a fire wall.

In a twin, the danger of allowing an engine fire to continue is equally serious. Once a fire wall begins to fail, the very structure of the wing is in jeopardy. And should the flames attack a nearby fuel tank, the results are likely to be explosive.

Once the decision has been made to shut down the offending engine, it must be done without hesitation, even when flying over inhospitable terrain in a single-engine aircraft. A controlled crash landing is preferable to cremation.

The purpose of a shutdown is to deprive the fire of additional fuel and is accomplished by closing the throttle and retarding the mixture control to the idle-cutoff position. Additionally, turn off the electric fuel pump (if applicable), and turn the fuel selector valve to the Off position. Do not, however, be in a rush to turn off the magnetos. Leaving on the ignition for a moment or two may allow residual downstream fuel to be burned in the safest possible place, the cylinders.

With some luck, starving the engine compartment of fuel may cause the fire to die naturally. But even if the flames, smoke, and heat seem to disappear, do not assume the problem has been resolved. The fire may only have diminished temporarily, or the smoke and flames may be coming out the bottom of the cowling.

Under no circumstances should a pilot attempt a restart. The fire may rekindle with even greater intensity.

Several aircraft operating handbooks also suggest that the master switch be turned off during the shutdown procedure. Unless the fire is electrical in nature or a crash landing is imminent, this is of dubious value. Deactivating the electrical system precludes the possibility of transmitting a Mayday message (assuming a pilot has the time, desire, and presence of mind to make such a broadcast). More importantly, this prevents the use of electrically operated flap and landing-gear systems during the subsequent descent and landing.

The possibility of asphyxiation also is of immediate concern. To prevent smoke from entering the cockpit, close all fresh-air and cabin-heat vents located either in the fire wall or along the sides of the fuselage. (Some aircraft have a fire wall shutoff that should be closed as well.) Air vents located in the wing roots of high-wing aircraft or in other locations free of streaming smoke or flame should be opened to increase the flow of fresh air through the cabin. (Those not thoroughly familiar with the sources of air for ventilation and cabin-heat ducts should review the plumbing of the environmental control systems for their aircraft. Vents and the like often are taken for granted and given only cursory attention but can be vitally important.)

If the cabin does fill with smoke, the air often can be cleared expeditiously by opening a door or a window on the right side of the cockpit (away from the pilot) as long as the opening is clear of trailing smoke and flame. Do not open the pilot's door or window because this may cause the smoke to pass in front of him on the way out and compound his breathing problem. (The smoke-removal checklist of a Boeing 727 calls for depressurizing the aircraft and opening the first officer's sliding-glass window when airspeed is less than 250 knots indicated, a procedure that seems to have the unanimous approval of captains.) In any event, pilots should be familiar with the smoke-removal procedures developed by the manufacturer for the aircraft they fly.

Howard Hughes was said to be almost paranoid about the possibility of asphyxiation. This probably stemmed from his fiery crash landing of the XF-11 photoreconnaisance-plane in 1946. Prior to flying his HK-1 "Spruce Goose" a year later, he had a large-diameter tube installed near his seat that would allow ambient air from outside the aircraft to blow in his face in the event smoke filled the cockpit for any reason. (None of the other crewmembers was provided such emergency equipment.)

Occasionally pilots are told that it is possible to dive an airplane to blow out an engine fire. This technique may be successful. On the other hand, the effect of increasing the airflow across the engine might cause fire intensity to increase. It all depends on the combustible mixture. For example, increasing airspeed encourages the burning of a rich mixture but may extinguish a lean mixture. Since a pilot has no way of assessing the combustible mixture, he cannot know whether to combat the fire by increasing or decreasing airspeed. (If some sixth sense suggests that a dive is in order, do not forget to open the cowl flaps—if available—to maximize airflow through the cowling.) One thing is certain, however: An oil-fed fire is much more difficult to blow out than one fed by fuel.

It is not particularly difficult to distinguish between fuel and oil fires. Burning avgas produces bright orange flames and leaves a smoke trail that often can be seen only by looking behind the airplane. An oil fire, however, is characterized by a profusion of dense, black smoke and may be accompanied by indications of low oil pressure and high oil temperature, depending on the size of the oil leak.

Although oil dripping on a hot exhaust manifold is sufficient to cause ignition, an oil fire also may be the result of a fuel fire that burns through an oil line. So it is quite possible that an engine fire that begins as one type may develop into another.

This indicates further the urgency of engine shutdown. If a

fuel-fed fire is denied a supply of avgas soon enough, it may die of starvation before igniting an oil fire. This latter type can be much more persistent and difficult to extinguish. This is because an engine-driven oil (or hydraulic) pump continues to pump flammable liquid and feed the fire as long as the propeller windmills. In this respect, the pilot of a multiengine aircraft has a decided advantage. He can feather the propeller, resulting in a stilled engine and an impotent oil pump. Although this does not guarantee that the fire will go out, it limits its destructive potential.

If the pilot of a single-engine airplane is sitting behind a raging oil fire, he too can combat the inferno by halting propeller rotation. However, he must raise the nose and reduce airspeed until the resistance of engine compression overcomes the waning aerodynamic forces that cause a propeller to windmill. (Stopping a constant-speed propeller can be assisted by fully retarding the pitch-control lever to the minimum-rpm position.)

This process of arresting engine rotation has the disadvantage of temporarily reducing the sink rate and increasing the time required to lose altitude. If a pilot does only one thing correctly when faced with an engine fire, it should be an expeditious descent and landing. This is not the time to stretch the glide in an attempt to reach some optimum landing site unless the fire is *known* to be out. Instead, select a *nearby* piece of terrain and plant the aircraft on it as quickly as is possible and survivable. One must adopt the attitude that the airplane has been lost, that it can be sacrificed if necessary to preserve the lives of those inside. When confronted with a persistent engine fire, the element of time is extremely critical. Give a fire enough time and it will consume you.

The message is particularly important to the pilot of a twin, who may be tempted to use the remaining engine to hobble to some distant haven. When fire rages, the only value of an operative engine is the assistance it can provide in accurately placing the airplane on a selected touchdown point.

The method of descent is at the discretion of the pilot, but most experts agree that the airplane should be configured so as to achieve the maximum rate of descent consistent with keeping the wings and tailfeathers firmly attached. With some aircraft, this may necessitate extending the landing gear or the flaps, or both, and then diving at the maximum-applicable airspeed.

Although pilots correctly are taught never to exceed various limiting airspeeds, this may not be the time to be so conscientious. If the aircraft is on fire, who cares whether the maximum-allowable landing-gear-extended airspeed is violated? Besides, airplanes are built with enough of a safety margin so as to be able to withstand a one-time emergency violation of structural limits. (But do not get *too* carried away.)

When descending at high speed in a single-engine airplane after propeller rotation has been stopped, consider that the increased aerodynamic forces may overcome engine compression and cause propeller windmilling to resume.

When discussing engine fires in single-engine airplanes, the subject of slipping usually arises. Presumably this is recommended when smoke from an oil fire obscures forward visibility or when flames lick the cockpit. Slipping may divert the smoke and flames toward one side of the airplane, but it is essentially a low-speed maneuver that results in less of a sink rate than diving, factors that must be weighed. A pilot might decide that diving initially would be more beneficial and that slipping would be more appropriate on final approach when forward visibility is more critical.

There comes a point during the descent when a pilot must shift mental gears and make the transition into the landing approach. This requires slowing the airplane and planning for the safest possible landing. It is of little benefit to survive an engine fire if the flight terminates in a lethal crash landing.

If a pilot is so fortunate as to be landing at a controlled airport, he should not hesitate to request that emergency equipment stand by, even if the fire appears to be out. The reduction of airspeed during an approach and landing could cause a smoldering fire to rekindle with a vengeance. This also explains why an orderly evacuation should be conducted as soon as the aircraft comes to rest and why everyone should get away from it as quickly as possible.

Many engine fires can be avoided by methodical preflight inspections. Pilots should be on the alert for puddles, streaks, and stains of fuel, oil, and hydraulic fluid, both under and inside the cowling. They also should be able to locate the various fuel and oil lines and know how to check their security and condition. Sometimes a good sniff under the cowling can detect a slow fuel leak before it develops into one that can be seen. Be sure also to check exhaust manifolds for security by tugging gently on the ends of the stacks. Exhaust leaking from a cracked stack can be an ideal source of ignition.

Of course, many pilots do not take the time to inspect the engine properly, trusting the statistical infrequency of in-flight engine fires and modern powerplant reliability to insulate them from a horrifying airborne emergency. But in so doing they give up one of the only two weapons against fires that we have: the preflight inspection and procedural proficiency. The rest is luck. And a sudden gush of flame is harsh notice that your luck has run out.

4

INSTRUMENT POINTERS

It is said that truth is stranger—and a thousand times more interesting—than fiction. This adage certainly applies to the true airspeed at which airplanes fly, perhaps more than we realize.

A case in point involves a pilot from southern California who complained resignedly that he had to fight a headwind no matter where or when he flew his S-model Bonanza. "Impossible," claimed an instructor. "If you want a tailwind that badly, just turn around and you'll have one."

But even that did not work. The Bonanza pilot genuinely believed that the wind was malicious and would turn against him no matter which way he flew.

Sensing his frustration, a few of us agreed to fly his wingtip in a similar airplane on a short flight toward San Diego. We believed that a forecast 15-knot tailwind would silence the pilot's frustrations once and for all.

After leveling off at 5,500 feet, both airplanes were established in cruise at 23 inches MAP and 2,300 rpm. But then a strange thing happened. The S-model Bonanza began to fall

162

behind, even though the indicated airspeeds of both airplanes were identical.

No wonder the pilot was frustrated. His airplane had a built-in headwind due to various errors in his airspeed indicator and engine instruments. His true airspeed was not even close to what he thought it was. (When both airplanes were flown side-by-side with everything pushed to the fire wall, they did have approximately the same airspeed, but the gauges were in serious disagreement.)

The pilot had the faulty gauges calibrated at an instrument shop, and he never again complained of headwinds conspiring against him.

Although somewhat extreme, this example illustrates why very few pilots really know the true airspeed (TAS) of their aircraft.

Determining TAS should be a simple matter of converting indicated airspeed (IAS) to calibrated airspeed (CAS) and then correcting the result for outside air temperature (OAT) and pressure altitude. Unfortunately, this can be much more difficult than it seems because of system errors that are either unconsidered or unknown.

A pilot often makes his first mistake when noting indicated airspeed. He glances at the gauge and sees 140 knots, for example. But this may not be the correct IAS, even though the airplane is stabilized in cruise flight. This is because longitudinal stability causes an airplane to exhibit a very slight nose-up/nose-down cycle that is repeated every 20 to 100 seconds. This phugoid oscillation may not even be noticeable, but it does cause airspeed to increase and decrease while the aircraft apparently maintains a constant altitude (even with the autopilot on and altitude hold engaged). Depending on the airplane, IAS variations of five knots or more are not unusual.

To derive a useful figure for IAS, it is important to observe the airspeed indicator for a minute or so and then note its *average* indication.

Although such an error may seem unimportant, consider

that each knot of IAS error is equivalent to more than one knot of TAS at altitude.

To obtain true airspeed, IAS is converted to CAS to compensate for errors in the airspeed indicating system. The first of these is position error. This occurs because it is almost impossible for an aircraft designer to position the static ports and pitot tube in a way that allows them to sense ambient and ram-air pressures with 100-percent accuracy. The second is instrument error, the result of an inaccurate gauge.

To obtain CAS, a pilot first must refer to the airspeed calibration chart in the aircraft operating handbook. Unfortunately, this chart is provided only for relatively new aircraft. Handbooks for older aircraft may not contain this information. But even when available, many pilots fail to use the correction. Instead, they assume that IAS and CAS are the same, which, of course, they are not.

A calibration chart, however, compensates only for position error. It does not consider instrument error, which can be substantial. Even when new, an airspeed indicator is guaranteed accurate only to within a few percent. A new gauge indicating 150 knots, for example, could be in error by five knots or more.

Known indicator errors cannot be included on the calibration chart provided in the handbook because, like the deviation errors of magnetic compasses, they vary between one instrument and the next.

Airspeed indicators do not age gracefully. Moisture and other contaminants entering the pitot tube further erode accuracy. This partially explains why the airspeed indicators of aircraft in formation (or those dual instruments installed in the same aircraft) often differ so greatly.

Another link in this chain of error is the OAT gauge, which also is not as accurate as it may appear. An error of 10°C is not uncommon and could be responsible for another few knots of erroneous airspeed.

The final factor is pressure altitude, the altitude indicated when the altimeter is set to 29.92 inches Hg. Failing to set the

altimeter properly induces a slight additional error, but this error normally may be disregarded unless the local altimeter setting is unusually high or low.

Considering the potential for error, it is easy to understand
why some pilots have only an approximation of the true airspeed of their aircraft (even though they may believe otherwise).
After all, what else is there to go by?

When the data used to compute TAS are in doubt, a pilot
can refer to the performance charts to determine what the true
airspeed is supposed to be. Unfortunately, projected and actual
true airspeed also can differ substantially. This has nothing to
do with the manufacturer's honesty; despite accusations to the
contrary, manufacturers really do attempt to provide the most
accurate data available. The trouble is, it may be *too* accurate.

When a new model is flight-tested, it is equipped with highly
calibrated instrumentation, including calibrated engine gauges.
Subsequent production aircraft are not so elaborately equipped.
In other words—and because of inaccurate power gauges—the
engine(s) of a given airplane may produce more or less than
what the engine instruments indicate. This also explains why
the fuel consumption of an aircraft may be consistently more or
less than anticipated.

Engines supplied to airframe manufacturers are guaranteed
(by the engine manufacturer) to produce between 100 and 105
percent of rated horsepower. A new 260-hp engine, for example, produces anywhere from 260 to 273 hp. If, by chance, one
of the more powerful engines is installed in the prototype aircraft used to gather performance data, the resultant airspeeds
may be higher than would be possible in many other "identical"
models.

Even when aircraft have equally powerful engines, they may
perform differently because of manufacturing variables. Differences in rigging, for example, can make one aircraft slower or
faster than another.

As an airplane ages, its performance is likely to decline because of airframe and wing dents, propeller nicks, gear doors

that do not close as tightly as they should, engines that lose some muscle, and so forth. Additional antennas and other exterior modifications also take their toll.

This helps to explain why two seemingly identical aircraft may perform so differently. Not being able to accurately determine true airspeed adds to the confusion.

Those who are more than passively curious about the accuracy of their airspeed indicators may be wise to periodically take their aircraft to a certified instrument shop and have a calibration card prepared. The process takes less than an hour and involves attaching a finely calibrated air compressor to the pitot tube, then pumping in pressures that correspond to known indicated airspeeds. These results are compared to actual airspeed indications, and the differences are plotted on a calibration card that can be kept in the aircraft. (The static pressure system test that is required every 24 calendar months on those aircraft used for instrument flight does not include a test of pitot pressure.)

To check the OAT gauge, just compare its indication (while in the shade) to a reliable thermometer.

The manifold pressure gauge is equally easy to check. First, determine barometric pressure at the airport. This is equal to the local altimeter setting minus one inch per 1,000 feet of airport elevation. The result is what the manifold pressure gauge should indicate when the engine is shut down.

These OAT and manifold pressure gauge checks determine their accuracy (or lack of it) at only one point on their scales, but this may be all that is needed.

The easiest way to determine tachometer accuracy is to buy an inexpensive device that uses stroboscopic principles to measure propeller rpm. Tachometer errors of 50 to 100 rpm are not uncommon.

Fortunately, there is a way to determine true airspeed that does not rely on instrument accuracy. It does, however, require careful attention to detail.

The procedure is described using the example shown in Figure 32. A pilot selects a pair of VORs (Santa Monica and Van

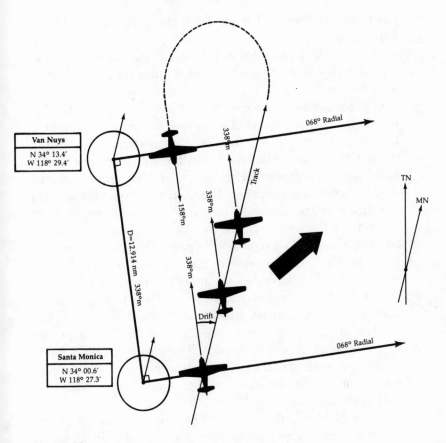

FIGURE 32

Nuys, California) that are separated by several minutes of flying time. He then needs to accurately measure the distance between them. Since a plotter is not accurate enough, he notes the coordinates of each station and uses a suitable computer (such as a Jeppesen Prostar) to calculate the distance, which is 12.914 nm in our example. He then measures the magnetic course, which is 338 degrees.

As you may have guessed, the pilot is going to determine the time required to fly the test aircraft from one station to the other, turn around, and repeat the flight in the opposite direction.

One problem associated with VOR navigation—especially at high altitude—is the difficulty in determining the precise instant of station passage. The To/From indicator does a jig as the aircraft passes overhead and does not settle down until the VOR is behind the tail. So instead of flying directly over the station, the pilot in this example will fly a mile or so abeam of it. Before doing this, however, he will adjust the course selector to the radial that is perpendicular to the course between the stations. As the aircraft passes abeam of the VOR and crosses the selected radial, the course deviation indicator will swing rapidly from one side of the instrument to the other. Timing of the speed run begins as the left/right needle passes through the centered position. This explains why the aircraft must not pass too far from the VOR. The farther the aircraft is from the station, the slower the needle will move, which reduces timing accuracy and allows VOR-accuracy errors to affect the flight test results.

The aircraft should cross the "starting line" on a precise magnetic heading of 338 degrees. The idea is for the pilot to maintain a heading that exactly parallels the course between the stations and is perpendicular to the radial used to determine station passage.

Prior to passing the second VOR, the pilot tunes it in and selects the same radial used to determine when the aircraft passed abeam of the first VOR. He stops timing the speed run as the left-right needle zips through the center of the instrument.

This procedure is repeated in the opposite direction (and at the same altitude and power setting) while the pilot maintains a reciprocal magnetic heading of 158 degrees.

After the outbound and return legs have been flown and timed, the groundspeed encountered on each leg is computed using the distance between the stations in each case. For example, if the times required to fly between the radials were 4:05 and 5:25, these would be used with a distance of 12.914 nm to arrive at groundspeeds of 189.7 and 143 knots, respectively.

The final step requires averaging the outbound and return groundspeeds (not the times), which results in an average groundspeed of 166.4 knots. Conveniently, this also is the average true airspeed experienced during the outbound and return flights.

The average groundspeed results in true airspeed because, when a heading is held as explained, forward progress (as measured parallel to the course between the VOR stations) is affected only by the headwind component (if any) while flying one way and the tailwind component while flying in the other direction. Since the headings flown are exact reciprocals, the headwind component exactly equals the tailwind component. When averaging groundspeeds, therefore, these components—being equal and opposite—cancel out one another.

This technique works equally well in any wind condition as long as the wind is steady. This is particularly convenient because the pilot does not need to know wind velocity while performing such a flight test.

If a pilot tried to do this while maintaining a given course and its reciprocal (instead of a given heading), he would have to crab the aircraft while flying in each direction to prevent drift. Turning into the wind would reduce groundspeed in each direction. By maintaining a heading (and not a course), the pilot allows the aircraft to drift. In this way, whatever crosswind exists has no effect on forward progress (as measured along the course line separating the VOR stations).

Prior to beginning each speed run, be certain that the air is smooth. Any turbulence—even light ripples—cannot be tolerated. Also, approach each run after several minutes of straight-and-level flight at a constant altitude and power setting to be certain that airspeed has stabilized. If a turn has just been completed, for example, the airplane is probably still recovering the airspeed lost while maneuvering.

Other tips include using the aircraft's autopilot to maintain altitude and heading (when applicable), bringing along an observer to help watch for traffic, and obtaining the cooperation

of air traffic control, since one of the out-and-return flights will
be at an illegal cruise altitude (if operating above 3,000 feet agl).

The procedure described also can be used to fly between
parallel roads or other checkpoints. To do so, however, requires
knowing the precise distance between the chosen points; measuring distance with a plotter is not sufficiently accurate. Also,
such a flight test must be at a relatively low altitude to accurately determine when the aircraft passes each checkpoint.

Whether using VOR radials or ground references, log the
indicated airspeed at 30-second intervals during each speed run.
Then, use the average of these to compute true airspeed conventionally. Compare the result of your computation to the true
airspeed determined by the flight test. You are likely to be surprised.

ALTIMETER AND AIRSPEED FAILURE

One of my first instructors was a genuine sadist. Whenever I
demonstrated progress and confidence, he would simulate some
emergency calculated to completely rattle me. For example, he
once covered the Stinson's only compass while I was attempting
to complete a fade-parallel, low-frequency range orientation; this
was *before* VORs blossomed along the airways.

"Hey, that's unfair," I reacted.

"Perhaps. But it also could happen during an actual IFR
flight," was the smug reply.

Another time, he simulated the failure of the airspeed indicator. But the emergency that really unnerved me was when he
covered the altimeter.

"Damn," I said, "altimeters don't fail."

"Are you willing to bet your life on that?" My response was
a meek, "Negative." My disdain for that instructor gradually
evolved into respect and finally into gratitude. He taught me
never to take anything for granted and that sooner or later even
the most trustworthy component could be a cause for concern
and possibly alarm.

During my instrument training, I had to contend with almost all imaginable instrument and system failures (not always successfully, I should add). But it was the simulated altimeter failure that caused the most consternation. It took only a few minutes of flying on instruments to appreciate that the altimeter is the single most important instrument on the panel. It is the only instrument that an IFR pilot absolutely, positively must have. It seems incongruous, therefore, that an airplane has any number of redundant features but usually only one altimeter. Some countries recognize the necessity of a functioning altimeter and require a pair of them (each with an independent static system) in any airplane flown in IFR conditions.

Although altimeter failure is rare, it does happen. Not long ago, television actor Lloyd Haynes and his instructor Mischa Hausserman were on an actual IFR departure from Santa Monica Municipal Airport in California, in Haynes's Bellanca Viking. At 4,100 feet, the hands of the altimeter froze. Fortunately, high ceilings prevailed. Haynes simply picked up the mike, requested a descent clearance from departure control and quickly returned to visual conditions.

But what if they had been engulfed in cloud while flying in an area of widespread low ceilings and visibilities? What procedure could they have used to successfully complete an IFR approach to low minimums? Anyone giving this what-if problem serious thought will conclude rapidly that there are no easy solutions available.

If altimeter failure occurs in cruise flight, it may go undetected for a while, leading you to believe you are doing a magnificent job of holding altitude. However, as soon as the failure is detected, tap lightly on the face of the instrument. Chances are the hands have stuck momentarily, and tapping may be all that is necessary to free them. The airframe vibration common to piston airplanes normally is sufficient to prevent the hands from sticking, but not always. If tapping the gauge fails to free the hands, then rotate the altimeter-setting knob to force the hands free. If this resolves the problem, regard the incident as a warning of a potentially more serious failure; trade the faulty altimeter for another.

(Sticking altimeter hands were a common problem on early jets. This is because they were relatively free of the airframe vibration normally needed to prevent the hands from sticking. The problem was resolved on these and subsequent turbine airplanes by equipping each with an altimeter vibrator, an electrical device that constantly and rapidly taps the instrument case.)

Another warning of impending failure is an altimeter-setting knob that becomes progressively more difficult to twist. This usually indicates that moisture entering the instrument through the static system has begun to corrode the internal mechanism. This or any hint of altimeter malfunction warrants expeditious replacement.

In addition to jamming or sticking, the hands of an altimeter also can become loose and swing to the bottom of the instrument face like pendulums. If the medium-length hand of a three-pointer altimeter falls loose, nothing really is lost. A pilot can keep track of the revolutions of the large hand to maintain a constant awareness of altitude. If the large hand flops loose, only the medium-length pointer is of value. Since one revolution of this hand represents 10,000 feet, it is difficult to determine altitude with much more precision than 200 feet. Although this is suitable for approximately maintaining an assigned altitude, avoid low approaches in IFR conditions.

Before concluding that an altimeter has failed mechanically, verify that the stuck hands are not the result of static-system icing. Although this is rare (except when the static source is located in an unheated pitot tube), it can occur even when ambient conditions normally would preclude such a possibility. For example, water entering the static sources during a recent wash or while taxiing through large, deep puddles can freeze when the airplane is flown to a sufficiently cold altitude.

If the altimeter failure is due to icing, the vertical speed indicator (VSI), which also relies on open static-air sources, will be inaccurate, too. To correct the problem simply turn on the alternate static source to restore system integrity. The alternate static source rarely is needed. Although this is indeed a testimony to static-system reliability, it also breeds complacency. Pilots not only tend to ignore the alternate static source, but also sometimes forget it even exists.

During the last seven biennial flight reviews that I administered, I asked each pilot to pretend he had encountered static-system icing. "As a result," I said, "your altimeter is unreliable. What should you do?"

The results were shocking. Three of the pilots proceeded to turn on the alternate-air (induction) sources for their fuel-injected engines. Two others simply conceded that they did not know what to do. Only the two remaining pilots opened the appropriate petcocks. (Water drained from one of these.) Sadly, all of these pilots were flying their own airplanes. Years of never having to use the alternate system allowed five of them to forget about it completely. (Admittedly, the alternate static source usually is installed inconspicuously under the panel, but this is no excuse to ignore it).

To remain aware of the alternate static source and its effect on the instruments, you are encouraged to operate the system at least once a month. If you rent airplanes, make a point of finding where the valve is hidden, just in case.

Owners of airplanes without an alternate source have only themselves to blame for static-system difficulties. An alternate source can be installed inexpensively by any competent instrument shop. Otherwise the only solution to static-system blockage is to break the glass face of the VSI to allow cockpit static air to enter the static system and reach the altimeter. (Breaking the glass of the VSI may damage the instrument, but it is worthwhile to sacrifice this one to restore the altimeter.)

If the altimeter fails and the VSI is operating normally, the problem clearly is caused by a mechanical failure of the instrument. If the airplane is equipped with a blind (altitude) encoder (an altitude-sensing device that operates independently of a conventional, panel-mounted altimeter), the transponder then is capable of continually transmitting aircraft altitude to air traffic control. If necessary, controllers can inform you at appropriate intervals of your altitude as indicated on radar. Bear in mind, however, that an altitude encoder is known to be accurate within 300 feet only at the time of the previous biennial system check. Encoder accuracy should be verified periodically by comparing the altimeter indication with the altitude superimposed on a controller's radar screen.

Many airplanes are equipped with encoding altimeters. Should an encoding altimeter fail, the altitude-reporting capability of the transponder would fail also. Many others have no altitude-reporting feature at all. In either case, altimeter failure can be catastrophic.

The simplest escape is to request a clearance to VFR conditions. Often, a simple climb or descent is all that is required. But if a considerable distance must be flown, the problem increases in proportion to the time required. Simply maintaining an assigned altitude without an altimeter is difficult. During prolonged flight, altitude is bound to vary, even when you do your best to keep the VSI zeroed. And in an effort to avoid an undesirable descent, you most likely will overcorrect and gain altitude. To appreciate the difficulty of such an exercise, simulate the problem and try it (especially during a turbulent flight).

There is one clever way to maintain an *approximately* constant altitude and prevent an untimely descent, but only in airplanes with normally aspirated (nonturbocharged) engines and constant-speed propellers. When altimeter failure is detected, note the indicated manifold pressure and tighten the friction lock on the throttle(s) to avoid inadvertent power changes. A significant altitude gain will register as a decrease in manifold pressure; a descent, as an increase in power. Propeller pitch (rpm) should not be varied because this has an effect on the reference manifold pressure. (Increasing rpm reduces manifold pressure and vice versa.) In effect, the power gauge can be used as a crude, nonsensitive altimeter.

Although many pressurized airplanes are equipped with dual altimeters, pilots of airplanes that do not have a second altimeter can resort to a unique emergency technique. In case of altimeter failure, simply depressurize the airplane and substitute the cabin altimeter for the malfunctioning instrument.

Ultimately, descent is necessary. In VFR conditions, this poses little more than inconvenience; fly the traffic pattern at whatever altitude seems comfortable. If necessary to descend from IFR to VFR conditions, try to do so directly over the point where the surface weather observation was made. The ceiling and visibility between weather-reporting points can be considerably worse than anticipated because of precipitous terrain and the vagaries of weather. Usually, it is best to descend over an airport with an operating control tower where potentially hazardous changes can be reported.

But if the clouds bottom out close to the decision height (DH) of an ILS, or the minimum descent altitude (MDA) of a nonprecision approach, you are in at least as much jeopardy as a long-tailed cat in a room full of rocking chairs. This is one of the most serious emergencies a pilot can encounter.

It is difficult to appreciate how frightening and unnerving it can be to descend IFR to a DH or an MDA without an altimeter. Rather than attempt to shoot the instrument approach, you could head for the nearest air force base or naval air station and request an emergency ground-controlled approach (GCA), the military equivalent of a precision radar approach. Once on final, you continually are kept informed of your altitude.

Without an altimeter, executing a nonprecision approach is virtually impossible, leaving an ILS approach as the only remaining option. Although the guidance offered by a glideslope can relieve much apprehension when descending toward the ground without an altimeter, you first must cope with an intriguing problem: glideslope intercept. Normally, this is achieved by flying beneath the glideslope at an appropriate and constant altitude until intercept occurs. But how can you descend safely to intercept altitude without an altimeter?

The best technique is to maintain a reasonably high cruise altitude until reaching the outer marker. Once there, enter a holding pattern outside the marker and on the localizer. Then, using the VSI for reference, descend slowly (and carefully) in the holding pattern. Ultimately, the airplane will wind up inbound on the localizer and slightly below glideslope. At this time, attempt to maintain altitude until glideslope intercept occurs. Once descending safely inbound on the glideslope, you then should recite the appropriate prayer (silently if passengers are on board) and hope that visual conditions are established before reaching the middle marker. Otherwise, a missed approach is mandatory, and the whole procedure will have to be repeated elsewhere.

Most instrument repairmen regard the altimeter as an almost "bulletproof" instrument. But they do acknowledge its potential for failure. Since the altimeter is the single most important IFR instrument, you must be extremely conscientious about not tolerating even the slightest malfunction. This, after all, can be a prelude to catastrophic, total failure.

The ideal solution is to install a second altimeter, which also can be used as a cross-check on the primary instrument. Or, consider carrying a hand-held, auxiliary altimeter. The most reliable models are accurate to within 50 or 100 feet and can be adjusted to the current altimeter setting.

The airspeed indicator also is regarded as "bulletproof," but this does not guarantee that the pitot heat will not fail during IFR conditions or that insects will not plug the pitot tube during VFR conditions. In either event, the results are the same: an inoperative gauge.

Having acquired the sadistic tendencies of my early instrument instructor, I have made it a practice to simulate failure of the airspeed indicator during some biennial flight reviews. This has led me to conclude that instrument-rated pilots seem to cope with the problem far better than do noninstrument-rated pilots. This probably is because IFR pilots are accustomed to flying with reference to airplane attitude, and this is the key to managing without an airspeed indicator.

The biggest challenge, of course, is to ensure that an approach to landing is not flown too slowly. Even a student pilot appreciates the need to maintain a safe airspeed to prevent a low-altitude stall. Unfortunately, the inability to read the airspeed indicator invariably results in excessive airspeed and the possibility of overshooting the runway. It might even result in exceeding the maximum-allowable airspeed with flaps extended.

Should the airspeed indicator actually fail, there usually is no immediate need to land. Instead, stay away from the airport and become familiar with flying without an airspeed indicator.

First, establish the airplane in a power-off, level-flight attitude. Once established in this glide, extend the flaps (and landing gear) while simultaneously allowing the nose to drop about five degrees. Then, very slowly, raise the nose until the airplane is nibbling at a stall. Note well the attitude of the airplane at this time. This is the attitude to avoid while on final approach.

Next, return the airplane to a slightly nose-down attitude and add only enough power to achieve a normal sink rate (about 500 fpm), simulating final approach. Execute a few turns. Become adept at flying by reference to airplane attitude. After 15 minutes or so of this type of familiarization, you will have developed some confidence and be better prepared for the approach and landing. You also will realize that an airspeed indicator really is not all that necessary in a lightplane as long as you pay attention to aircraft attitude.

Once in the pattern, avoid steep turns and an excessively nose-high attitude to prevent overtaking a slower airplane. Instead, execute a go-around and try again.

Perhaps the best technique is to develop an awareness, before the airspeed indicator fails, of the attitude and power setting required to maintain a normal final-approach speed. Like so many of aviation's problems, this one is best handled when the pilot is prepared.

――――――――――――――― GYRO FAILURE

Coping with the failure of one or more gyroscopic flight instruments may not seem particularly difficult. After all, every instrument-rated pilot has had to demonstrate the ability to control an airplane without them. An instructor or examiner simply covers the attitude and heading indicators, and the student is left with the basics: needle, ball, and airspeed.

But FAA accident records indicate that many pilots are incapable of making the transition from full panel to partial panel when an actual gyroscopic failure occurs during instrument flight. Although such accidents are uncommon, they do have a relatively high fatality rate. Often, the victims are experienced and highly qualified.

Most pilots have little difficulty making the transition from full panel to partial panel while *practicing* because they are provided a foolproof way of identifying a malfunctioning gyro. After all, if someone covers the gauge, it definitely is no longer usable. Shifting one's attention to the remaining instruments becomes logical and automatic.

Unfortunately, the *actual* failure of an attitude or heading indicator in the real world of IFR flight often is not as easily detectable. First of all, most air-driven instruments are not equipped with fail flags or other warning devices. Secondly, the misleading data provided by failing gyro instruments often develops gradually, making detection more difficult. A pilot lacking a well-developed, *habitual* scan pattern may become unwittingly lured into a potentially hazardous attitude by an erroneous instrument display.

Several years ago, for example, a pilot departed a coastal, northern California airport toward an overcast, night sky in a Cessna 182. Although conditions were technically VFR, the natural horizon was not visible. After a normal takeoff toward the ocean, the pilot climbed to what witnesses estimated to be about 500 feet. The aircraft was then observed entering a shallow, power-on, descending turn to the right. A moment later, the aircraft impacted the water in a slightly nose-down, banked attitude.

Although his passenger-bride was killed instantly, the pilot survived with serious injuries. Subsequent investigation revealed that the vacuum pump shaft had sheared (possibly when takeoff power had been applied), which allowed the attitude indicator to decelerate and tumble *gradually*. By apparently focusing his attention on this single instrument, the pilot became an unsuspecting victim of gyro-system failure and blithely flew his craft into the Pacific. He followed the gyro's erroneous display because (1) there was no *immediately apparent* indication of gyro malfunction, and (2) he failed to respond to the contradictory attitude information available from other instruments.

Was this pilot a novitiate to instrument flight? Hardly. He was a 22,100-hour airline captain and general-aviation pilot with considerably more than 1,000 hours of actual instrument flight recorded in his stack of log books.

This and other similar accidents demonstrate clearly that even professionals can be guilty of excessive dependence on a single instrument, an instrument that could be failing gradually and subtly.

Let's be realistic. The attitude indicator, which also is called an artificial horizon, is the center of attention. Through this single device, we have been taught to envision the outside world, to see "through" the panel to the natural horizon. But since the device is ordinarily so reliable, it tends to breed a form of complacency that promotes laziness. The discipline of scanning and cross-checking begins to decay. When the Cessna 182 pilot followed a failing gyro into the sea, other instruments shrieked silent warning of his neglect. But these were either unseen or ignored.

In addition to the attitude indicator, three other instruments should be used to confirm or determine variations in pitch: the

VSI, the altimeter, and the airspeed indicator. If all three suggest a descent, for example, while the attitude indicator displays otherwise, the gyro indicator must be regarded skeptically.

The direction and angle of bank, however, may not be quite as easily determined, especially during cross-controlled or "uncoordinated" flight. For example, if the turn needle (or coordinator) indicates a left yaw and the ball is slewed right, what is the direction of bank? This *seems* to describe a skidding left turn and therefore a bank to the left. But not necessarily. The airplane could be yawing to the left with the wings level or even banked slightly right. Coincidentally, this is the presentation of a turn-and-bank indicator during a climb in a single-engine airplane when no corrective rudder is applied to compensate for the left-turning tendency.

The situation can become particularly hazardous when the pilot does not recognize gyro-system malfunction prior to the development of an undesirable flight attitude when at a relatively low altitude.

Unfortunately, such a predicament is impossible to simulate in flight because an instructor cannot gradually fail one or both gyros. Nor can he fail them without his student being aware of it. Either the gyros are covered or they are not.

Given enough time, a pilot ultimately becomes aware of the display discrepancy between an actually failing gyro system and the raw-data instruments. But can he determine and reject the erroneous data prior to becoming spatially disoriented in some unusual attitude? Perhaps. But if the failure occurs while the pilot is preoccupied with other cockpit chores at a relatively low altitude, the probability increases of his becoming a tragic statistic.

One of a pilot's best defensive weapons is to routinely practice partial-panel flying, develop an efficient scan pattern, and apply these skills to every IFR flight. An effective scan pattern also should include an occasional glance at the vacuum (or pressure) gauge, since this can be one of the few valid clues of an impending gyro failure. Include the ammeter as well because a loss of electrical power can cripple the electrically driven gyro of a turn indicator or coordinator.

Scanning alone, however, is insufficient. The indication of each flight instrument should be correlated to the attitude indicator to corroborate this vital instrument's validity.

All of this goes to reinforce an IFR adage: "If an instrument pilot isn't doing something at all times, he's doing it wrong."

If a gyro-system failure does occur, it is recommended that the pilot cover the affected instruments so that he will not be tempted to look at these gauges and be misled by their erroneous and contradictory indications.

If in instrument conditions, he should consider heading toward VFR conditions so that an instrument approach is not required while operationally handicapped with only a partial panel. An ILS approach to minimums without the benefit of attitude and heading indicators is extremely difficult (especially when a bit of turbulence is thrown in for good measure). Many pilots are incapable of mustering the necessary skill. (Anyone who doesn't include himself in this category should try a partial-panel ILS to minimums while under the hood. It can be a humbling experience.)

If VFR conditions are not within range, try to find a nearby airport that has a radar approach facility and request an Airport Surveillance Radar (ASR) approach. Without gyros, such an approach is simpler (and probably safer) than flying a published ILS, VOR, or NDB approach procedure. And don't worry if an ASR approach plate for the airport of your choosing can't be located; it may not be a published procedure. But this does not mean that such an approach cannot be executed. During emergencies, an ASR can be provided by most radar-equipped approach facilities. When an ASR approach plate is not available, the controller provides information such as descent altitudes, the missed approach point, the missed approach procedure, and so forth.

An instrument approach to a north-south runway is most troublesome because of the magnetic compass's northerly turning error. Whenever the airplane is banked while on a northerly or southerly heading, the seemingly ornery compass responds by sashaying up to 30 degrees away from the actual heading. (The compass indication lags when turning from a northerly heading and leads when turning from a southerly heading.) Quite obviously, this makes it even more difficult to either maintain or change heading accurately without the assistance of a gyroscopic heading indicator. Given the option, it is preferable to execute an approach to an east-west runway because on these headings the northerly turning error of the compass is nil.

If the destination airport does not have an east-west runway, it might be possible to execute a letdown to visual conditions on an easterly or westerly radar vector (assuming the ceiling is sufficiently high). Once the airport is in sight, a visual, circling approach to the available runway can then be executed.

To obtain this kind of radar assistance, however, it is suggested that a pilot advise the controller of the gyro-system failure. If a gyro failure occurs in IFR weather, and VFR conditions are out of range, declare an emergency.

If a pilot prefers not to be responsible for turning to and maintaining specific headings, he can request a no-gyro approach. This procedure requires that a pilot begin and recover from turns in response to commands from the radar controller. For example, a controller might say "turn left," pause the appropriate period of time (depending on the amount of turn required), and then say "stop turn." All turns are to be executed at the standard rate (three degrees per second). After intercepting the final approach course, however, the pilot will be advised to execute subsequent turns at half the standard rate.

Some accidents attributable to gyro failure occur when pilots enter IFR conditions with known instrument malfunctions such as abnormal fluctuations or unusual vibrations. Improprieties cannot be tolerated because these often are symptomatic of an impending instrument failure.

Even when the gyros appear to be functioning normally,

there is a series of recommended operational checks that should be performed prior to every IFR flight:

- Check the vacuum (or pressure) gauge shortly after engine start to confirm that system output is within limits. Consider that an excess of vacuum (or pressure) can be damaging because this may force gyros to exceed their rated speed (about 24,000 rpm).
- Be alert for unusual noises that signal internal bearing damage or wear. (This is best perceived in a quiet cockpit immediately after engine shutdown.)
- Watch the instruments after engine start for abnormal vibrations and erection time, which should take no longer than five minutes for air-driven gyros and three minutes for electrical gyros.
- Cage the heading indicator, and set it to coincide with the heading indicated by the compass. Then uncage the gyro and twist the knob. If the compass rose continues to turn, the instrument is malfunctioning.
- During taxi to the runway, the heading indicator normally should not precess more than five degrees.
- While taxiing, execute gentle S-turns. During a left turn, confirm that the heading indicator and turn indicator (or coordinator) indicate a left yaw and that the slip-skid ball moves right. These indications should be similar but opposite during a right turn.
- During all taxi maneuvers, the attitude indicator should not change in pitch or roll unless maneuvering on sloped or bumpy taxiways.
- Some instructors teach a method of stomping on the brakes while taxiing to demonstrate that the resultant pitching down of the nose is properly shown on the attitude indicator. This is ill-advised because of the damaging loads that abrupt braking imposes on gyro bearings.
- Prior to cloud entry, be attentive for possible gyro malfunc-

tions and glance again at the vacuum (or pressure) gauge for normal output.

- In flight, be aware that three degrees of gyroscopic precession every 15 minutes is normal for a heading indicator. Substantially more warrants caution and investigation.
- Consider that the root cause of most air-driven gyro failures or malfunctions is contamination by impurities in cabin air. These include moisture, dirt, and tobacco smoke tar. To prevent such damage, keep smoking to a minimum and change gyro filters regularly. This applies to vacuum-driven gyros, not those powered by pressure or electrical systems.
- Minimize aerobatic maneuvering in those aircraft with gyros that cannot be caged.
- Consider that slight decreases in indicated vacuum (or pressure) over a period of several flights can indicate a decline in air pump efficiency and possibly an impending pump failure.

Fortunately, gyroscopic failure is uncommon, but uncommon does not mean never. Being aware of the possibility, however, is half the battle.

TURN INDICATOR VS. TURN COORDINATOR

Prior to the end of World War I, pilots who valued their lives had to remain clear of cloud. This was because the instrument technology required for what was then called blind flying had yet to be developed. But by 1918, the Sperry Gyroscope Company, building on the success of Elmer Ambrose Sperry's earlier gyroscopic ship compasses and stabilizers, introduced the revolutionary turn indicator. This was the first instrument to incorporate a gyroscope to detect the motion of an airplane about one of its three axes.

Thus was born the science of instrument flight. Pilots soon began to develop the skills needed to maintain control of an aircraft in instrument meteorological conditions. In those days, the technique of flying solely by reference to instruments was commonly known as the "needle-ball-and-air-speed" method— a reference to the primary group of flight instruments.

The needle refers to the pointer of the turn indicator (Figure 33a), which—when properly calibrated—indicates the direction and rate of a turn. In reality, the turn indicator is a yaw-rate indicator that responds only to motion about an airplane's vertical axis. Although the difference between a yaw and a turn may not be immediately obvious, it is significant. Assume, for example, that it were possible for a general aviation airplane to perform a 90-degree banked turn while maintaining altitude. What would the turn needle indicate at such a time? Although the turn rate would be rather startling, the yaw rate would be nil, and the turn needle would be centered. This is because an airplane in a knife-edge turn is not yawing at all; it is only pitching. In effect, the airplane is performing a loop on a horizontal plane.

Since its inception, the turn indicator was combined with an inclinometer, or slip indicator (the "ball" component of the primary flight instruments), so that a pilot not only would be informed of turn rate, but turn quality as well. The trick was— and still is—to coordinate the flight controls so as to keep the ball of the slip indicator centered at all times. A ball leaning in the direction of turn indicates a slip; a ball leaning opposite to the turn indicates a skid. With respect to nonturning flight, a

FIGURE 33a

ball "out of its cage" (not between the lubber lines on the curved glass tube) with the wings level also indicates a skid.

Technically speaking, skids and slips are the same; each is regarded by engineers as a slip and represents a misalignment of the relative wind with the airplane's longitudinal axis. This explains why the proper name for the instrument is a turn-and-slip indicator, even though it is known colloquially as a turn-and-bank indicator.

The turn indicator reigned supreme for 11 years, but on September 24, 1929, a young Army Air Corps lieutenant named James H. "Jimmy" Doolittle made a dramatic demonstration of two new gyroscopic instruments, the artificial horizon and the directional gyro. Doolittle covered the open rear cockpit of his Consolidated NY-2 biplane with a canvas hood and made an instrument takeoff from Mitchell Field near New York City. He climbed to 1,000 feet and flew several miles before returning to the airport, making the first landing solely by reference to instruments. (A safety pilot, Lieutenant Benjamin S. Kelsey, occupied the front cockpit during this historic flight.)

The advent of these revolutionary instruments, now called attitude and heading indicators, resulted in the full-panel matrix of six flight instruments. Although the turn indicator is still included in this cluster, it is often regarded by some pilots as of secondary importance, to be used as a standby instrument or as a reference for trimming. The need to make timed turns, or turns at a specific rate, is usually required only in case of a pneumatic-system failure that renders air-driven attitude and heading indicators inoperative.

Because most attitude and heading indicators are air-driven, the turn indicator usually is electrically powered so that all gyroscopic instruments do not have a common power source. In this way, the failure of one power source still leaves operational at least one of the three gyroscopic flight instruments. (Failure of the primary gyros, the attitude and heading indicators, leaves available a "partial panel," which includes the turn-and-slip indicator, the airspeed indicator, the altimeter, the vertical-speed indicator, and the magnetic compass.)

In 1966, the turn indicator's position on the panel was challenged by a different kind of instrument. New airplanes began incorporating turn coordinators (Figure 33b) in place of turn indicators. The change was made with little fanfare, and pilots were told little about it. Most assumed—and many still do—that the turn coordinator was nothing more than a turn indicator with a new look and a new name. But it was not the same, and few pilots—then as now—appreciated the differences. Before discussing the technical aspects of the turn coordinator, however, it is worthwhile to understand how and why it evolved.

In the mid-1960s, the late Dr. Karl Frudenfeld, an obstetrician and aviation entrepreneur, headed Brittain Industries, which was in the process of developing a single-axis autopilot, or wing leveler. To hold costs down, Frudenfeld wanted to utilize an airplane's turn indicator to sense roll. The theory was that a deflection of the turn needle would signal the autopilot to apply aileron in the opposite direction to maintain a wings-level attitude. This technique was unsatisfactory because it soon was realized that an airplane banks before it turns. As a result, the corrective action of the autopilot lagged well behind the rolling motion of the aircraft.

Allan Mills, a Brittain engineer (and inventor of the turn coordinator), suggested that a turn indicator would do the job if it were modified to detect roll as well as yaw. In this way, the

FIGURE 33b

autopilot could react to the first indication of a roll and keep the wings level.

The turn indicator was modified successfully, but since the result did not behave like its predecessor, Brittain decided to change the instrument's appearance and name so as to alert the pilot that there was something different about the new presentation. Thus was born the turn coordinator. Shortly thereafter, it received FAA approval and began to appear in all kinds of aircraft, even those without Brittain autopilots.

The advantage of the turn coordinator is that—following failure of the attitude indicator—a pilot can maintain a wings-level attitude just the way the Brittain autopilot did. All he has to do is monitor the symbolic airplane on the face of the instrument and apply whatever aileron input is required to keep it on an even keel. This is easier than waiting for a turn to develop (as indicated by a turn needle) because a pilot can arrest a bank before the airplane has an opportunity to turn. Such an easy method of control did not escape the airframe manufacturers, who were quick to substitute the new turn coordinator for the old turn-and-bank indicator.

Perhaps the best way to understand a turn coordinator is to discuss separately its ability to detect yaw and its ability to detect roll. For example, if the airplane is yawed left while keeping the wings level (a flat, skidding turn similar to a taxiing turn), the symbolic airplane banks left to indicate the yaw rate. Notice that the coordinator displays a bank even though the wings are held level. When the yaw is arrested, the symbolic airplane rolls level.

Similarly, if the airplane is made to roll left while opposite rudder is applied to prevent yawing (such as when entering a forward slip), the symbolic airplane tilts in the direction of roll. It remains tilted only while the airplane is rolling and indicates only the roll rate, not the bank angle. When the rolling motion ceases and the airplane is held in a banked attitude, the symbolic airplane returns to neutral (wings level).

The turn coordinator presents the same indication for a roll as it does for a yaw. All of this can make the turn coordinator somewhat confusing, especially during recovery from unusual attitudes when only a partial panel is available. For example, if the symbolic airplane is leaning right, is the airplane rolling or yawing? Since the coordinator responds to both motions, the action of the symbolic airplane does not answer the question. The airplane could be rolling or yawing or both. It is even possible for someone manhandling the controls to induce a yaw in one direction and a roll in the other so that the two opposite-direction motions cancel each other in a way that prevents the symbolic airplane from moving at all.

Another disadvantage of the turn coordinator is that the face of the instrument looks like a small attitude indicator. This has victimized more than a few unsuspecting pilots who anticipated attitude information that they had no right to expect. This led turn-coordinator manufacturers to apply a NO PITCH INFORMATION placard to the face of the instrument. There is little they can do, however, to prevent pilots from reacting to the instrument as if it were a bank-attitude instrument, which it is not.

The turn coordinator is at its best when used to maintain a wings-level attitude or when entering and recovering from coordinated turns. Upon entering a turn, the coordinator first indicates roll rate, but when the roll rate stops the symbolic airplane indicates yaw rate. (When the airplane is both yawing and rolling, the symbolic airplane indicates a combination of both motions.)

The turn coordinator is at its worst during unusual attitudes when slipping or skidding. Because they are not as well-damped as turn-and-slip indicators, turn coordinators may cause overcontrolling or miscontrolling, which can lead pilots into unusual attitudes. With a turn coordinator, it is difficult to tell at a glance precisely what the airplane is doing. In turbulence, interpreting the instrument is nearly impossible. At times like this, many would prefer to have a conventional turn indicator. (Although most airframe manufacturers provide a turn coordinator as standard equipment, a turn indicator usually is an available substitute.)

The best way to fly instruments is to visualize aircraft attitude and apply the same coordinated corrections as when flying visually. The airplane, of course, does not know whether or not it is in cloud and responds the same in either event. Unfortunately, visualizing attitude while flying instruments on a partial panel is not always easy, particularly for those who seldom practice. Consequently, many instrument pilots rely on certain rules to maintain aircraft control and recover from unusual attitudes in instrument meteorological conditions.

There are two conflicting schools of thought regarding how this should be done. Those with military backgrounds were taught the "1-2-3" method. This involves: (1) centering the turn needle with the rudder, (2) centering the ball with aileron, and (3) controlling airspeed with elevator. Others counter with the claim that "stepping on the ball" (using rudder to recover from a slip or skid) and using aileron to roll in and out of a turn (centering the needle) is much preferred. This seems most logical because this is the way an airplane is normally flown.

In most cases, both techniques work equally well, especially when control inputs are smoothly coordinated. The use of a turn coordinator, however, muddies the water because such hard and fast rules are not as applicable when it is not known whether the symbolic airplane is indicating roll or yaw. Only one of the two techniques will work at all times, whether a pilot is referring to a turn needle or the symbolic airplane of a turn coordinator.

Assume, for example, that an airplane is entering a spin or has become stabilized in one. Whether the pilot is looking at a needle or a symbolic airplane, the rapid yaw rate will cause an indication in the direction of spin rotation. There is no way to know, however, where the ball will be at such a time; it could be dead center or off-center in either direction. The only technique one can use safely during a spin is the "1-2-3" method, applying rudder opposite to the direction of rotation as indicated by the turn needle or the symbolic airplane. If a pilot were to use the other method and apply aileron against the indicated yaw, he might unwittingly flatten the spin and place the airplane in an unrecoverable maneuver. Sadly, this is what those with turn coordinators tend to do because they develop the habit of leveling the symbolic airplane with aileron input. Similar aileron usage during slow flight at minimum airspeed can induce a spin, especially when applied hurriedly to counter a pro-spin yaw.

Just as the arguments about how to fly partial panel will undoubtedly continue to rage, so too will the debate about whether the turn indicator or the turn coordinator is most advantageous.

SWINGING A COMPASS

The magnetic compass is an ancient instrument. Although its origin is unknown, the earliest example seems to have consisted of a magnetized piece of metal resting on slivers of straw that floated in water. This was about 1,000 years ago, and those who observed such a compass believed that the needle was attracted by the North Star.

The compass card, upon which is printed a compass rose, is credited to Flavio Gioja of Amalfi, who attached a card to a piece of lodestone in the early 14th century. Christopher Columbus's compass reportedly consisted of a "single needle supporting a paper compass rose that pivoted on a steel point."

The modern magnetic compass consists of two parallel steel-bar magnets that are mounted on a float and surrounded by a compass card, or indicator, that hangs pendulously and behaves like a plumb bob. This is one reason the compass card tilts relative to the instrument case during changes in aircraft attitude.

The instrument is filled with a liquid that dampens compass card oscillations, provides buoyancy to reduce internal friction, and lubricates the bearings. Compasses originally were filled with alcohol, which led to their being called "whiskey" compasses. They now contain acid-free white kerosene and are often referred to as wet compasses.

Aircraft magnetic compasses are less accurate than those used on ships because they are smaller, lighter, and subjected to more vibration, acceleration, and shock. Yet they are so reliable that they often are taken for granted. Pilots make it a point to check virtually everything on the instrument panel, but the magnetic compass often is given short shrift. The gyroscopic heading indicator is set to match the compass heading; that is about the extent of most pilots' interest in this instrument.

We cannot afford to be so complacent about the magnetic compass because it can contain serious errors that can lead us astray.

Those who fly aircraft equipped with an HSI (horizontal situation indicator) slaved to a remote flux-valve compass, which usually is installed in the wingtip or tail, often are most guilty of compass complacency. Such a slaving system maintains the heading indicator's proper setting, reducing the need to reset the heading indicator manually to conform with the magnetic compass's indications. Because these pilots rarely refer to the magnetic compass or reset the heading indicator to match the magnetic compass's indications, they tend to ignore the instrument. But should a slaved compass or electrical failure occur, they suddenly will wish they had paid more attention to the status and accuracy of the "lowly" magnetic compass.

Assuming that a magnetic compass is in good operating condition, errors in level flight are caused by magnetic deviation, a localized magnetic field in an aircraft that attracts a compass "needle" and causes it to *deviate* from the proper magnetic heading. Such deviation is the result of aircraft parts that become magnetized when the aircraft is manufactured, electrical wiring and current flow, magnetized engine components, and the operation of magnetos and alternators (or generators).

Deviation, of course, does not have a fixed value; it varies with the magnetic heading of the aircraft. This is because the local magnetic field responsible for deviation turns with the airplane while the compass needle remains pointed in approximately the same direction, magnetic north. Part 23 of the Federal

Aviation Regulations (Airworthiness Standards) requires an airplane to have a deviation card that displays the amount of deviation on heading increments of no more than 30 degrees. Deviation must be determined with the compass in level flight attitude and with the engine(s) running. The radios may be on or off. Maximum allowable deviation is 10 degrees. More than 10 degrees is allowed if the deviation is known to be caused by the operation of a specific piece of equipment and the aircraft also is equipped with either a gyroscopic or magnetically stabilized heading indicator (e.g., operating the windshield heat of a Piper Cheyenne I causes a deviation error of as much as 25 degrees).

If a magnetic compass has a deviation card, a similar placard is not required of a slaved HSI. But even though the compass portion (usually a flux valve) of such a system is subject to less deviation than a magnetic compass (because it is located remotely from normal causes of deviation), it is not without some deviation of its own and should be checked periodically for error.

The airframe manufacturer prepares an aircraft's first deviation card, but it is accurate only at that time. Localized magnetic fields and their effect change as the aircraft and compass age. Deviation also can change significantly with the addition, removal, and exchange of electrical equipment and avionics. As a result, magnetic compasses typically are out of adjustment and placarded with deviation errors that bear no similarity to reality.

During an inspection of 43 randomly selected airplanes at Santa Monica Airport in southern California, 40 were found to have deviation cards prepared when the aircraft were new. Fourteen of these aircraft were more than 20 years old. Six had no cards at all. If this is representative of the general aviation fleet, many pilots have no idea how much in error their compasses may be.

There is an easy way to check compass accuracy at least once during every flight. Simply line up with the runway, add some power while the brakes are locked (to insure that the alternator or generator is charging and producing its normal effect), and note the compass heading. By doing this on a number of different runways, a new deviation chart can be constructed with little bother.

It is important to know that the exact magnetic direction of a runway cannot be determined simply by adding a zero to the runway number. Runway 11L at Tucson, Arizona, for example, has a magnetic direction of 123 degrees. The exact direction of a runway can be obtained from an instrument approach plate or a tower controller.

The most accurate method to determine all of the deviation errors at one time involves a procedure called swinging the compass. This consists of turning the airplane to various magnetic headings (usually in 30-degree increments) and noting the compass headings. The difference between each compass heading and its related magnetic heading, of course, is the deviation error.

A swing can be accomplished on the ground or in the air. When done properly, the air swing has the potential to be more accurate because the aircraft can be placed in a level attitude with the engines developing cruise power and the landing gear (when applicable) retracted. (Yes, landing-gear position can affect deviation.) A ground swing, however, usually is sufficient for most purposes. It also is a simpler, less expensive procedure because an aircraft on the ground can be held rock-steady on a given heading and the compass reads more accurately. A ground swing often is performed using a compass rose painted on the ground. Many airports, however, do not have a compass rose. When one is available, the job often requires two people, because someone usually must be positioned outside the aircraft to help the pilot precisely align the aircraft in the proper directions.

There is, however, a more convenient way to ground-swing a compass, one that requires neither a compass rose nor an assistant. All that is needed is a reliable gyroscopic heading indicator (directional gyro). First obtain the precise magnetic direction of any runway associated with a long, parallel (or perpendicular) taxiway that has a centerline stripe. Then taxi the aircraft onto the stripe (the one on the taxiway, not the runway) so it is headed in exactly the same direction as the taxiway. This is relatively easy as long as the stripe is at least 100 yards long. Be certain that the aircraft is not near any magnetic disturbances such as electric generators, large motors, iron cables, or steel structures. Be sure that all extraneous tools and equipment have been removed from the cockpit. Turn on all electrical equipment, including radios, that normally would be used in cruise.

The next step involves setting the heading indicator to the exact magnetic direction of the runway. (If the aircraft is equipped with an HSI, unslave it from the remote, flux-valve compass and use it as a conventional gyroscopic heading indicator.) Then turn the aircraft to the first 30-degree heading increment (such as 60, 210, or 330 degrees, for example) as indicated on the heading indicator. With the aircraft so aligned, note and record the compass heading. Continue turning the aircraft in 30-degree increments while recording the compass heading at each stop along the way. When the aircraft has turned 180 degrees, realign it with the taxiway stripe while heading in the direction opposite the one used initially. This is to check that the gyroscopic heading indicator has not precessed while the aircraft was being maneuvered. Precession can be avoided by making taxiing turns slowly, not jerking the aircraft with the brakes and accomplishing 180 degrees of ground swinging in minimal time (about two or three minutes).

Complete the swing by continuing the taxiing turns until the compass headings at all twelve 30-degree increments have been recorded. After the aircraft has completed a full circle, check the heading indicator once more for precession. (A normal gyroscopic heading indicator precesses about three degrees every 15 minutes; more than four degrees in 10 minutes indicates a probable gyro malfunction.) A second ground swing should be performed with the radios off. Accurate compass guidance takes on even more significance in the event of avionics or electrical failure.

The final step requires entering the results of the ground swing on a new deviation card (available at any instrument shop) and substituting it for the old. A pilot also might want to plot deviation on a graph, as shown in Figure 34. The deviation shown on this graph is acceptable because it does not exceed 10 degrees on any heading, and the total amount of positive deviation (where the compass heading is greater than the magnetic heading) is equal to the total amount of negative deviation (where the compass heading is less than the magnetic heading). However, if the deviation on any heading exceeds 10 degrees or if there is considerably more deviation in one direction than in the other, a pilot should have the compass adjusted by a certified repairman so that it indicates more accurately.

The magnetic compass contains two small compensating magnets that are used to counteract the local magnetic fields in the aircraft that affect it. The process of adjusting these magnets so as to reduce deviation to acceptable levels is called compass compensation and is not difficult.

The only tool required is a small screwdriver made of non-magnetic material like brass, plastic, or aluminum. Prior to compensating, there must be nothing on the person's body that might affect the compass, such as a penknife, keys, or steel-rimmed eyeglasses.

As when swinging, the aircraft is aligned on a line of known magnetic direction and the gyroscopic heading indicator is set to that heading. Then the aircraft is turned to a magnetic heading of exactly due north and the brakes are set. The engine rpm must be high enough to insure that the alternator or generator is charging (to create the magnetic field normally induced by the aircraft's charging system).

Next, the small rectangular plate (usually on the bottom of the face of the compass) is removed. This will expose two screws, one labeled N-S (north-south) and the other labeled E-W (east-

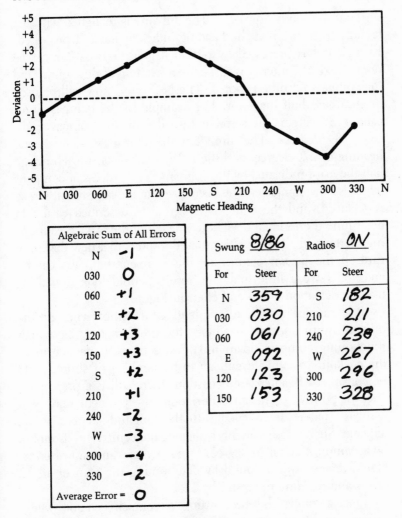

Algebraic Sum of All Errors	
N	−1
030	0
060	+1
E	+2
120	+3
150	+3
S	+2
210	+1
240	−2
W	−3
300	−4
330	−2
Average Error =	0

Swung **8/86**   Radios **ON**

For	Steer	For	Steer
N	359	S	182
030	030	210	211
060	061	240	238
E	092	W	267
120	123	300	296
150	153	330	328

FIGURE 34

west). While on the north heading, the N-S screw is turned until the compass indicates exactly 360 degrees. Then the aircraft is turned to a magnetic heading of due east, and the E-W screw is adjusted until the compass reads exactly 090 degrees.

Half the job is now over. The airplane is realigned with the taxiway to insure that the heading indicator has not precessed. Even if it has precessed by only a degree or two, it must be reset. Next, the aircraft is turned to a heading of due south, and the compass heading is noted. The N-S screw now will be used to eliminate half the error. For example, if the compass indicates 188 degrees, the screw is turned until the compass indicates 184 degrees. The aircraft is then turned to a magnetic heading of 270 degrees and the E-W screw is used to eliminate half the error indicated by the compass. The process of compensation is now complete. The plate covering the adjustment screws is replaced, and the compass is swung as described earlier to determine the residual deviation on each of the 30-degree heading increments. The results are used to prepare a new deviation card. If the person performing the compensation was careful and you have a little luck, the results should look something like the deviation graph and chart in Figure 34.

If it was not possible to eliminate all deviation when on the original north and east headings, the problem may be a malfunctioning compass or an unknown source of magnetism in the cockpit. In either event, an instrument repair shop should be consulted. If, after compensation, there still is a preponderance of positive or negative deviation, the problem may be a compass that is not aligned with the longitudinal axis of the airplane. Such a case warrants realigning the compass in its mount by an amount equal in degrees to the average amount of error. (The average error is found by determining the sum of all 12 errors and dividing the result by 12.)

Once a compass has been swung, or compensated and swung, a pilot should turn various pieces of equipment on and off to determine which, if any, adversely affects the compass. Gas-combustion heaters, ventilation fans, cassette players, portable transceivers, and other pieces of equipment have the potential to cause surprisingly large compass errors. (In some Cessna 172s, for example, the fore-aft movement of the control wheel produces as much as 15 degrees of compass movement.)

In addition to unanticipated deviation errors, pilots also should be on the alert for an ailing compass. A compass card touching the glass of the instrument, for example, requires remedial attention. A sticking compass card is a sign of excess friction in the bearing at the pivot point. A vibrating compass card could be caused by an internal problem but often is eliminated by changing propeller rpm slightly. A compass with a low fluid level is not a serious problem, but it should be refilled and resealed by an instrument repairman. Bubbles in the fluid? This might indicate that the fluid is swirling and can result in an incorrect heading indication.

The "ancient" magnetic compass is not particularly exotic or exciting, yet it is one of the most necessary and reliable instruments. It does, however, require care and attention that it all too often fails to receive.

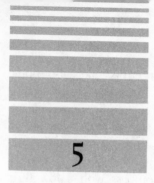

5

SYSTEMS MANAGEMENT

──────────── **GEAR-UP LANDINGS**

About three times a week some U.S. pilot finds his airplane impossible to taxi because it is sitting on its belly instead of its wheels. Many of these embarrassing, and costly, incidents are the pilot's own fault—forgetting to lower the gear before landing, inadvertent retraction on the ground, premature retraction during takeoff, failure to verify proper gear extension—but the majority, 58 percent, are the result of genuine mechanical malfunction.

What can you do to minimize the repair bills if you are faced with the necessity of landing with the gear up?

Consider, for example, a documentary film produced by the U.S. Air Force more than 20 years ago. It showed an F-86 pilot using the leading edge of a wingtip to nudge and lock into position the dangling nosewheel of an Aero Commander twin.

Also shown was a high-wing, single-engine military plane with a stubborn main-gear leg that refused to drop into position. What did this imaginative pilot do? He simply landed on the main leg that would extend and gingerly laid the opposite wing on the back of a pickup truck racing in formation along the runway.

Although general aviation pilots aren't encouraged to employ such extreme measures to protect an airplane, there are several techniques that may be useful when the gear cannot be extended conventionally or with the emergency system.

First confirm that the landing gear really has malfunctioned. Often, the lack of a gear-down light is the result of a burned-out bulb. If possible, exchange this bulb for another (red or green) that is already illuminated. (Retractable-gear airplanes should be equipped with spare bulbs.) Also, be certain that the navigation lights haven't been turned on inadvertently during a daylight flight. On many aircraft, that automatically dims the landing-gear lights and makes them difficult to see in daylight.

On electrically controlled or operated gear systems, the problem could be a popped circuit breaker, which could be reset one or more times to get the gear down and locked; just make sure the fault is traced and corrected before you take off again.

Then, if possible, *confirm* that one or more gear legs have failed to extend by having someone outside the aircraft make a visual inspection. This can be done by flying slowly past the control tower or requesting the pilot of a chase plane to move in for a close look. Accept these visual observations with a grain of salt, however. The gear may appear to be extended properly, but this doesn't necessarily mean that the legs are *locked* into position. If there is any doubt about the actual status of the landing gear, attempt recycling the system one or more times. If this fails to provide the desired gear-down indications, revert to the aircraft's alternate extension system.

There is no substitute for an intimate knowledge of emergency systems. But if a pilot is in doubt about this method of gear extension and a pilot's operating handbook is not immediately available, he might consider swallowing his pride and request that the tower locate someone who might provide assistance.

When dealing with such an emergency, however, pilots must be cautious not to become excessively distracted so as to create a more serious crisis. Maintaining a safe altitude and airspeed is paramount; extending the landing gear is secondary. This is particularly important when flying in clouds. *Fly the airplane first.*

If one of more landing gear legs refuse to respond to conventional or alternate methods of extension, their stubbornness often can be overcome by applying some brute force. One way to do this is to dive the aircraft to the red line (in smooth air only) and execute a rapid pullup—within the limits of safety. For most aircraft this means creating a 3.8-G load factor. In effect, the landing gear is made to weigh almost four times its normal weight, and this might force the lagging leg into the down-and-locked position.

Inducing rapid yawing also may be helpful. After stabilizing at or slightly below the maneuvering speed, alternately and abruptly apply rudder one way and then the other until either the misbehaving leg falls into place, or the procedure proves ineffective.

Another useful technique requires considerably more skill and should not be attempted by inexperienced pilots. It involves making a firm landing, followed by a bounce and a climbout, on the main landing gear leg that is *known* to be down and locked. Hopefully, the resulting jolt will encourage the crippled leg to drop into position. Normally, this maneuver should be attempted with flaps up. In this way, the touchdown will be relatively nose-high; it precludes landing on and possibly damaging the nosewheel. This technique absolutely requires that a pilot be intimately familiar with the aircraft. Otherwise, more serious problems could result.

If all efforts fail to stiffen the legs, a pilot is then faced with deciding where to land. If possible, he should select an airport with crash-and-rescue facilities. Although a gear-up landing rarely is harmful to those on board, injuries are possible—and so is fire.

When the tower controller asks a pilot if he'd like to have emergency equipment standing by, he should not be shy about replying in the affirmative. The sight of fire trucks racing after a landing aircraft may rattle the passengers, but this is no time to worry about their anxiety. Take advantage of all the free insurance you can get.

Also consider selecting an airport with sufficient maintenance facilities to repair the potential damage.

There is a widely held belief that a gear-up landing on grass or sod results in less airframe damage than one on concrete or blacktop. This is not necessarily so; a smooth hard-surface runway usually causes less damage than rough, unimproved grass strips. A hard surface does, however, create sparks that can ignite fuel.

Until recent years, many airport authorities coated their runways with foam to reduce frictional damage and fire potential during a gear-up landing. But the U.S. Navy has concluded that foam has questionable advantages and usually isn't worth the effort and the expense. And most authorities agree. A pilot still can request foam at certain airports. He should be prepared, however, to pay a handsome fee for this service.

While proceeding toward the nearest suitable airport, remember that fuel consumption is considerably higher with the gear extended than when the wheels are tucked neatly in the wells. Don't compound the problem by running out of fuel.

Also consider burning off excess fuel, especially if the tanks are relatively full. This reduces landing speed, and fire potential.

If the problem is a crippled main landing gear leg, consider consuming as much fuel from that side of the aircraft as is feasible. By reducing the weight of that wing, it is possible to delay the unsupported wing from touching the ground during the landing roll. And reduced impact speeds reduce damage.

If one leg fails to extend, should the landing be made with all wheels retracted or on the available legs? The answer is dictated by airport conditions. If ditches or other obstacles line the runway and maximum directional control is needed during the landing rollout and one of the main legs has failed to extend, consider landing gear-up. Landing on only one main gear usually causes the aircraft to veer strongly in the direction of the faulty leg after touchdown.

Many accident investigators suggest also that landing with all wheels up and on the belly minimizes damage to the wings, although such advice is debatable.

If a pilot elects to land with available legs extended, he has three possible configurations to consider. The first involves a hung-up main gear, which necessitates landing on the other main leg and nosewheel. If possible, the landing should be made in a nose-high attitude with wings level. As airspeed decays, apply whatever aileron control is necessary to keep the unsupported wing airborne. Once that wing touches down, be prepared for a strong yaw in that direction. Anticipate the need to apply full opposite rudder and braking to maintain some degree of directional control.

Landing with a retracted nosewheel is much easier. Simply hold the nose off the ground until *almost* full up-elevator has been applied. Then gradually release back pressure and allow the nose to settle slowly toward the surface. This usually is preferable to waiting until the nose drops after holding the control wheel full aft, because of the additional damage this might create. To minimize burrowing, do not apply any brake pressure during the landing roll, unless absolutely necessary.

The third consideration involves landing with only the nosewheel extended. The initial contact should be made on the aft fuselage structure with the nose held high to prevent wheelbarrowing, porpoising, and possible loss of control. As the nosewheel touches down, keep the wings level, and apply nosewheel steering as necessary. Conventional braking, of course, will be unavailable.

Although these procedures apply primarily to landing gear difficulties, notice that with very little modification they also apply to a landing with one or more failed tires.

Another question often asked concerns the flaps. Should they be used during a gear-up landing? Generally, flaps should be extended on high-wing aircraft to reduce touchdown speeds. One exception is when landing with a dangling or retracted nose-wheel. It is much easier to keep the nose from dipping when the flaps are retracted.

With respect to low-wing airplanes, it usually is best to leave the flaps up and sacrifice the slower touchdown speeds in favor of protecting internal wing structures. Extended flaps dragging a runway surface can destroy both wings. Flaps may be employed safely, however, if the main gear legs are down and locked.

Prior to making a gear-up landing, be certain that all passengers are properly buckled, all loose objects have been stowed, and everyone has been briefed about the need to expeditiously and calmly evacuate the aircraft *after* it has come to a stop. (Yes, nervous passengers have been known to leap out while an aircraft is still in motion.) While on final approach, shut off all unnecessary equipment—which includes disarming the ELT (emergency locator transmitter) at controlled airports. (Don't worry, you'll be found) When the landing is assured, turn the fuel selector to the "off" position, pull the mixture control to "idle cutoff," and turn off the magnetos.

Most pilots contemplate using the starter to position the propeller horizontally to protect props and powerplants from ground damage. This is much more difficult than one might imagine because most engines continue to windmill at approach airspeeds. Slowing to near-stalling airspeed might stop the prop, but the resultant hazards far outweigh the benefits.

The prop might stop, however, during the landing flare or while rolling on the supporting landing gear legs. This would be the time to crank the engine and position the propeller but only if a pilot doesn't become so obsessed with the challenge that he loses control of the aircraft.

Finally, turn off the master switch.

A pilot usually is aware of a landing gear difficulty and can take the appropriate steps to minimize the problem . . . but not always.

Consider this set of circumstances that befell a southern

California pilot who made a routine departure in his Piper Comanche 250. Shortly after liftoff, he attempted to raise the landing gear. Although everything seemed normal, the "gear unsafe" light wouldn't extinguish. At a safe altitude, the pilot lowered the legs conventionally. Again, he attempted retraction, but the stubborn "unsafe" light remained lit.

Rather than continue to his destination, the pilot lowered the gear once more and turned toward home to have the problem repaired.

While on short final, he double-checked the gear lights—three green. Not anticipating any difficulty, he prepared for a routine landing. But as soon as the mains touched, the aircraft swerved violently and uncontrollably to the right. For a few dizzying seconds, the pilot became his own passenger.

After the dust settled, the bewildered pilot stepped out of his undamaged airplane only to find that his right main wheel was 90 degrees out of phase with the other two wheels. An alignment pin somehow had come loose, which allowed the wheel assembly to twist about the strut axis; that explained why the right leg could not be coerced into its wheel well.

The pilot conceded later that he probably was better off not knowing about the condition of his landing gear. Otherwise, he claims, apprehension might have worsened the outcome.

Although failure of gear to retract generally is not a serious problem, it can be to a pilot who has just made an IFR departure from an airport with less than landing minimums. He'll be forced to continue to another, possibly distant airport at reduced airspeed, high-powered setting, and reduced range.

One way to avoid some landing gear problems is to adequately preflight the system before departure, even though this may require a bit of crawling. Make sure the wheel wells are clear of mud and debris that can affect the operating mechanism and the electrical microswitches used to activate various gear warnings. Once airborne, be careful to observe maximum-allowable gear retraction and extension speeds; violating these limits can induce long-term metal fatigue and possibly damage one or more of the relatively fragile wheel-well doors.

Although mechanical failures account for most difficulties, do remember that 42 percent of landing-gear-related accidents are caused by pilot error. Should you become a victim of your own inattentiveness, here's one piece of advice—when something begins to scrape the runway during landing, do not attempt to go around. Applying power to a possibly damaged propeller, engine, and airframe can result in a far more serious accident than simply skidding on your belly. Instead, shut down the engine and go along for the ride. Chances are it will be a short one.

PRESSURIZATION

There probably are more absurd misconceptions about aircraft pressurization than about any other aircraft system.

Consider, for example, the popular belief that a bullet shot through a pressurized fuselage will cause explosive decompression and loss of aircraft control. This is, after all, what happened to Pussy Galore and James Bond in *Goldfinger* when a stray bullet went through the cabin wall of their Lockheed Jetstar. Not only did they experience explosive decompression, but the aircraft went into a spin, forcing Pussy and James to parachute to safety. Totally ridiculous, but it made for good drama.

And how about the myth perpetuated by the motion picture *Airport '77*? After the Boeing 747 came to rest at the bottom of the Caribbean, the intrepid captain (Jack Lemmon) allayed his passengers' fear of drowning by proclaiming authoritatively, "Don't worry, folks; this airplane is pressurized!" Apparently pacified, the naive passengers headed for the piano bar to sip martinis until rescued.

Someone should have nominated this movie for the "Best Comedy of the Year" award.

Unfortunately, many general aviation pilots also are unrealistic about pressurization. Modern technology enables them to cruise nonchalantly at 25,000 feet (or higher) in living-room comfort without fully appreciating that only inches away is an alien, hostile environment that can challenge their very survival. Man cannot tolerate such extremely frigid temperatures and oxygen deprivation for very long without suffering partial or total incapacitation.

Pressurization failure is unusual, but considering the proliferation of these systems in the general aviation fleet, it is appropriate to consider the potential hazards. But first, let's review some basic principles.

Pressurizing an aircraft cabin (the pressure vessel) is similar to pumping air into a tire that has a controllable leak. In the case of piston-powered aircraft, pressurizing air is provided by the engine turbochargers (as shown in Figure 35). The "leak" consists of one or more outflow valves at the rear of the cabin. These valves allow air to escape continuously. This prevents excessive pressure from causing structural damage and provides an exit for venting stale air overboard. Pressurization is maintained by pumping in as much air as is allowed to escape.

Many believe that cabin pressure is determined by varying the amount of air pumped into the aircraft. Not so. The flow of incoming air is approximately constant. Cabin pressure is determined by the outflow valves, which modulate automatically to vary the amount of air flowing overboard and maintain the selected degree of pressurization.

In effect, the cabin always has at least one open "hole." The addition of a bullet hole, therefore, would have no effect on cabin pressure. The outflow valve(s) would compensate by closing slightly and automatically to maintain a constant flow of air through the cabin. Larger holes in the structure, however, may result in depressurization.

In the case of jetliners, the outflow valves are so large that the loss of an entire cabin window may not affect cabin pressure significantly. (It would not be pleasant, however, to be seated next to such a window.)

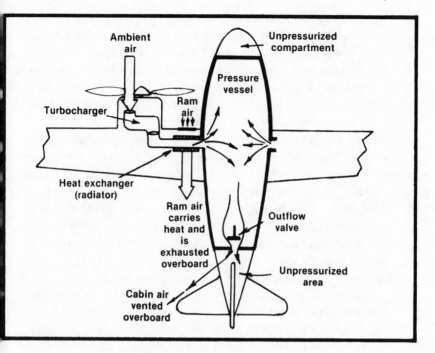

FIGURE 35

Should an outflow valve stick closed, an emergency relief valve opens automatically to prevent excessive cabin pressure and possible structural damage.

Maintaining cabin pressure obviously relies on a continuous source of air from the turbochargers. At least one engine, therefore, must always be developing a moderate amount of power. Retard the throttle(s) excessively and cabin pressure will be lost. (One can only wonder how the Boeing 747 in *Airport '77* was able to provide sufficient engine power while underwater to maintain cabin pressure and prevent sea water from flooding the aircraft.) Engine power, therefore, should always be maintained until the cabin has been depressurized conventionally.

This raises an interesting point regarding pressurized singles such as the Cessna P210N. An engine failure at altitude would result in rapid decompression. Although the outflow valve would close automatically in a vain attempt to preserve cabin pressure, other leaks in the aircraft would allow cabin pressure to escape. There is no such animal as a completely airtight cabin. Allowing one fuel tank to run dry before switching to another, therefore, is not recommended when operating a pressurized single.

Since air used for pressurization is compressed by the turbochargers before being pumped into the cabin, it is much warmer than ambient air outside the aircraft. As a result, pressurized air often must be cooled before entering the cabin, especially when flying at low altitudes on a warm day. This is done by ducting the high-pressure air through a heat exchanger (or radiator) where it is cooled by ram air (see Figure 35).

When ambient temperatures are well below freezing, the pressurized air may not be warm enough to maintain a cozy cabin. At such times, a conventional cabin heater is used.

Although a turbocharged, pressurized airplane allows flight above *much* of the weather, it certainly can't get above *all* of it. Anything that flies can expect to encounter some form of weather, no matter how high the altitude. In his book, *Operation Overflight*, Francis Gary Powers related how he gazed upward at the nearly 100,000-foot top of a Middle Eastern thunderstorm while cruising near the operational ceiling of his Lockheed U-2. And what pilot can ever forget the quip transmitted by one of America's pioneer astronauts after being established in earth orbit: "Another thousand feet and we'll be on top."

It can be said, however, that as one flies higher, he will experience increasingly less weather. But one must be careful not to become complacent. Weather at the middle altitudes can be damnably inhospitable.

During one recent winter, for example, a 160-knot jet stream was found as low as 18,000 feet msl over the United States. The associated clear air turbulence (CAT) varied from light to severe.

Although similar turbulence can be found in the lower layers, it can be more hazardous at altitude. Consider, for example, the 145-knot maneuvering speed of a Cessna 414A Chancellor. When cruising at 25,000 feet (FL250) on a standard day, true airspeed is 200 knots. But at this altitude, indicated airspeed is only 134 knots, 9 knots below the maneuvering speed. During a turbulence encounter, the aircraft would not have the stall protection it has at the lower altitudes. Above 25,000 feet, indicated airspeed and the available stall margin become significantly less. The obvious solution to such a problem is to descend.

One advantage of flying in the frigid climate of the middle altitudes is that structural icing is usually less of a problem than when flying at lower altitudes. This is because the indicated outside air temperature usually is less than −15°C. Such air usually is too cold for water to exist in the liquid state. Most clouds consist only of harmless ice crystals, which do not cling to an airplane. (Do not rely on an ice-free flight, however; there are exceptions to the rule.)

Although the lack of moisture often eliminates icing worries, the arid air can be physiologically concerning. This is because long flights at altitude result in some dehydration. The pressurized air in the cabin may have the density normally found at lower altitudes, but it is woefully dry nevertheless. The adverse effects of dehydration can be avoided by drinking water (not coffee!) during lengthy, high-altitude flights.

Pilots are accustomed to dealing with atmospheric pressure in terms of inches of mercury. Standard pressure at sea level, for example, is 29.92 inches Hg and decreases with altitude.

Pressure also is measured in pounds per square inch (psi). At sea level on a standard day, atmospheric pressure is 14.7 psi. The chart in Figure 36 provides the standard pressure (and temperature) for various altitudes.

The degree to which an airplane can be pressurized safely is expressed in terms of a "differential." For example, the Cessna 414 has a maximum allowable pressurization differential of 5.0 psi. This means that the airplane can be pressurized to a point where pressure inside the cabin is 5.0 psi greater than atmos-

Standard Atmosphere		
Altitude (feet)	Pressure (pounds/ square inch)	Temperature (degrees Fahrenheit)
Sea Level	14.7	59
1,000	14.2	55
2,000	13.7	52
3,000	13.2	48
4,000	12.7	45
5,000	12.2	41
6,000	11.8	38
7,000	11.3	34
8,000	10.9	31
9,000	10.5	27
10,000	10.1	23
11,000	9.7	20
12,000	9.3	16
13,000	9.0	13
14,000	8.6	9
15,000	8.3	6
16,000	8.0	2
17,000	7.6	− 2
18,000	7.3	− 5
19,000	7.0	− 9
20,000	6.8	−12
21,000	6.5	−16
22,000	6.2	−20
23,000	5.9	−23
24,000	5.7	−27
25,000	5.5	−30
26,000	5.2	−34
27,000	5.0	−37
28,000	4.8	−41
29,000	4.6	−44
30,000	4.4	−48
35,000	3.6	−66
40,000	2.7	−70
50,000	1.7	−70

FIGURE 36

pheric pressure outside the aircraft. Additional pressurization is not permitted because of system or structural limitations.

The maximum allowable differential of an airplane becomes considerably more meaningful when used in conjunction with the chart in Figure 36.

Assume that a pilot wants to fly his Cessna 414 at 25,000 feet. According to the chart, atmospheric pressure at that altitude is 5.5 psi. But when the aircraft is pressurized, pressure within the cabin is 5.5 psi (outside pressure) plus 5.0 psi (the pressure differential) which equals 10.5 psi.

According to the chart, 10.5 psi equates to an altitude in the free atmosphere of 9,000 feet. In other words, when a Cessna 414 is at 25,000 feet, the "cabin altitude" is only 9,000 feet.

Now assume that a 414 pilot wants to fly as high as possible, but doesn't want the cabin altitude to exceed 5,000 feet where standard atmospheric pressure is 12.2 psi. Subtracting the pressure differential of 5.0 psi from 12.2 psi equals 7.2 psi. Referring again to the chart, it is found that 7.2 psi is normally found at about 18,000 feet. In other words, by flying no higher than 18,000 feet, the pilot can maintain a cabin altitude of 5,000 feet.

The chart can be used similarly with the pressure differential of any airplane. A Boeing 747, for example, has a maximum-allowable pressure differential of 8.6 psi. At 29,000 feet, the ambient pressure is 4.6 psi. Adding the pressure differential to the outside pressure results in a cabin pressure of 13.2 psi, which equates to a cabin altitude of 3,000 feet.

Anyone who has ever flown commercially is aware of how flight attendants brief passengers on the use of the emergency oxygen system. This is because pressurization systems can fail. And if supplemental oxygen isn't *immediately available*—especially to the pilot—the airplane and everyone on board may be in jeopardy.

Unfortunately, many general aviation pilots apparently consider oxygen to be immediately available as long as the tank is full and the masks are *somewhere* on board. But if rapid decompression occurs, sufficient time may not be available to find the masks, connect the hoses, and turn on the system. Cockpit masks should be connected and *tested* before climbing to altitude.

At 25,000 feet, someone deprived of an oxygen mask in an unpressurized aircraft has only three to five minutes of useful consciousness; if oxygen deprivation is caused by rapid decompression, the time available is reduced by 50 percent; if the pilot is a smoker, he may have less than a minute of useful consciousness. At 30,000 feet, these times are cut in half.

With an oxygen mask at hand, decompression usually is not a serious problem (unless caused by airframe failure); without a *handy* supply of oxygen, it can be disastrous.

Rapid decompression—inaccurately called explosive decompression—is not as dangerous physiologically as it sounds unless the victim is suffering from blocked ears or sinuses. The feeling is that of a sudden expansion of air in your lungs followed by an outrush through your nose and mouth. It's sort of like having the wind knocked out of you without being hit. Your cheeks and lips may flap somewhat as the wind goes out, but that's about it. No one is incapacitated or knocked out.

Decompression can cause a few anxious moments. For example, the cabin may become temporarily IFR as moisture in the aircraft condenses into a cloud and uninformed passengers begin to panic. But first, to thine own self be true. Calm down and do not allow hyperventilation to worsen the problem. Rapid breathing not only can cause dizziness and spots to appear in front of your eyes, it also can result in numb fingers and toes and expedite unconsciousness. Control breathing before and after donning the immediately available oxygen mask. (Be certain that no one is allowed to smoke while supplemental oxygen is being used because of the obvious hazard this creates.)

One of the pilot's first considerations is to determine whether an emergency descent to a lower altitude would be appropriate. Modern or heavy icing reported in the clouds below, for example, might make it more prudent to remain aloft and suffer the indignities of an oxygen mask until conditions below improve. In such a case, be certain to determine that all passengers are properly masked.

An untimely descent also could affect range adversely because of increased fuel consumption and loss of a tailwind, an unfortunate set of circumstances when over large bodies of water.

If decompression is caused catastrophically by a blown-out window or other structural failure, it's possible for someone on board to have been injured from flying debris; an emergency descent could be dictated by medical reasons. Also, be aware that a large hole in the fuselage can decrease cabin pressure to *less* than that outside the aircraft because of Venturi effect.

If the decision is to remain aloft for a while, be extremely careful about opening a thermos of hot coffee. When at altitude, the boiling point of water can be so low that opening the thermos could result in an explosion of steam that can have serious consequences to those nearby.

Decompression is not always involuntary. There may be times when it is desirable. One way to fight a cockpit or cabin fire, for example, is to starve the fire of oxygen. A controlled decompression does this nicely. It is also a handy way to remove smoke caused by an electrical or air-conditioning malfunction. With the outflow valves open, the cabin can be cleared almost immediately. Depressurizing the airplane also is advisable if an impending window failure is noticed or if the turbochargers are pumping contaminated air into the cabin.

If a rapid decompression dictates an emergency descent, be careful about simply lowering the nose and accelerating to the never-exceed (red-line) airspeed, as is usually recommended. Consider the possibility and (sometimes the probability) that turbulence may be encountered when penetrating the lower altitudes. Such an encounter while diving at red-line airspeed could cause structural damage. Also, if structural failure was responsible for the decompression, such a high-speed descent could further damage the airplane—even in smooth air.

When at high altitude (20,000 feet or above), indicated airspeed is so much below the red line that a large, negative body angle may be required for timely acceleration. But don't be in too much of a hurry to dump the nose lest the negative G-load toss objects (and unbuckled passengers?) against the ceiling. One technique to help avoid this is to roll into a moderately steep bank during the pitch-down. In this way, the positive Gs of the turn help to offset the negative Gs created when pushing forward on the yoke. When the desired pitch attitude has been established, the turn can be stopped.

Be aware that as altitude loss progresses during an emergency, high-speed descent, air density increases. For a given body angle, therefore, indicated airspeed will increase steadily. This requires gradually reducing the nose-down attitude to prevent airspeed from creeping beyond the red line.

If the descent is made in turbulence, maintain at or less than the maneuvering speed (V_a) and extend flaps or landing gear, if airspeed permits, to obtain a respectable rate of descent. A clean descent (gear and flaps up) at V_a resembles a glide and hardly qualifies as an emergency descent necessitated by rapid decompression.

Time permitting, notify air traffic control (ATC) about your predicament and squawk transponder code 7700. A midair collision with other IFR traffic would be even more disturbing than a sudden loss of cabin pressure.

Fortunately, pressurization malfunctions are rare. But a professional attitude demands system familiarization and emergency preparedness.

―――――――――――――― ELECTRICAL FAILURE

In most respects, single-engine aircraft can be marvelously equipped with accurate, redundant navigation and communications systems; modern powerplants can be relied upon to get an airplane across oceans and continents. But there is a weak link: the electrical system. Like an automobile, it has no redundant features (except in a twin that has dual generators or alternators). When a major component fails, the electrons—sooner or later—will cease to flow, subjecting a pilot and his passengers to considerable apprehension.

Although such an emergency is most serious at night or when flying IFR, the consequences of an electrical failure during a VFR flight at high noon should not be taken lightly.

The loss of electrical power can deprive the pilot of numerous critical systems. Depending on the airplane, these could include the auxiliary fuel pump, heater fan, landing-gear and flap motors, stall warning system, other visual and aural warning systems (including landing-gear position indicators), avionics, fuel gauges, and some engine instruments.

One way for a pilot to prepare for electrical failure is to be thoroughly familiar with the aircraft. He should know which devices are electrically powered and which are not. While a transmitter clearly is electrically dependent, other items may not have such obvious power sources. For example, stall warning systems on some aircraft are electrical; on others they are not. The same is true of fuel gauges, fuel valves, and cylinder-head temperature gauges.

Once aware of the systems affected by electrical failure, a pilot can predetermine how to cope with these losses and thus be better prepared for an emergency. (Of course, he should know how to compensate for the loss of any system, electrical or not.)

Electrical difficulties at night are especially nerve-racking because of the loss of cockpit and exterior lighting. A flashlight is an absolutely necessary piece of equipment for night flying. In the event of an electrical failure, a pilot must otherwise control every system strictly by feel and fly his aircraft to a safe landing using little more than the seat of his pants for guidance.

Most pilots believe that reference to the instrument panel can be maintained easily with a flashlight. With respect to climbing, cruising, or descending at a relatively constant power setting, they're right; the flashlight can be held conveniently in the right hand. But during a landing approach, when one hand is on the yoke and the other is on the throttle, how does one hold and manipulate the flashlight? This is one of those challenges that doesn't seem difficult until attempted.

One solution is to hold a small flashlight between the palm of the left hand and the control wheel. Another is to hold a small flashlight in your mouth. In this way, both hands are unencumbered and a slight head movement allows scanning of the full panel.

Although it is more powerful, using a larger, heavier, conventional flashlight requires the agility of a three-armed paper hanger. The well-equipped pilot, however, carries both a small and a large flashlight. The small one is most useful in flight while the other is best suited for preflight inspections. (Spare batteries and bulbs also are suggested.)

The most traumatic and shocking electrical failure occurs during an IFR flight, especially at night. Not only does a pilot lose all avionics and other accessories, he also loses anti-ice and deice protection (including pitot heat), since these devices are dependent on electrical switches.

When fate pokes its finger into the wiring and incapacitates the electrical system, the IFR pilot has no choice but to revert to dead reckoning and hope to find visual conditions before fuel runs out or icing becomes critical. Without avionics, he'll have primarily his wits with which to work. (With any luck, he will not be flying one of those rare birds equipped with electrically powered gyros.)

Unless an expensive, auxiliary Nicad battery is installed, there's nothing that can be done to improve system reliability. Certainly, this should be a consideration to those who fly extensive single-engine IFR (especially at night).

It is fortunate, however, that total direct current failure is rare. When it does occur, it usually is the fault of the pilot who either has failed to heed warning signals or has completely mismanaged the system.

The items most likely to fail are the alternator (the generator in older aircraft) and the voltage regulator. These control the flow of electrical power to aircraft systems and the battery. But such a failure is not necessarily catastrophic. The battery, after all, usually is available as a standby reservoir of electrical energy that can be tapped until depleted.

The problem, however, is recognizing alternator or regulator failure. On older aircraft, such a loss initially is recognizable only by a discharge indication of the ammeter. Unfortunately, this gauge usually is not included in a pilot's scan, and its silent warning often goes unnoticed until the battery almost is dead and the lights are fading. Then, of course, there is little to be done about it.

Newer-model aircraft often are equipped with a red, low-voltage warning light designed to call the pilot's attention to an alternator failure. But even this improvement frequently is misunderstood.

Simply stated, the warning light indicates that the alternator no longer is supplying electrical power; the battery automatically has become the power source for as long as it can last. This does not necessarily mean that the alternator or voltage regulator has failed. Sometimes a temporary surge of excessive voltage has shot through the electrical system, which is protected by an over-voltage relay. The relay causes the alternator to disengage from the system and the warning light to illuminate. In this case, electrical integrity can be restored by turning off the alternator switch, waiting for the warning light to go out, and turning the alternator back on. If the light doesn't extinguish, however, the charging system probably has failed. (None of these suggestions are intended to replace specific advice found in the pilot's operating handbook.)

Also, a seemingly failed alternator might be brought back to life by resetting the "alternator field" circuit breaker that has popped. But before resetting a circuit breaker—any circuit breaker—touch it to be certain that it is not hot, a condition that could indicate a serious short. If it is hot, the breaker should not be reset.

If the breaker is not hot to the touch, reset it. But if it pops again, consider accepting the loss of that item protected by the breaker. Resetting a circuit breaker more than once or forcing a circuit breaker closed when it keeps popping out can lead to more serious difficulties, such as an electrical fire.

Occasionally, two devices are protected by a single circuit breaker. If one of these breakers pops after being reset once, turn off both items protected by that breaker. Then reset the breaker and turn on the two items one at a time to determine which is responsible for causing the breaker to pop. Then turn off the ailing device. reset the breaker, and restore the other device to service.

The alternator's warning light unfortunately may go unnoticed during daylight flight, especially when sunlight washes the instrument panel. In daylight, a pilot who is not paying attention to the ammeter may be unaware that the battery is being drained until electrical devices begin failing en masse.

There are two types of ammeters in popular use, and unless a pilot knows the differences between them, their messages can be misinterpreted.

The first is the zero-center ammeter, which indicates only whether electrical energy is being deposited into or taken out of the battery. A needle deflected to the right indicates that the battery is being charged; a deflection to the left indicates a discharge. A normal indication in cruise flight is for the needle to be *very slightly* right of center because the battery receives a constant trickle charge to keep it full. If the ammeter indicates a *considerable* charge after more than an hour of cruise flight, the battery may be incapable of accepting a charge and should be checked on the ground.

Whenever the engine is developing 2,000 rpm or more and everything is functioning properly, the ammeter should *never* indicate a discharge *even when everything in the airplane has been turned on*. This is because FAA regulations prohibit installation of an electrical system capable of drawing more current than can be produced by the generating system. This kind of discharge indication should be regarded as an alternator or generator failure.

The second type of ammeter is the zero-left variety (also called a loadmeter), which is found predominantly on Piper aircraft. This gauge has nothing to do with the battery and indicates only the total number of amperes (current) being drawn from the alternator. In other words, the loadmeter indicates alternator output to the electrical system: The greater the electrical load, the larger the indication. Unlike the zero-center ammeter, the loadmeter should not indicate zero *unless the alternator has failed.*

If a warning light or ammeter indicates the probability of an alternator or generator failure while flying a single-engine aircraft (or a twin with only one operable generating system), the pilot may have precious little time available from the battery. The first step is to turn off everything electrical that is not necessary. This might include exterior lighting, the autopilot, and extraneous avionics. It is even recommended that the failed alternator be turned off (if possible) because it could impose an unnecessary drain on the battery. When flying at night or IFR, plan to land at the nearest suitable airport, irrespective of how inconvenient this may be. The alternative of continuing to a more distant airport and having to approach and land with a dead battery can be very risky.

The rating of the aircraft battery (as indicated in the pilot's operating handbook) provides a clue as to how long it *may* last. For example, a 35-amp battery is really a 35-ampere-hour battery. In other words, when fully charged this battery has the potential to deliver 35 amps of current for one hour, 17.5 amps for two hours or seven amps for five hours. But this is true only of a relatively new, fully charged battery. If the battery has been in service for a few years, its power may be reduced substantially because of internal resistance. Or if the alternator failure was not detected immediately, much of the stored energy already may have been used. So here's a rule of thumb: Once the electrical load has been reduced, avoid having to depend on battery power for more than one hour.

The amount of current used by various appliances can be

determined by a glance at their respective circuit breakers or fuses. A given device uses up to approximately half the current indicated on the circuit breaker. If an anticollision light is protected by a ten-amp circuit breaker, for example, it probably draws a five-amp current. The transistorized receiver (nav or com) uses only about 1.5 to two amps, so not much current is sacrificed by leaving one on. Transmitting, however, may use up to six or seven amps, so avoid lengthy conversations. An autopilot in straight-and-level flight in smooth air uses very little current, but avoid using the autopilot in turbulent air or for changing attitude. At such times, autopilot actuators are used, which increases electrical load. Radar, distance-measuring equipment (DME) and transponders also use substantial electrical power and should not be used unless absolutely necessary.

If alternator failure occurs during an IFR flight (day or night) and a nearby airport is unavailable, advise ATC that you'll be turning everything off (including the transponder and transceiver) and that you'll be incommunicado until nearing the destination airport. Then do just that; turn off everything except one VOR receiver and other critical items such as a fuel pump (when required) and pitot heat. It is absolutely imperative that sufficient battery power be preserved to execute a safe IFR approach.

Prior to descent, reestablish communications with air traffic control and turn on only those electrical devices required for approach and landing.

Fortunately, electrical difficulties usually are not so extreme. Often, only a single appliance has failed. But before giving up on its usefulness, be sure to first determine that it has been turned on properly and that its circuit breaker has not popped (or its fuse has not failed).

One type of electrical failure occurs on the ground but really isn't a failure at all. If the battery is completely dead and a ground power unit is used to start the engine, chances are the alternator will not work once the external power source has been removed. This is because an alternator (not a generator) requires some current from the battery to operate properly. Since the battery is still dead, the alternator will not perform, even with the engine running. The only solution is to recharge the battery on the ground or replace it.

This difficulty should be kept in mind when the battery is weak or the weather cold. Rather than deplete the battery trying to start the engine, consider using ground power at the outset to prevent the kind of alternator problem just described.

With respect to battery health, consider that a lead-sulphuric acid battery may discharge itself by up to 50 percent during a month of inactivity. Also, a fully charged, new battery is capable of delivering full power only when the outside temperature is 80°F or more. At 32°F, 0°F, and −30°F, it produces only 65, 40, and 10 percent, respectively, of its rated power capacity. During these conditions, the use of ground power is strongly recommended for engine start.

In the final analysis, the ability of a pilot to cope with any form of electrical failure often depends on his knowledge of the system. Otherwise, the results can be electrifying.

WHAT'S ALL THE FLAP ABOUT?

The safety of an airplane usually is determined not by how fast it will fly but, rather, how slowly. In addition to the obvious advantages of slow flight—such as reasonably short takeoff and landing distances—crash survivability varies in proportion to the square of the impact speed. Slow flight and controllability, therefore, become two of the designer's primary considerations.

The principle of stall-speed reduction is simple enough: increase wing area or camber (curvature), or both. Enlarging the wing obviously increases lift, but the effect of varying wing camber is not understood as readily.

Consider a high-speed airfoil with very little camber. Very little downwash is produced behind the trailing edge of the wing, and since lift is directly proportional to downwash, such a wing generates relatively little lift. An airfoil with more camber has a greater downwash angle, (Figure 37a), and consequently, increased lift.

Now consider a wing that has a deflected, trailing-edge flap, a device used to increase wing camber (and sometimes wing area) as the need arises. In other words, downwash (and subsequently, lift) can be controlled by the pilot at will. But increasing camber also has the fringe benefit of increasing the upwash of air flowing toward the wing. As a result, additional quantities of air are forced to flow over the wing. This increases the amount (or mass) of air that ultimately becomes downwash. Since the amount of downwash air is increased (in addition to the downwash angle), the reaction to it—or lift—also increases, as does drag.

Although many contrivances have been devised to increase lift, the principles involved are common: increased wing area, or camber, or both.

The *plain flap* (Figure 37b) is the simplest of all and is quite effective. It is merely a hinged portion of the wing's trailing edge that is used on many general aviation aircraft, such as the Piper Warrior and Beechcraft Bonanza. When extended, the flap increases wing camber, which results in additional lift.

The *split flap* (Figure 37c) consists of an essentially flat plate that deflects from the lower surface of a wing's trailing edge. It produces a slightly larger increase in lift coefficient than the plain flap and for the same basic reason: effective wing camber is increased. A disadvantage of the split flap is the large increase in drag that occurs during even small angular deflections.

When the flap "splits" from the wing, airflow beneath the wing is deflected downward, which increases lift. Air flowing above the wing, however, is almost unaffected and flows smoothly rearward. This divergence of airflow at the wing's trailing edge creates an undesirable, turbulent wake behind the flap. The split flat, however, is suited ideally for thin, high-performance wings containing little room for the construction of a more complex flap mechanism. This is one reason why such a flap was chosen for the Cessna 310, for example.

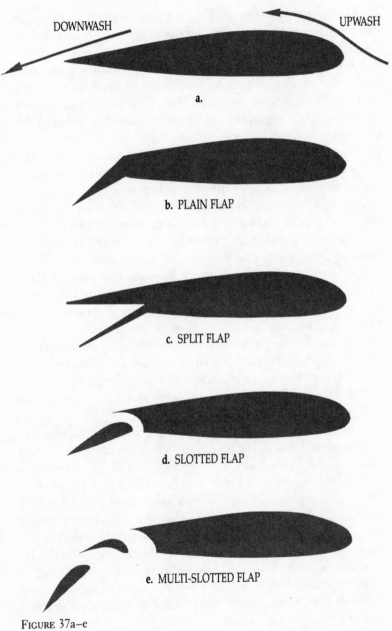

DOWNWASH   UPWASH

a.

b. PLAIN FLAP

c. SPLIT FLAP

d. SLOTTED FLAP

e. MULTI-SLOTTED FLAP

FIGURE 37a–e

The *slotted flap* (Figure 37d) is similar to the plain flap, but the difference between the two produces dramatic results. When the slotted flap is extended, a carefully designed gap forms between the wing's trailing edge and the flap's leading edge. This gap, called a slot, allows high-pressure air from beneath the wing to be ducted through the slot so as to increase airflow along the flap's upper surface. This considerably increases lift availability at large angles of attack.

The effect of the slot, *plus* the increased wing camber, *plus* the increased wing area created when the flap travels rearward during extension, enables the slotted flap to achieve greater increases in lift than either the plain or split flap. Such a flap is employed on the Navion and most high-wing Cessnas.

The *multi-slotted flap* (Figure 37e) is an ingenious improvement of the single-slotted flap. As this flap extends, a small airfoil, or vane, is positioned neatly between the wing's trailing edge and the flap's leading edge. The vane serves two purposes: It creates an additional slot and, because of its unique shape, directs airflow through the slots with greater efficiency. Although the double-slotted flap is an outstanding method of lift enhancement, it is mechanically complex and therefore used primarily on large aircraft, such as the Boeing 707. Triple-slotted flaps (with two vanes and three slots) are used on the 727.

The *Fowler flap* (Figure 37f) is one of the most efficient trailing-edge devices, but it is expensive and complex. When retracted, the Fowler flap is an integral part of the wing structure. When extended, it first slides almost directly aft to increase wing chord and area, resulting in a tidy increase in lift with a minimal increase in drag. Such a scheme is ideal for use during takeoff. As the flap is extended farther, it begins to deflect downward, which increases wing camber. Fully extended, the Fowler flap creates more lift and slightly less drag than a slotted flap of similar size and design. The unmodified Fowler flap is not used on small aircraft because of mechanical and cost disadvantages resulting from its complexity.

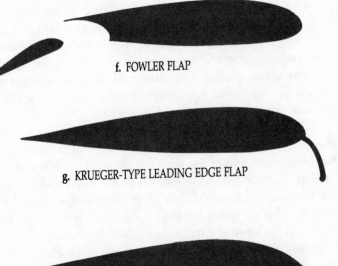

f. FOWLER FLAP

g. KRUEGER-TYPE LEADING EDGE FLAP

h. DROOPED LEADING EDGE

i. LEADING-EDGE SLAT

j. PERMANENT SLOT

FIGURE 37f–j

A relatively new family of flaps consists of leading-edge devices. Although primarily used on jetliners, leading-edge flaps, slats, and slots have been applied to a few general aviation aircraft and promise to become more popular in the future. As wings become smaller and more fuel-efficient, designers must dig deeper into their bag of aerodynamic tricks to retain slow-flight performance and controllability.

The *leading-edge flap* (Figure 37g), which also is known as a Krueger flap, is essentially a flat plate that is normally flush with the underside of the wing's leading edge. When this plate, or flap, is extended, wing camber is increased and some of the air that normally would flow under the wing is forced to flow over it. This increases lift and reduces stall speed. The leading-edge flap is almost always extended simultaneously with trailing-edge flaps. Such a flap has no intermediate position; it is either up or down. The leading-edge flap can extend along the entire wing or along a portion of it. It usually is found, however, on inboard wing sections.

The *drooped leading edge* (Figure 37h) is a form of leading-edge flap. Drooping the wing's leading edge not only increases wing camber at large angles of attack, but causes the oncoming relative wind to change direction gradually and flow more smoothly above the wing. The same wing with a conventional leading edge cannot be flown as slowly or at as large an angle of attack.

While only a few early aircraft incorporated a controllable "drooped snoot," a modern modification of this technique is to build a lesser, permanent droop into the wing's leading edge (usually accomplished by adding a circular-radius cuff). Examples include several high-wing Cessnas.

The *slat* (Figure 37i) is a small auxiliary airfoil that normally is flush with, and forms, the wing's leading edge. When extended, the slat reveals a slot that serves essentially the same purpose as a slot formed by extending slotted trailing-edge flaps: relatively high-pressure air from ahead of and beneath the wing is ducted so as to flow smoothly above the wing and increase lift. But, since the slat also is a lifting surface (an airfoil), it adds to wing area and dramatically increases lift at large angles of attack. The slats of a Helio Courier, for example, are so effective that they create most of the total lift at very low airspeeds. Another lightplane, the French-built Rallye, takes similar advantage of slat technology.

The notion of a slotted wing is not new; only the slat-formed slot is a relatively recent innovation. A glance at any Globe Swift or Stinson Voyager reveals a permanent slot (Figure 37j) about two feet long near the outboard, leading edge of each wing.

As with other slots, permanent ones delay the stall and, because of their location forward of the ailerons, increase roll controllability at reduced airspeed. Fixed slots, however, are not practical on modern machines because of their detrimental effect on cruise performance.

(When it was discovered that the stabilator of a Cessna Cardinal could be made to stall—and lose effectiveness—during the landing flare, a fast fix had to be found. Since the stabilator is essentially a small, upside-down wing, Cessna modified the surface by adding a permanent slot, which cured the problem. The stabilator no longer could be made to stall.)

Slats, too, originally were fixed in position. They couldn't be retracted, which resulted in unacceptable drag losses in cruise flight. Inevitably, slats became movable so that they could be tucked away when not needed. At appropriately low airspeeds, slats usually are extended either hydraulically (as on the Boeing 727) or automatically as a result of the center of pressure shifting forward along the top of the wing at increasingly larger angles of attack (as on a Rockwell Sabreliner and a Helio Courier).

Boundary Layer Control (BLC) has has not found its way into general aviation yet, primarily because of unacceptable weight and cost penalties. But, since experimental BLC systems constantly are being developed, they are worthy of mention.

The layer of air that flows *immediately* adjacent to the wing's upper surface is relatively inefficient; it is slowed down by the skin friction of the wing. One way to increase its efficiency is to blow high-energy air into this boundary layer through tiny holes in the wing's upper surface. Another technique is to suck away the near-stagnant boundary layer through similar holes in the wing. This forces the higher-velocity air immediately above the boundary layer to flow closer to the wing and increase lift. A third contrivance literally and powerfully blows air over whatever lifting surface needs to be made more effective (for example, a flap).

Complex? Yes. Impractical? So far. The difficulty of providing an appropriate power source (within the wing?) does not hold any bright promises for general aviation. But then, neither did the turbocharger nor the autopilot.

Fortunately, flap *management* is a relatively simple affair. It requires, simply stated, only heeding advice offered by the airframe manufacturer. However, there are other useful tips worth considering.

- Do not taxi or execute an engine runup with the flaps extended (especially when operating from unimproved surfaces in low-wing aircraft). This prevents possible flap damage from pebbles or other debris.
- Avoid taxiing through puddles during near-freezing temperatures. Otherwise, water that may splash into the flap tracks and mechanism could freeze and prevent retraction after takeoff.
- After takeoff, generally avoid flap retraction until above the influence of ground effect and at an airspeed well above the flaps-up stall speed (the bottom of the green arc).
- When checking out in an unfamiliar aircraft, be alert for possibly strong pitching moments when retracting flaps after takeoff, and when extending flaps for landing.
- When slow-flying along the downwind leg of a traffic pattern prior to landing, extend flaps partially. This usually results in a flatter attitude, which improves over-the-nose visibility.

- Remember that most airplanes are limited to fewer Gs when flaps are extended as opposed to the clean configuration. In order to prevent the possibility of overstressing the flap structure, avoid flap extension during approaches in severe turbulence.
- Avoid making full-flap, IFR approaches (unless necessary to comply with a steep descent profile) because of the difficulty this may create during the initiation of a missed approach. Extend flaps fully when the landing is assured (unless known pitch-trim changes make this inadvisable at low altitudes).
- If—following an engine failure—it appears the plane is only a few feet short of gliding over the runway threshold, extend a minimal amount of flaps (the first notch, for example). This may provide sufficient "ballooning" to reach the threshold safely. This technique can be effective as a last-ditch effort during the last few seconds of flight. For longer periods, flap extension usually erodes glide performance.
- Flaps can be retracted immediately after touchdown to improve braking performance on short or slick runways, but be careful not to grab the landing-gear switch by mistake. Otherwise, the rollout may be much shorter than anticipated.
- Retracting the flaps immediately after touching down on the main-gear tires allows the nose to be held off the runway longer, if necessary (as when the nose gear fails to extend or the nosewheel tire is known to be flat).
- A technique that can be used (but only by experienced pilots who know their aircraft) is to retract the flaps after the sink rate has been arrested during the landing flare and when the tires are only inches above the runway. The aircraft will settle firmly onto the runway almost instantly. This is an excellent way of preventing excessive floating and helps to place the aircraft precisely on a preselected spot during a short-field landing. This technique requires practice, however, under the watchful eye of an instructor.
- Should flaps be used during a crosswind landing? By all

means. But do retract them after touchdown to help prevent a subsequent and unexpected liftoff and to reduce the airplane's natural weathervaning tendency.

- Some self-styled bush pilots suggest making the takeoff roll with flaps retracted and then, immediately prior to liftoff, extending them to the takeoff position. Theoretically, this technique eliminates the drag of extended flaps during a short-field takeoff roll, but makes them available during rotation. Don't believe it. The drag caused by takeoff flaps at such low airspeeds is almost undetectable. And, since there is the possibility of extending flaps to the incorrect position during a critical phase of flight, this technique of "popping" the flaps is far more dangerous than any presumed benefit might warrant.

UNDERSTANDING THE AIRSPACE SYSTEM

In the early days of aviation, aeronautical charts were simple. With the exception of displaying widely scattered airports and a few navaids, they were little more than topographical charts. In some cases they were road maps. A pilot could fly from one place to another in total freedom. The airspace through which he flew was all the same: uncontrolled and essentially unregulated.

But as aviation grew, the Civil Aeronautics Authority, and then the Federal Aviation Administration, found it necessary to smother a pilot's chart with more than 20 types of overlapping and intertwining airspace (with more coming, no doubt).

Each type of airspace requires its own rules. The result can be confusion and conflict. There are certain places—especially in the vicinity of terminal control areas (TCAs)—where it is not difficult to inadvertently violate one regulation or another.

The most common mistakes made by pilots are the result of confusing airspace requirements. Many flight instructors and

Airspace Quiz

See if you can match each type of airspace on the left with the most accurate clue listed on the right. A score of 90% or better is excellent. A score of 70% or less suggests that a review of the Airman's Information Manual (AIM) is in order. Answers appear at the end of this chapter.

1. ___ Control area

2. ___ Positive Control Area (PCA)

3. ___ Control Zone (CZ)

4. ___ Continental Control Area

5. ___ Transition area

6. ___ Airport Traffic Area (ATA)

7. ___ Terminal Control Area (TCA)

8. ___ Airport Radar Service Area (ARSA)
9. ___ Warning area

10. ___ Prohibited area

11. ___ Restricted area

12. ___ Military Operations Area (MOA)
13. ___ Air Defense Identification Zone (ADIZ)
14. ___ Military Training Routes (MTRs)
15. ___ Airport advisory area

16. ___ Alert area

17. ___ Uncontrolled airspace

18. ___ Special conservation area

19. ___ Temporary flight restriction

20. ___ Controlled firing area

A. Flight service station provides service

B. Extends to 4,000 feet agl (usually)

C. NOTAM

D. Victor airway

E. U.S. Capitol Building lies within one
F. Not below 2,000 feet, please

G. Special VFR allowed (in most locations)
H. IRs and VRs

I. VFR minimums are clear of clouds and one-mile visibility at low altitudes
J. Instrument rating required

K. Substantial soaring activity, for example
L. Five-mile visibility

M. A piece of (inverted wedding) cake

N. 156 and 200 knot speed limits

O. It stops when they see you coming

P. Outside the three-mile limit

Q. Invisible hazards to navigation, usually
R. VFR flight plan may be required

S. Aerobatics and high-speed maneuvering
T. Usually begins at 700 feet above ground level

examiners do not know as much about the subject as they should. Consequently, misconceptions are legion.

One reason for the confusion is that the National Airspace System has been developed piecemeal over the years. As each new layer or chunk of airspace was added, the FAA provided a legal definition and the justification, but often failed to explain the need adequately or clearly. It provides pieces of the puzzle but often fails to paint the Big Picture. (Rumor has it there is no Big Picture.) How many pilots, for example, understand the purpose of the continental control area or why a control zone extends to 14,500 feet msl?

Rather than discuss the components individually, it is better first to stand back for an overview. Once the fundamentals are understood, everything else tends to fall into place.

The most important concept to understand is that of controlled airspace. What is it? What is its purpose? The one characteristic common to *all forms* of controlled airspace is that this is where ATC exercises control over all IFR traffic for the purpose of providing separation. VFR pilots are allowed in controlled airspace as long as they abide by the weather minimums required for VFR flight within controlled airspace, as shown in table 1 of Figure 38. An instrument pilot popping out of a cloud should be offered the opportunity to use the see-and-be-seen concept of traffic separation to prevent entanglements of the worst kind.

If the visibility and cloud-clearance requirements cannot be maintained, pilots operating VFR must not enter or operate in any form of controlled airspace, period. It is that simple.

There are seven types of controlled airspace: control areas, the continental control area, control zones, transition areas, terminal control areas (TCAs), airport radar service areas (ARSAs), and the positive control area (PCA). The important point to remember about these is that—despite their different names—they all are controlled airspace. Another point to remember is that if VFR weather conditions exist, a pilot may enter the first

Minimum VFR Visibility and Distance from Clouds		
Table 1: Controlled Airspace		
Altitude	Flight Visibility	Distance from clouds
1,200 ft agl or less, regardless of msl altitude	3 sm	Clear of clouds
more than 1,200 ft agl, but less than 10,000 ft msl		500 ft below 1,000 ft above 2,000 ft horiz
more than 1,200 ft agl, and at or above 10,000 ft msl	5 sm	1,000 ft below 1,000 ft above 1 sm horiz
Table 2: Uncontrolled Airspace		
Altitude	Flight Visibility	Distance from Clouds
1,200 ft agl or less, regardless of msl altitude	1 sm	clear of clouds
more than 1,200 ft agl, but less than 10,000 ft msl		500 ft below 1,000 ft above 2,000 horiz
more than 1,200 ft agl, and at or above 10,000 ft msl	5 sm	1,000 ft below 1,000 ft above 1 sm horiz

FIGURE 38

four types of controlled airspace without communicating with anyone. Pilots, however, must communicate with ATC prior to entering terminal control areas, airport radar service areas, and the positive control area, all of which are discussed later.

Control areas are outlined on VFR aeronautical charts in blue shading and consist predominantly of the en route airspace structure. In other words, control areas consist of the low-altitude federal airways (and their extensions and enlargements). They usually begin at 1,200 feet agl, which means that the space beneath the floor of an airway is uncontrolled (unless some other form of controlled airspace underlies the airway). The low-altitude airways extend up to but do not include a pressure altitude of 18,000 feet msl (FL180). (In Hawaii, control areas have no upper limit.)

Although en route IFR operations usually occur within control areas (separation from other traffic is not provided outside of controlled airspace), they are given considerably more elbow room when at or above 14,500 feet msl. At these higher altitudes, IFR traffic can get clearance more regularly to navigate via direct routes or radar vectors that do not follow federal airways. Consequently, all airspace at 14,500 feet msl and above is designated as one mass of controlled airspace, and that is called the continental control area (CCA).

As its name implies, the continental control area exists only over the continental United States, except for Alaska's Aleutian Islands. Excluded also is all airspace less than 1,500 feet agl.

There is no operational difference between a control area and the continental control area.

IFR operations need separation from other traffic not only while en route but also during arrivals and departures. Transition areas and control zones are designated for these purposes. Control zones usually are outlined on aeronautical charts by dashed blue lines and surround one or more airports that have published instrument approaches. This type of controlled airspace extends from the ground up to the base of the continental control area (14,500 feet msl), as shown by example A in Figure 39. Such an airspace configuration consisting only of the CCA and control zones, however, is not practical because there are no low-altitude airways leading to the control zone. The only way to fly IFR to such an airport and remain within controlled airspace would be to remain within the CCA (at or above 14,500 feet msl) until almost directly above the airport and then spiral downward within the usually 10-mile-wide cylinder of controlled airspace (the control zone).

For all practical purposes, control zones terminate at the base of some lower, overlying layer of controlled airspace. In example B, the control zone extends from the ground to the

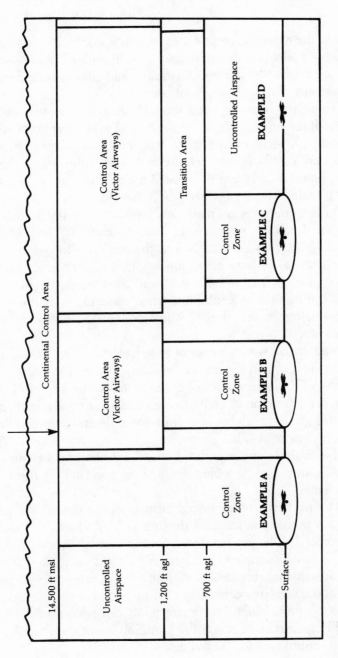

FIGURE 39

237

base of the overlying control area, which is only 1,200 feet agl.

May a pilot pass through a control zone without permission? Yes, as long as the minimum-visibility and cloud-clearance requirements of table 1 are maintained.

There are, however, a few special rules pertaining to control zones. If the primary airport in the control zone is reporting less than a 1,000-foot ceiling, pilots operating under visual flight rules may not fly below such a cloud layer within the control zone; however, they can fly through the control zone as long as they remain at least 1,000 feet above the cloud tops.

VFR minimums normally are predicated on flight visibility—the distance a pilot can see from the cockpit. The control zone, however, is an exception to the rule. A VFR pilot may not operate to or from an airport within a control zone unless the reported *ground* visibility is at least three miles. Flight visibility can be used as a substitute when operating to or from an airport within a control zone when ground visibility is not reported at that airport.

If an airport within a control zone has less than a 1,000-foot ceiling or less than three miles visibility, a pilot can request a special VFR clearance to operate to or from that airport. This clearance is unique to control zones and requires a minimum reported ground visibility of at least one mile and that the pilot remain clear of clouds.

If a control zone is outlined on a VFR chart by a chain of blue Ts instead of by a blue dashed line, special VFR flight is not allowed.

The next type of controlled airspace is the transition area, which is outlined in magenta shading on VFR charts. It is used to help bridge the gap between a control area (an airway) and a control zone (example C in Figure 39). In this way, the transition area, which begins at 700 feet agl and terminates at the base of the overlying control area, provides additional controlled airspace within which instrument pilots can maneuver during an IFR approach. In effect, the transition area lowers the floor of the control area to 700 feet agl.

Is there any difference between a transition area and the overlying control area? Only in size and shape. The rules of controlled airspace apply equally to both.

An interesting case is shown in example D, which consists of an overlying control area and a transition area, but no control zone. The transition area implies the existence of an instrument approach to this airport, but the absence of a control zone implies otherwise. This is not an uncommon situation in mountainous areas. The airport does have an instrument approach, but the IFR minimums are so high that an instrument pilot must reach VFR conditions prior to reaching the floor of the transition area (700 feet agl) or execute a missed approach. Upon reaching VFR conditions, the instrument pilot is on his own in avoiding other aircraft that may be under the floor of the transition area. In this case, the airspace beneath the transition area is uncontrolled. (Table 2 in Figure 38 shows VFR operations in uncontrolled airspace require only one mile visibility.)

These four types of controlled airspace, the control area, the continental control area, the control zone, and the transition area are what is unofficially referred to as *weather-related* airspace. In other words, a pilot may enter any of them without permission as long as VFR conditions for controlled airspace can be maintained.

Permission from air traffic control is required prior to entering the remaining three types of controlled airspace. The first of these is the positive control area (PCA). This blanket of airspace extends from Flight Level 180 (approximately 18,000 feet msl) to FL600, a pressure altitude of 60,000 feet. (Imagine the freedom one could enjoy above 60,000 feet where all airspace—and space—is uncontrolled.) The PCA covers the 48 continental states as well as the mainland of Alaska and is restricted to IFR operations. Admission to this lofty layer also includes certain aircraft equipment requirements. The highest en route altitudes available for VFR operations, therefore, are 17,500 feet msl eastbound and 16,500 feet msl westbound.

The second type of controlled airspace requiring an ATC

clearance is the TCA, colloquially referred to as the inverted wedding cake because of the way its layers expand, mushroom-like, with altitude. Since the TCA is controlled airspace, pilots must maintain VFR conditions while in the TCA, unless they are on an IFR flight plan. (Operating within a TCA requires that pilots abide by specific rules, as specified in Part 91 of the Federal Aviation Regulations.) The purpose of a TCA is to enable ATC to provide adequate separation between all aircraft operating in the vicinity of particularly busy airports.

The third type of controlled airspace requiring ATC approval is the airport radar service area (ARSA), which is similar to but much less restrictive than a TCA. VFR pilots are required to communicate with ATC prior to entering an ARSA. This affords ATC the opportunity to provide traffic separation and advisories to all traffic operating in the vicinity of those airports within the ARSA.

Closely related to the ARSA is the terminal radar service area (TRSA), which technically—and by itself—is not a form of controlled airspace. When flying within a TRSA, which overlies some busy airports, VFR pilots are provided traffic advisories on a workload-permitting basis. Although VFR pilots operating in a TRSA are not required to communicate with ATC, they are strongly urged to do so. (TRSAs gradually are being replaced by ARSAs.)

Last, but not least, is the airport traffic area. Although traffic is controlled by tower controllers within an ATA, the ATA technically is uncontrolled airspace as far as weather requirements are concerned.

An airport traffic area extends from the ground up to but not including 3,000 feet above the airport elevation and has a radius of five statute miles. The lateral dimensions of an ATA are not shown on aeronautical charts, but their presence is indicated by a blue airport symbol, which indicates that the airport is tower controlled. Pilots must be in contact with the tower prior to entering or operating within the traffic area, but they may overfly the ATA at or above 3,000 feet agl without calling anyone.

When the tower is closed, the ATA ceases to exist, and the airport becomes uncontrolled.

All airspace that is not controlled obviously is uncontrolled. Pilots may fly in such airspace as long as they maintain the minimums required for VFR flight in uncontrolled airspace, as shown in table 2 of Figure 38.

Instrument flying (without a flight plan) is allowed in uncontrolled airspace, but those who operate in this manner are strictly on their own. Uncontrolled instrument flight requires that the pilot assume all responsibility for terrain avoidance and altitude selection (although he must abide by the hemispherical altitude rule, in case another aircraft is heading the other way). Also, there is no assurance of navaid quality or availability. Communications with ATC might or might not be possible, but, even if a pilot can contact ATC, there will be no attempt by a controller to separate IFR traffic in uncontrolled airspace.

Is it legal for an instrument pilot operating under FAR Part 91 to take off without an IFR clearance in instrument weather conditions from an airport not located in a control zone? Absolutely. He must, however, either reach VFR conditions or obtain a clearance prior to entering any controlled airspace that might lie above. This technique is used frequently by instrument pilots departing remote airports covered by a local layer of fog.

This is the basic structure and function of the regulatory hydra called controlled airspace. Not all of the various permutations and idiosyncracies of the National Airspace System have been covered. Pilots should recognize, also, that changes to the structure and function of controlled airspace are almost always in the works.

The purpose of this discussion has been only to provide a different perspective as a method of reviewing a subject that often receives inadequate attention.

Curiously, pilots operating under visual flight rules need to know more about airspace requirements than when operating IFR. This is because it is the VFR pilot's responsibility to determine where and under what conditions it is permissible to fly. IFR pilots simply operate in accordance with clearances from ATC. In this respect, the greatest demand is placed on the VFR pilot, for it is he who must thread his way alone through the FAA's airspace maze.

Answers to airspace quiz:

1 (D), 2 (J), 3 (G), 4 (L), 5 (T), 6 (N), 7 (M), 8 (B), 9 (P), 10 (E), 11 (Q), 12 (S), 13 (R), 14 (H), 15 (A), 16 (K), 17 (I), 18 (F), 19 (C), 20 (O).

6

FLYING IFR

There is something about instrument flying that conveys a sense of inflexibility. Inexperienced pilots as well as many veterans view the IFR system as a set of rigid rules that require absolute adherence at all times. To them, instrument flying is cut-and-dried, with little or no tolerance for deviation.

But this is an unrealistic view of the practical world of IFR. Experienced pilots know that there is much more involved than simply following the dictates of an IFR chart. They have discovered that instrument flying is a thinking man's game and allows for more operational flexibility than generally is appreciated.

This is not to suggest that instrument pilots should take unwarranted liberties and jeopardize safety. But there is an almost unlimited number of techniques and procedures that can be applied within the constraints of the system to simplify IFR flights and make them more efficient. All that is required is an understanding of the rules and a cooperative, professional attitude toward controllers.

Consider, for example, a pilot who has just received a clearance from ground control (or clearance delivery). Unfortunately, the routing or altitude provided is undesirable. Should this pilot restate his request to the ground controller? No, not if he is capable of complying with the instructions. Requesting a revised clearance (as many pilots do) only delays departure. The ground controller, after all, is only a middleman who must convey a pilot's request to the center (unless a tower en route clearance is involved) and wait for a reply. In most cases, the pilot should accept the clearance, depart, and request changes after he is handed off to a center controller. Of course, he should not accept a departure clearance if it poses a hazard, such as flight into a thunderstorm or icing conditions.

Accepting a clearance does not guarantee an expeditious departure. The pilot may have considerable delay while waiting to be admitted into the IFR system, a common problem when departing high-density traffic areas. Ground delays of 15 to 30 minutes are not unusual. But there are ways to reduce the effects of such inconvenience.

To prevent operating and possibly overheating their aircraft engines, pilots might consider shutting down until the tower controller provides a five-minute warning, for example. The pilot can either monitor the tower frequency on one receiver (which does not drain the battery very much) or wait for a prearranged, discrete light signal from the tower before restarting. Such a technique, which is common practice at some airports, saves considerable fuel, engine wear and tear, and numerous ticks of the Hobbs meter, a particularly valuable benefit for those who rent. (This technique is not recommended for those not adept at hot-starting fuel-injected engines.)

Substantial time can be saved by not using the IFR system until it really is needed. For instance, if actual IFR weather conditions are not anticipated until en route or nearing the destination, a pilot can eliminate much or all of a ground delay by departing VFR and picking up the IFR clearance when underway.

One of Murphy's Laws claims that the departure runway inevitably points a pilot away from his destination. A pilot does not have to put up with the inconvenience; he can request permission to use another runway.

If such a request is refused, a pilot then can alter his departure technique to minimize the penalty of taking off in the "wrong" direction. The idea, of course, is to reverse course as soon as possible. But to do this, it is necessary to know what conditions must be met before ATC will allow an aircraft to turn in the "right" direction. For example, if it is first necessary to reach a specific fix, a pilot might consider a shallow, high-speed climb to reach that fix in a relatively short period of time; a low airspeed would only prolong flight away from the destination. Or if a specific altitude must be attained before course reversal is allowed, then consider using the airspeed for maximum climb rate (V_y). Remember the rule of thumb: Every minute or mile flown in the "wrong" direction adds two minutes or two miles to the flight.

In certain radar control environments, a pilot departing can expect to be routed away from terrain obstructions until he attains a sufficient crossing altitude. Such detours add considerable time and distance to a flight, but there is a way to reduce or eliminate them when the initial phase of an IFR departure can be conducted in VFR conditions. If the terrain responsible for the lengthy departure routing can be negotiated *safely* in visual conditions, simply advise the controller that you can maintain visual separation from the obstructions and that a visual climb is requested until reaching some specific point at or above the published minimum en route altitude (MEA).

This is particularly useful when flying in the west because it allows a pilot to negotiate a mountain pass without having to clear the adjacent peaks by the altitude or distance margins required when flying IFR.

Once beyond or above the obstacles, the pilot can then resume the IFR portion of his flight. Note, however, that this technique requires a pilot to be familiar with the terrain in the vicinity of his departure route. Strangers to the area would be ill-advised to accept this recommendation.

When making a local departure through an overcast to VFR conditions, many pilots report "VFR" immediately upon breaking out of the clouds. This is both illegal and hazardous. According to regulation, a pilot is not VFR until 1,000 feet on top. This height above the clouds is necessary if a pilot is to visually keep his aircraft safely separated from all others. But by reporting "VFR" too soon, he not only is too low to see and avoid other aircraft, he may cause the controller to cancel radar service, which would deprive the pilot of potentially critical traffic advisories.

Once on course and climbing to cruise altitude, a pilot's attention usually begins to shift toward the en route phase of flight. He also may begin to wonder about the validity of the winds aloft forecast and whether the actual winds really do justify climbing so high. But there may be no reason to wonder. Simply pick up the mike and ask the controller to ask other pilots that may already be at your intended cruise altitude for wind reports. You may discover that the forecast tailwind really does exist. Or, you may learn that the actual winds do not justify such a prolonged climb and a lower, time-saving altitude can be requested.

Once at cruise altitude (IFR or VFR), do not be in a hurry to fiddle with the "go" knobs. Allow climb power to accelerate the aircraft to cruise speed *before* reducing power. Allow the engine to cool *before* closing the cowl flaps (especially in the summer). Allow oil and cylinder-head temperatures to stabilize before leaning the fuel-air mixture.

The en route phase of IFR flight also provides numerous opportunities to increase flight efficiency. One of the easiest is to request direct routings whenever practical. There is, after all, no reason to fly doglegs just because the airways are laid out that way. To shorten flights, some pilots continually tune in distant, en route VORs that might enable them to eliminate all or part of a dogleg. The request for "present position direct" is made as soon as a navigable signal is received (or if the aircraft is equipped with an IFR-approved, long-range navigation system).

Miles can also be shaved from a flight by proceeding toward a VOR that cannot yet be received. Simply request a radar vector toward that VOR. Controllers usually are happy to oblige and will reply with something like, "Turn right, heading zero-five-five, vectors to Chutzpah VOR. Proceed direct when able." At times, a pilot might even be able to obtain a vector from Los Angeles direct to Kansas City, for example (as long as fuel and bladder capacities are sufficient to comply).

Once the distant VOR signal is received and identified and the course deviation indicator (CDI) is centered, many pilots make the mistake of turning immediately to the heading indicated by the course selector. This is a mistake because the pilot has yet to determine whether or not the aircraft is tracking directly toward the station. In other words, the heading last assigned by the controller may have incorporated drift correction. So, rather than turning directly toward the VOR, simply maintain the assigned heading and wait to see what effect this has on the course-deviation indicator. Make heading changes only in response to needle movement and to save unnecessary maneuvering.

Many pilots also do a lot of unnecessary S-turning in the vicinity of a VOR. In an attempt to remain precisely on course, they chase the CDI needle to the station, through the cone of confusion, and beyond, a complete waste of time and energy. Other pilots are more relaxed about en route tracking. When within a few miles of the station, they simply hold a heading and wait for the needle to settle down *after* station passage, before attempting to resume tracking. If station passage dictates a course change such as 12 degrees, turn half that number of degrees when approaching the station and interception of the outbound radial is guaranteed with a minimum of fuss and bother (unless a dramatic wind shift occurs directly over the VOR).

Since many general aviation autopilots (including many of

the high-priced models) do not track VOR radials very well and become excessively sensitive near a station, a comfortable flight suggests using the heading mode for en route navigation.

Although good flight planning demands remaining clear of restricted airspace, controllers are kept informed about when these areas are not in use. A considerable amount of unnecessary detouring might be avoided by asking the center controller if "R-two-five-zero-five is 'hot' this afternoon." If he responds in the negative, a clearance directly through the area usually is possible, a perfectly safe procedure.

En route IFR often finds a pilot flying in VFR conditions for long periods of time. When this occurs, a pilot on an IFR flight plan can request a VFR-on-top clearance for at least a portion of the flight, an infrequently used procedure that can simplify many problems.

A pilot cleared to fly VFR-on-top must remain in VFR conditions, fly at an appropriate VFR altitude (above the MEA and below Flight Level 180), and track along the routing prescribed by the last IFR clearance. The advantage of VFR-on-top (even when there are no clouds in sight) is that a pilot has considerably more altitude flexibility at a time when desired IFR altitudes may not be available because of conflicting IFR traffic. The pilot of a Cessna 172, for example, might not want to climb to an assigned altitude of 12,000 feet on a warm day and instead might prefer to maintain VFR-on-top at 6,500 feet. Altitude changes, crossing restrictions, and other requirements of IFR flight also are simplified vastly when VFR-on-top.

Assume that a pilot is cruising at 6,000 feet but would like to climb higher to take advantage of more favorable winds. He is concerned, however, about the possibility of icing conditions at the higher, colder altitude. Can he climb to 8,000 feet and have the option to return immediately to the warmer altitude should the need arise? Frequently, he can. All he has to do is request "an altitude block from six to eight." If approved, the pilot can climb and descend within this altitude block to his heart's content. Or he can maintain any altitude in between. It simply is a matter of knowing what to request.

As he approaches the destination airport, a pilot may be advised to expect holding at some point down the road. Is there anything he can do to minimize this penalty? Of course. All he has to do is advise ATC that he is reducing airspeed to consume part (or perhaps all) of the delay while en route. This technique can save considerable fuel and reduce (or eliminate) the holding time required. After all, why be in a hurry to hold?

Once in a holding pattern, a pilot below 14,000 feet must time the pattern legs and adjust the outbound leg (if necessary) to result in a one-minute-long inbound leg. What a pain. Instead, why not request five- or 10-mile-long DME (distance measuring equipment) legs and eliminate some of the mental gymnastics? Such a request is almost always approved (assuming that the aircraft is DME equipped).

Once released from the shackles of a holding pattern and again en route toward his destination, a pilot eventually may notice that he is being radar vectored either away from or beyond the airport, ATC's method of spacing arrival traffic. When this occurs, reduce airspeed again, a convenient way to reduce the length of a delay vector and save fuel in the process. At times, a delay vector can be avoided altogether by volunteering to the controller that a speed reduction would be preferred to an out-of-the-way vector.

It should be apparent that many IFR options are the result of imaginative and timely headwork. But none of this flexibility may be available unless a pilot has established some rapport with the controller. Usually all that is necessary is a professional approach to communications and a considerate attitude toward a controller's problems. For example, special requests should be held in abeyance when the frequency is congested and the controller obviously is pressed. At times, a bit of give-and-take is required, and a pilot should be equally prepared to comply with a controller's request. Learn to work with ATC, not against it.

A controller quickly recognizes and rewards with favor those who are most cooperative and least insistent.

But never be so cooperative as to compromise safety. You are the pilot-in-command and are solely responsible for the safe operation of your aircraft.

Perhaps the real key to taking advantage of the IFR system is to recognize that air traffic control was designed to serve pilots, not enslave them. Only after he learns to appreciate this can a pilot really begin to extract the operational benefits. The number of options available are limited only by a pilot's imagination and his knowledge of how the system works.

A DIFFERENT APPROACH

How would you like to shoot a VOR approach to Zamboanga, an NDB approach to Rangoon, or a localizer approach to Singapore? Well, you can do just that using your own airplane and without ever leaving the local flying area.

These locations may be romantically appealing to most pilots, but the reason for suggesting such adventuresome flying is not to give vent to your wanderlust. Rather, the suggestions that follow, in addition to adding some spice to your flying, are methods to help a pilot become more thoroughly acquainted with the vagaries of nonprecision approaches.

The ILS approach is, in a sense, easier to master than VOR, NDB, and localizer approaches. Once a pilot has learned to move the CDI and glideslope needles slowly and keep them in place, he can feel justifiably confident about shooting a similar approach anywhere in the world. This is because one ILS approach is essentially the same as every other.

Nonprecision approaches, on the other hand, are not so similar. They are like people; each has a unique personality with which to reckon, procedures that somehow differentiate one approach from another. This is one reason why nonprecision approaches annually claim more victims than do ILS approaches even though the latter permits a pilot to descend to considerably lower minimums.

The NDB (ADF) approach to Runway 13 at Hong Kong is an excellent example of just how unique a nonprecision approach can be. The actual approach plate has such a profusion of hieroglyphic notations that it looks more like an Aresti aerobatic chart.

The approach begins when the pilot is at cruising altitude and is cleared direct to the Cheung Chau NDB for an ADF approach to Runway 13. (English-speaking pilots refer to this as the "Charlie-Charlie" approach.) Upon reaching the beacon, the pilot must descend over it in a series of precise figure eights so as to cross the beacon inbound at 1,000 feet. After passing "Charlie-Charlie," he descends to 750 feet (the MDA) and tracks across 10 miles of the South China Sea toward the Stonecutters NDB.

After passing Stonecutters, the pilot plunges straight ahead and purposefully heads toward a 1,518-foot-high obstacle. Continuing, he should spot the hill on one side of which are two large, brightly-colored, illuminated, orange-and-white checkerboards. The pilot aims for these warning signs and gets as close to them as he dares. He must not overfly the checkerboards, however, because if he is fortunate enough to miss the towering obstacle nearby, he might wind up in China. Instead, he banks sharply right and heads toward the RW NDB at the approach end of Hong Kong International's Runway 13. Theoretically, the pilot then will be on short final and should have little difficulty descending over (and through) concrete canyons of high-rise buildings to a successful landing.

This is an extreme example of what can be expected during a nonprecision approach, but it does demonstrate that a pilot who has learned to shoot a VOR approach at Santa Monica, for example, may not be prepared for what may await him elsewhere.

Unfortunately, the average pilot becomes proficient in exe-

cuting only those approaches within a relatively short distance
of his home airport. This can build false confidence because he
may not be sufficiently familiar with the nonprecision approach
procedures used elsewhere. But there is a solution to this problem, a different approach to nonprecision approaches.

Since the typical VOR approach incorporates only one VOR
station, it is possible to use a local station as if it were distantly
located. For example, if a pilot lives in beautiful downtown
Burbank, California, he can practice shooting a VOR approach
to Kansas City International Airport by substituting the nearby
Van Nuys VORTAC for the MKC VORTAC shown on the
Kansas City "VOR Rwy 27" approach plate. A pilot can practice the Kansas City approach without ever leaving Southern
California.

There is one obvious problem with this suggestion, but it is
actually a blessing in disguise. After executing the Kansas City
approach (while using the Van Nuys VOR), there's no way that
a pilot will find a runway at the missed approach point. So, let's
turn this liability into an asset. What does a pilot do when he
cannot find the runway? He executes a missed approach. So
here's a way to practice both the approach and the missed approach.

Since a pilot knows in advance that he will have to execute
a missed approach, he will be forced to prepare for that maneuver, something most pilots don't do when relatively certain of
finding a runway under the overcast. Learning the pull-up procedure prior to *every* IFR approach is a habit most of us need
to develop further.

Another problem easily solved is that of adhering to the altitudes published on an approach plate. Assume, for example,
that a Denver-based pilot wants to practice the "VOR Rwy 22L"
approach to Knoxville, Tennessee, while using the Denver VOR.
According to the Knoxville approach plate, the pilot is supposed
to cross the final approach fix (the VOR) at 3,000 feet (or above).
There is obviously no way to fly over the Denver VOR at 3,000

feet msl because this station is situated more than a mile above sea level.

The solution is obvious. Simply add some convenient altitude to every altitude shown on the Knoxville approach plate. The lowest altitude shown on the Knoxville plate is 1,500 feet msl which, of course, is the MDA. The Denver-based pilot should mentally add 5,000 feet, for example, to all the altitudes shown on the Knoxville plate. In this case, the MDA would be raised from 1,500 to 6,500 feet, the 3,000-foot altitude required over the VOR would become 8,000 feet msl, and so forth.

One must be cautious, however, to determine in advance that a practice approach of this nature will not cause the aircraft to barge through a local traffic pattern, TCA, ARSA, or other restricted airspace. If necessary, the altitudes can be raised farther so as to remain above a nearby airport traffic area during the procedure.

Conversely, if a Knoxville-based pilot wishes to use a nearby VORTAC to practice a "VOR-A" approach to Ely, Nevada, for example, he need not change the altitudes shown on the plate. The MDA at Ely is 8,800 feet, well above the relatively low terrain of east Tennessee. It might be desirable, in this case, to *lower* all altitudes by 4,000 or 5,000 feet.

One word of caution. When practicing IFR procedures, safety demands carrying a qualified safety pilot—even during CAVU (ceiling and visibility unlimited) conditions and when not wearing a hood. Conforming to the rigors of an IFR approach, especially an unfamiliar one, demands that considerable time be spent concentrating on the instruments. Without an additional pair of Mark IV eyeballs to scan the skies, safety is seriously compromised. To maximize the value of such practice, however, it would be wise to hire an instrument instructor.

In many parts of the country it is becoming more and more difficult to practice ADF approaches. This is because the FAA is decommissioning so many nondirectional radiobeacons. But for those who choose to use our "mock approach system," the lack of a local radiobeacon poses no problem. Simply use a convenient commercial broadcast station and pretend it is an NDB.

When training pilots in the Los Angeles area, I usually have them tune in KMPC (710 kHz), hand them a plate for the "NDB Rwy 1" approach to West Yellowstone, Montana, and relax to the accompaniment of soothing music and an on-the-hour newscast. West Yellowstone is perfect, in this case, because the published MDA is 8,000 feet. This keeps a training flight well above the jet traffic zipping in and out of the Burbank ARSA.

Occasionally, a problem arises that could prevent using a local VORTAC station in place of the one specified on an approach plate. This occurs when a cross-radial from a second VORTAC (or NDB) is required to define a fix such as in Figure 40, which is a simplified display of the "VOR Rwy 26" approach to El Paso, Texas.

If a pilot wanted to practice this approach while flying in the vicinity of Intercourse, Pennsylvania (yes, there really is such a place), for example, it's not likely that he would be able to find a pair of VORTACs in the same relative position as those needed for the El Paso procedure (ELP and EWM VORTACS). So, instead of using the Newman 131° radial to define Giffen Intersection, he would use a 7.0 DME indication from the Pennsylvania VORTAC being used to practice the approach.

Fortunately, more than one facility is rarely required for a nonprecision approach. A single VORTAC or NDB is usually all it takes to practice distantly-located procedures in your own backyard.

In addition to the experience gained from practicing an assortment of nonprecision approaches at altitude, there are numerous other reasons that make this technique more practical than shooting local approaches to "real" airports.

First of all, this procedure does not require working with approach control or the tower. As a result, there are no costly, time-consuming traffic delays. Also, the safety pilot (or instructor) does not have to be concerned with extraneous communi-

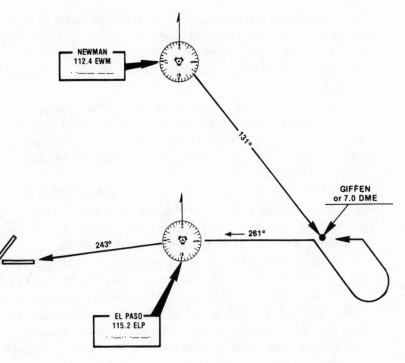

FIGURE 40

cations and watching out for other aircraft buzzing around the pattern. Since he is not so preoccupied, the instructor can spend more time observing and critiquing a pilot's technique.

Also, the instructor can allow his student to digress from the published procedure (like descending below the MDA) without worrying about wiping out someone's chimney with the landing gear. This allows a pilot more time to recognize his own errors and take positive, corrective action. Often, this results in a more meaningful lesson as compared to one in which an instructor must terminate the deviation because of conflicting terrain and/or traffic.

The high-altitude approach also gives the instructor a chance to present his student with a totally unfamiliar approach plate.

Having to study a procedure while en route (or holding) is excellent preparation for the real world of instrument flight. For many pilots, it is a shocking exprience to deviate to an alternate airport and execute an approach for which he has not planned.

Have you ever tried to practice a back-course ILS approach at a local airport only to find that the prevailing wind (and runway in use) invariably conspires against you? For similar reasons, most pilots rarely have the opportunity to shoot a "back-door" approach to an airport.

But that approach can be executed at altitude. After all, a localizer has virtually the same characteristics at 5,000 feel agl as it does at 500. Additionally, other rarely used, "back-door" approaches (VOR or ADF) can be practiced at altitude.

Difficulties can arise also when practicing a local approach that coincides with the runway in use. Because of excessive VFR traffic in the pattern, a pilot may not be allowed to continue an approach to both the MDA and the missed approach point. Instead, the tower controller may request that the approach be broken off at some point (or altitude) that defeats the purpose of the exercise. More frequently than not, pilots practicing approaches at a busy airport are not allowed to execute the missed-approach procedure because this, too, may conflict with traffic.

All such problems are eliminated by executing the procedure above the airport traffic area. It's a great way to beat the system.

When a pilot elects to use a local navaid as the nucleus for a distantly located procedure, he has the option of practicing any of thousands of approaches to "airports" all around the world. But perhaps he cannot find a published approach procedure to suit his needs. This problem, too, is easily resolved; the ambitious pilot can create his own procedure. A typical example is shown in Figure 41 and is a procedure that I sometimes give to an advanced instrument student. It helps me to determine if he knows how to prepare for and execute a strange approach.

So you see, you can shoot a nonprecision approach to Zam-

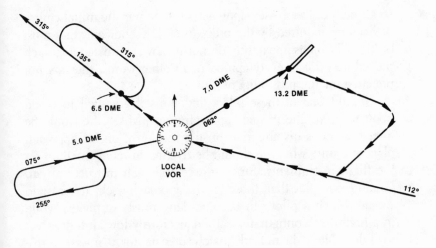

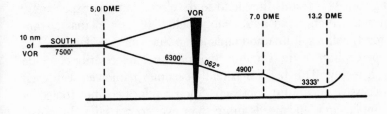

PULL UP: Climb HEADING 120° to 5800' then climbing RIGHT turn to 7500'
to intercept VOR 112° radial to VOR direct to 6.5 DME fix and
hold NORTHEAST, LEFT turns.

FIGURE 41

boanga, Rangoon, Singapore, or anywhere else in the world
you may care to venture—without ever leaving home.

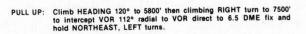

———————————— MISSED APPROACHES

At a recent FAA-sponsored safety seminar, 42 instrument-rated
pilots (all of whom were current) were asked to cite the missed-
approach procedure for the most commonly used instrument
approach at their home airports. Twenty-nine of them could

recall neither the missed-approach altitude nor the initial course or heading required by the procedure. This indicates that most of these 29 pilots apparently do not review the missed-approach procedure prior to every approach. In other words, they are not prepared for the possibility of a miss.

Should one of these pilots find himself engulfed in cloud upon reaching the missed-approach point (MAP), he would be forced to focus his attention on the fine print on his approach plate at a time when he should be riveting his concentration on the flight instruments. Since missed-approach instructions can be more complex than those for the approach itself, it is easy to see how such a pilot can become dangerously distracted while in a high-drag configuration at a dangerously low altitude.

Pilots often do not adequately prepare for a miss because they seldom are required to perform one (except during training flights). As a result, they tend to develop a landing expectancy, or set, which is an anticipatory belief (or desire) that an approach will result in a normal landing. Such an expectancy causes a perception of the situation that does not necessarily coincide with reality. This belief apparently becomes reinforced with each successive successful approach. Such a pilot becomes rooted in complacency and needs more than ever to consider the possibility of a missed approach. He and all other instrument pilots should be as prepared for a missed approach as they are for the approach itself.

There are several reasons why a pilot might have to miss. These include: (1) poor lateral alignment of the aircraft with the runway of intended landing; (2) aircraft or ground system failures or abnormalities; (3) the need for excessive or unusual maneuvering; (4) the probability of an undershoot or overshoot; (5) instructions by ATC to make a missed approach; (6) concern or discomfort about the way an approach is proceeding; and (7) any indication that a safe landing does not appear likely.

Notice that these reasons for a miss are in addition to those cited by regulation. FAR Part 91 states essentially that a pilot may not operate below decision height (DH) or a minimum descent altitude (MDA) unless: (1) the aircraft is continuously in a position from which a descent to landing can be made at a normal rate of descent using normal maneuvers; (2) the flight visibility is at least that prescribed for the approach; (3) the aircraft has reached the visual descent point (when applicable); and (4) one of the required visual references for the runway of intended landing is distinctly visible and identifiable.

These conditions must exist not only to descend below a DH or MDA but must exist continuously until touchdown. Otherwise a missed approach is mandatory. Regulations also dictate a miss when these conditions do not exist upon reaching the missed approach point or whenever an identifiable part of the airport is not distinctly visible during a circling maneuver (when at or above the MDA) unless this is a result of normal banking during the circling approach.

A pilot should prepare for a missed approach prior to every instrument letdown, even when the approach is conducted in a radar environment and even if weather reports indicate ceilings and visibilities above minimums. Although radar controllers frequently provide radar vectors following a miss, such relief should not be anticipated. Instead, study the missed-approach procedure and memorize at least the initial actions required. These normally consist of the missed-approach altitude and the initial heading or course. This should suffice until achieving a safe climb rate, aircraft configuration, and altitude. At this point a pilot can refer to the missed-approach procedure for further guidance.

Since almost every missed-approach procedure terminates in a depicted holding pattern, prepare for this as well. Determine in advance the method of holding pattern entry to be used and perhaps sketch the entry on the approach plate.

There seems to be some confusion among pilots as to the minimum weather conditions required to execute an instrument approach. Legally, the pilot of a noncommercial flight may begin and execute an instrument approach regardless of the reported weather. Such a look-see approach may be made even when the reported weather is zero-zero, or W0X0F (indefinite ceiling zero, visibility zero, fog). The likelihood of a missed approach at such a time is of course quite likely but the approach itself is legal even though descent below the DH or MDA may not be.

It is interesting that an approach clearance automatically and tacitly includes a clearance for a missed approach, which explains why (thankfully) the miss can be executed without a blessing from ATC. A clearance for a practice instrument approach in VFR conditions, however, does not include clearance for a missed approach. Anyone wanting to practice a miss must first obtain permission (when operating in an airport traffic area).

During the approach, maintain the mental discipline needed to execute a timely missed approach. The pilot should be as spring-loaded for this procedure as a multiengine pilot is for an aborted takeoff. Occasionally think to yourself: "I will execute a missed approach unless I see the required visual cues and am in a position to continue the approach to landing safely." In other words, program yourself for a miss.

Resist allowing ATC to talk you into doing anything that will destabilize the approach or make you feel uncomfortable, particularly after passing the final-approach fix. Also, do not be affected by overhearing that aircraft ahead of you have landed safely. Weather can be fickle and close an airport just before you get there. Consider, too, that when executing certain ILS approaches, some pilots might be authorized for lower minimums because they are Category II- or Category III-qualified and equipped. A decision to descend below DH or MDA must be made strictly on the basis of personally observed conditions.

During any approach when there exists the possibility of a missed approach, consider using only partial flaps until landing is assured. Recommended procedure in many airplanes is to deploy the first notch, or approach flaps. The transition from a descent to a climb will be much easier and the climb performance much better in most aircraft, and pilot workload during a critical segment of flight is significantly reduced. Consider also that the use of full flaps complicates level-off at MDA because so much power is required to arrest sink rate and maintain altitude.

Does an approach with only partial flap deflection significantly affect stall and approach speeds? Not really. On most airplanes, the initial flap setting produces more lift than drag and accounts for most of the stall-speed reduction. Extending the flaps farther produces more drag than lift and has relatively little effect on stall speed. In the case of a Cessna T210N, for example, the last 10 degrees of flap extension reduce stall speed by only four knots but add substantial drag.

The instrument approach often is regarded as the most critical phase of flight and has been loosely compared to the threading of a needle. The pilot flies through a decreasingly narrow channel until reaching a small "window" through which adequate visual cues and guidance must be available to justify continuation (legally and otherwise). When these cues are not found, the missed approach is mandatory.

With respect to nonprecision approaches, a pilot is permitted to fly along the final-approach course until reaching the MAP before being committed to a miss. Often, however, this only delays the inevitable. Once the aircraft passes a point (such as a visual descent point, or VDP) beyond which a straight-in approach to the runway cannot be made without either diving or risking an overshoot, there is no point in continuing. Bite the bullet and execute a miss.

A subject of some controversy involves the initiation of a missed approach at decision height. Because of aircraft inertia and the time required to make the transition from descent to climb, it is inevitable that an aircraft will dip temporarily below DH during such a transition. But it is legal for an aircraft to momentarily sink below DH as the missed approach is begun, or must a pilot anticipate the dip and initiate the miss prior to actually reaching DH?

According to FAA's Office of Flight Standards, a pilot may dip below DH as long as the missed-approach procedure is initiated at or above DH. Furthermore, FAA-designated flight examiners allow dipping during instrument flight tests. A final note: Airline pilots operating heavy aircraft are trained (with FAA approval) to initiate the miss at DH and accept any unavoidable sinking below DH. Such a procedure is considered safe because if the aircraft is on the glideslope at decision height, it will not sink beneath the glideslope during a properly executed missed approach.

The missed approach maneuver can be relatively simple. But according to NTSB, a delay in execution is as prominent a cause of accidents as is failure to perform the maneuver and is far more likely to result in serious injuries and fatalities. This means that the maneuver should be aggressively initiated as soon as conditions mandate the need or when a decision is made to execute an early miss prior to reaching the DH or MAP, whichever is applicable.

The maneuver requires three simultaneous steps. The first involves focusing attention on the flight instruments; once the decision to miss has been made, do not allow any peripherally sighted visual cues outside the aircraft to either alter the decision or affect the concentration needed to perform the maneuver. The second and third steps mandate raising the nose to the appropriate climb altitude and advancing the throttle(s) to obtain maximum-allowable power.

The last two items require aggressiveness. Since the aircraft is low on altitude and high on drag at such a time, timid attitude and power changes can result in unacceptable altitude and airspeed losses at a time when performance decay is least desirable. This does not mean that a pilot should yank back on the yoke so as to induce a stall. Nor does it mean that the throttle(s) should be rammed to the firewall (especially when operating turbocharged engines). Aggressiveness in this case means that these actions should be made in a positive manner and without delay.

Flap retraction should be handled in accordance with the pilot's operating handbook. The first step usually involves retracting them only to an intermediate position after establishing climb attitude. This eliminates most of the flap-created drag but has little effect on lift.

Do not be in a rush to raise the landing gear. Unless beginning the missed approach when relatively high above the ground, delay gear retraction until the aircraft has achieved a positive climb rate and conditions are such that the added drag created during gear retraction (on some aircraft) can be tolerated.

Finally, complete flap retraction when airspeed and altitude are such that the likely pitch change can be handled safely and the associated loss of lift poses no danger. (The greatest pitch-trim change usually is associated with the last increment of flap retraction.)

Although the missed-approach maneuver is not difficult, its proper execution under demanding conditions seems to require a series of almost reflexive actions. Proficiency in the maneuver can be developed and maintained by occasionally practicing at altitude during simulated IFR conditions.

Once the initial transition to a missed-approach maneuver is accomplished, the pilot should make whatever initial turn is required by the published procedure. One word of caution, however. If the miss is initiated prior to reaching either the DH or MAP, remain on the final approach course until reaching the MAP. An early turn could result in the aircraft heading for an obstacle. This is because obstruction clearances are provided only when such turns are made in compliance with the missed-approach procedure, which does not begin until passing the MAP.

Similarly, if conditions dictate initiating a miss when below either the DH or MDA (because a pilot loses sight of the required visual cues, for example), do not execute any required turns until the aircraft is climbing and is once again at or above DH or MDA.

One confusing aspect of missed approaches involves the procedure during the circling portion of a circling approach (after the aircraft has left the final-approach portion of the instrument-approach procedure). Should a miss become necessary at such a time, turn the aircraft toward the runway of intended landing (even though it no longer can be seen) until the aircraft is on a heading that will intercept either the final-approach course (which leads to the MAP) or the missed-approach course, whichever appears most suitable under the circumstances.

Since such a missed approach is not straightforward, a pilot might practice such procedures at home. Sketch some circling maneuvers on different approach plates and ask yourself how you would make the transition to a given missed-approach procedure from different points along the various circling tracks. It is an easy way to gain familiarity with these transitions and will simplify matters when the need arises in actual instrument conditions.

Is there any rush to communicate with ATC during a missed approach? Not really. This is because the airspace within which the missed approach procedure takes place is reserved for such an eventuality. Although a declaration to ATC should be made as soon as practicable, never let this distract you from the maneuver and the procedure. It is important that a pilot remember his priorities: The first is to aviate (control the aircraft); the next is to navigate (comply with the published procedure); and finally he should communicate. Once ATC is informed of the miss, a pilot should be prepared to cope with a barrage of instructions and questions that could include a complex clearance. Do not become involved in communicating until the aviating and navigating are comfortably under control.

After executing a missed approach, a pilot has three options: Hold until conditions improve, shoot another approach, or proceed to an alternate. The last option poses the greatest challenge because the pilot may not have an alternate in mind and may be pressured by a low-fuel condition. If this is the case, he will have to obtain the latest available weather reports, select an alternate, agree with ATC about how to get there, unfold the necessary en route chart, and pull out the appropriate approach plates. This can be quite a burden to someone who might be simultaneously entering the holding pattern that signifies the end of the missed-approach procedure. Do not hesitate to ask for assistance, such as vectors, or to declare an emergency if need be.

Whenever the possibility exists for a missed approach, pilots should pre-select an alternate, become familiar with at least the initial routing, and have all necessary charts at hand prior to initiating the approach at the original destination.

When filing an instrument flight plan, remember that an approved, suitable alternate airport must be designated when the destination is forecast to have a ceiling of less than 2,000 feet or a visibility of less than three miles within plus-or-minus one hour of the ETA (estimated time of arrival) at the destination airport (the "1-2-3" rule). Also, the weather at the alternate must be forecast (for the ETA at the alternate) to be at or above the alternate minimums as shown on the approach plate for the alternate airport.

This, however, is only a planning requirement. After executing a missed approach at the destination, the alternate airport becomes the new destination. The pilot may then proceed there regardless of actual or forecast weather. He may not land, however, unless the normal minimums are found to exist for the approach being made.

It is unfortunate that the missed approach carries with it the implication of failure, the unsuccessful result of a valiant effort. But this connotation is invalid. Placed in proper perspective, the missed approach is a powerful survival procedure that can be used to assure success whenever the outcome of any instrument approach is in doubt.

COMMUNICATIONS FAILURE

One requirement for the instrument rating is knowing how to conduct an IFR flight in the event of a two-way communications failure. Unfortunately, many pilots gradually forget the required procedures and are left with only a vague recollection of the principles involved. While writing this book, I gave a simple quiz about communications failure to 22 instrument pilots. All but three failed.

One reason for this is the reliability of modern avionics. Failures do not occur as frequently as when transceivers had vacuum tubes and whistle-stop tuning. In those days, pilots informed air traffic control of communications failure by tossing a fistful of aluminum chaff out of the window. The idea was to create a distinctive radar return that would signal the pilot's dilemma to controllers. Chaff gave way to flying the triangular pattern, another method of advising ATC that two-way communications were no longer possible. But even this procedure has been eliminated. The FAA now recommends that a pilot signal a communications failure by squawking the emergency transponder code of 7700 for one minute and then 7600 for 15 minutes. (This 16-minute sequence should be repeated throughout the flight or until the problem is resolved.)

The pilot then is expected to complete his IFR flight by tiptoeing through a mine field of regulations entitled "IFR Operations: Two-Way Radio Communications Failure." He had better be careful, too, because ATC will assume he is abiding strictly by regulation and handle other aircraft accordingly. This means that if a no-radio pilot is supposed to be at a specific altitude, he can expect opposite-direction traffic to pass 1,000 feet above and below. Contrary to popular belief, other altitudes (and alternate routes) are not kept clear for his exclusive use. A pilot not precisely aware of what is expected of him can pose a serious threat in an IFR environment.

The regulations dealing with communications failure do not consider all possibilities. They only provide guidelines that apply to most situations; at other times, a pilot must use sound judgment and common sense.

Before delving into required and recommended procedures, let us consider the most likely causes of communications failure. In the case of a pilot operating with only one transceiver, any of several component malfunctions can cause a communications breakdown. This is why extended IFR operations with only one radio should not be conducted even though they are legal. Those who insist on stretching their luck should at least consider carrying a hand-held transceiver. Many pilots carry them in even the most highly equipped cockpits.

The most likely cause for total loss of communications when flying an aircraft equipped with dual transceivers is the failure of either the speaker or the audio amplifier. Although the pilot still can transmit in the blind, he cannot receive. He is essentially incommunicado. All that is needed to prevent such a problem is to have a headset available for use when things get quiet.

A malfunctioning microphone, transmitter selector switch, or jack can prevent a pilot from transmitting no matter how many radios he might have. Although nothing can be done about a faulty switch, a spare mike often resolves this problem. An increasing number of aircraft are equipped with dual mike and speaker jacks.

The inability to transmit is usually a short-term problem. If the pilot squawks the appropriate sequence of transponder codes or simply waits long enough (if the aircraft is not transponder-equipped), the controller ultimately will recognize the loss of communications. After a period of time, a resourceful controller probably will ask the pilot to "ident" or "squawk stand-by." If the pilot responds, communications have been reestablished and the flight can continue more or less routinely. (By requesting different transponder responses, a controller can obtain from a pilot the answers to a variety of questions.)

The most catastrophic communications breakdown is the result of total electrical failure, including a drained battery. In instrument meteorological conditions (IMC) at night, a successful landing is left to the fates, since the pilot truly is flying blind. This is a principal reason why an increasing number of pilots carry portable transceivers.

In the event of an electrical system malfunction, the pilot immediately should turn off all but the most essential equipment to limit current drain on the battery and should notify

ATC of the situation. He also should limit transmissions to the barest essentials to prolong battery power.

In the event of an electrical system emergency such as indications of a Nicad battery overheat or an electrical fire, the pilot should notify ATC immediately that he will be off the air for up to 15 minutes and shut down the principal sources of electrical power (the master switch). In the ensuing radio silence, he should perform the appropriate emergency check list. Once the emergency is under control, the pilot should reestablish communications with ATC and negotiate an approach to the nearest suitable airport unless the fault has been corrected completely.

One of the reasons why prompt notification of ATC is important is that the transponder return will be lost in the event of total electrical failure or system shut-down; the controller may assume the aircraft has crashed if the blip or data block disappears from the screen and he has received no communication from the pilot.

Can an en route controller monitor the progress of an aircraft by observing its primary radar return? He often cannot. When a transponder fails, the aircraft may simply disappear from radar. Terminal radar facilities, however, can detect and track an aircraft with or without an operating transponder.

While there is debate as to whether the accumulation of ice on antennas can interfere with communications and navigation reception (radio manufacturers claim ice has too low a mineral content to affect reception or transmission, despite reports by pilots of difficulties), the build-up of static electricity in precipitation can cause the temporary loss of both navigation and communications reception.

Although unlikely, it is possible to lose both transceivers because of the independent failure of each. If this occurs and the nav receivers are operating normally, a pilot should be aware that ATC may transmit using the voice feature of navaids in the area.

Loss of communications is not always the result of equipment failure. There are times when a frequency is so jammed with traffic that a pilot cannot get a word in edgewise. Or perhaps the frequency is unusable because someone has a stuck microphone button. Or you may be handed off to another sector while out of range; or you may have been given an improper frequency. Try the previous frequency again first. These normally are only irritations, but not always. Consider a pilot being vectored toward high terrain or approaching a minimum en route altitude (MEA) that requires an immediate climb. If he is unable to obtain a revised clearance expeditiously, he should take matters into his own hands. This means that he should squawk 7700—which is bound to attract attention—and take *whatever* action is necessary.

If a pilot experiences communications failure and either is in or subsequently enters VFR conditions, the regulations require that he remain VFR and land as soon as practicable. One must be careful not to interpret this requirement too literally. When flying on an IFR flight plan, a pilot frequently is above an undercast in VFR conditions. Although it is possible for him to remain VFR indefinitely, the pilot might not be able to locate a VFR airport visually. At such a time, he might be better off continuing with his clearance, even if this means reentering IFR conditions and having to shoot an IFR approach. ATC will anticipate the pilot's actions and keep his route and altitude free of other traffic. This is preferable to a pilot executing an approach where he may not be expected.

If a VFR airport is found and the pilot opts to land there, he should find some way to inform the controller that he is abandoning his IFR flight plan. One way is to squawk the VFR transponder code (1200). Another is to turn perpendicular to the route of flight. An off-course turn is strongly recommended, especially when descending through the positive control area (PCA) that exists at flight level 180 and above. A pilot descending in the PCA while on an airway risks descending into other IFR traffic (even though they also are in VFR conditions).

Once on the ground, immediately telephone the nearest FAA

facility and explain what has happened. The disappearance of the transponder return from his radar may have caused the controller to assume a crash.

If, after communications failure, a pilot needs to continue in IFR conditions, he will be concerned with navigation, flying at the appropriate altitudes, and determining the most logical way to execute an approach.

Routing usually is the simplest problem to resolve. The pilot need only conform to his last clearance. If ATC advised him to expect a further clearance via a different route at some point, he should follow the course spelled out in the clearance he was told to expect.

If for some reason the last clearance does not provide a routing to destination, the pilot should comply with it for as long as possible and then use the route originally filed for the remainder of the journey. If the two routes do not coincide, the pilot must use his best judgment in making the transition from one route to the other.

If radio failure occurs while being vectored, the pilot should turn directly toward the fix or route to which he is being vectored. The only problem with this is that controllers do not anticipate the possibility of radio failure as they did in the past. They frequently issue vector clearances—especially in high-density airspace—without mentioning the point or route to which the aircraft is being vectored. If a communications failure should occur after receiving such a clearance, a pilot would have no idea where to go. Consequently, a pilot should not accept such a clearance without knowing the fix or route to which he is being vectored.

Assume that a pilot is flying the route specified in his last clearance. He then receives a new routing but experiences communications failure before he can reply. In this case, he can fly either route. Both will be kept clear of traffic until ATC determines which one the pilot has opted to fly.

Managing altitude can be tricky. The key is to remember that each route segment must be considered individually. *In each case,* fly either the last assigned altitude or the MEA, whichever is *higher.* The only exception occurs when a pilot has been told to expect a further clearance to maintain a different altitude upon reaching a specific fix (or at a certain time). Upon reaching that point, climb or descend to that altitude and maintain it or the MEA, whichever is higher, on each subsequent route segment.

This raises an interesting point. Figure 42 shows an aircraft approaching Gonif Intersection at 5,000 feet. The MEA for the next route segment is 8,000 feet. Should the pilot climb so as to cross Gonif at 8,000 and be at the MEA for the entire length of this route segment or should he wait until crossing the fix to begin the climb? Of those pilots surveyed, most indicated that the climb should begin prior to reaching Gonif Intersection. They were wrong. Do not climb until reaching the fix.

This leads to another question: If the pilot is flying a slow-climbing aircraft, how does he know that he can climb rapidly

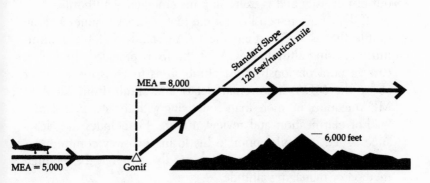

Standard Slope	Groundspeed in Climb					
	60 kt	90 kt	120 kt	150 kt	180 kt	210 kt
Sea level to 5,000 ft = 150 ft/nm =	150 fpm	225 fpm	300 fpm	375 fpm	450 fpm	525 fpm
5,000 ft to 10,000 ft = 120 ft/nm =	120 fpm	180 fpm	240 fpm	300 fpm	360 fpm	420 fpm
10,000 ft and above = 100 ft/nm =	100 fpm	150 fpm	200 fpm	250 fpm	300 fpm	350 fpm

FIGURE 42

enough to avoid the obstacle responsible for the higher MEA?

There are two ways for a pilot to ensure that he will not be in jeopardy. The first is to simply have faith in the system. The second is more assuring and involves the FAA's standard slope as shown in Figure 42. According to the table in the figure, an airplane will clear all obstacles safely as long as it can climb according to the gradients shown. For instance, when between 5,000 and 10,000 feet, the airplane needs to climb at only 120 feet per nautical mile. With a climb groundspeed of 120 knots, for instance, the required climb performance is only 240 fpm.

Most aircraft are capable of such a climb gradient. Exceptions might include twins with an engine shut down, heavily loaded aircraft with low service ceilings, or any aircraft laden with ice. If he is flying an aircraft that cannot meet these modest climb requirements, it is in the pilot's best interest to begin climbing prior to reaching the fix. He also should squawk 7700 to alert the controller that he is deviating from the regulations out of necessity and is exercising his emergency authority.

If the terrain responsible for the higher MEA requires a climb profile that is steeper than the FAA's standard slope, a minimum-crossing altitude (MCA) at the fix is provided. In such a case, a pilot obviously must climb so as to cross the fix at or above the MCA. The remainder of the climb (from MCA to MEA) requires no more than complying with the standard slope.

For clarification and review, Figure 43 includes the clearance issued to a pilot prior to his losing two-way communications. Also shown is the route he is to fly as well as the required method of managing altitude.

Arriving near his destination, a pilot who has experienced two-way communications failure is supposed to proceed to any appropriate IAF (initial approach fix) or the fix defining the beginning of the instrument approach procedure (the beginning of the bold course line shown on the plan view of the approach plate). As before, he must maintain the last assigned altitude or the MEA, whichever is higher.

According to regulation, he may not leave this fix to begin

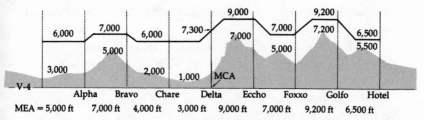

FIGURE 43 To illustrate altitude management, let us assume a pilot lost communication with ATC after being cleared to fly Victor 4 to Hotel Intersection. Last assigned altitude was 6,000 feet at Alpha intersection, the pilot would climb to 7,000 feet, since the MEA is higher than his last assigned altitude. The MEAs for the next two segments are lower than the last assigned altitude, so after crossing Bravo, the pilot would descend to 6,000 feet. Approaching Delta, he would start a climb sufficient to bring him to the intersection at at least 7,300 feet, the minimum crossing altitude for the segment. He would continue climbing to the new MEA, 9,000 feet. At Eccho, the pilot would descend to 7,000 feet, since the MEA is higher than his last assigned altitude. The next two segments would require 9,200 and 6,500 feet, respectively.

the approach or descend until the estimated time of arrival (ETA) for the destination (as filed or as last amended with ATC). If the pilot reaches the approach fix at or after the ETA, he simply descends to the approach altitude while holding or in a procedure turn—whichever is appropriate—and executes the approach. If the airport has more than one instrument approach procedure, the pilot should select the most appropriate. All approaches are cleared for use by a no-radio pilot for at least 30 minutes.

But what if the pilot is ahead of schedule upon arriving at the appropriate approach fix? Simple. He must hold at the fix until the ETA. But what if there is no holding pattern published for the fix? He then must hold on the same side of the approach course as the procedure turn. Aha, but what if a procedure turn has not been designated for the approach? At such a time the pilot is left to his own devices. He must use discretion in selecting a holding pattern that offers adequate terrain clearance and poses minimal potential conflict with other IFR traffic that might be in the area.

Things can get sticky in terminal airspace. Consider, for instance, the plight of a pilot flying VFR-on-top. He loses two-way communications just as he is about to call approach control for an approach clearance. If he is not within range of VFR conditions, he has no alternative but to squawk 7700 and shoot any available and appropriate IFR approach. He can only hope a radar controller will recognize his problem and clear the path ahead.

This discussion has one thing in common with the regulations governing two-way communications failure: Neither can be so presumptuous as to anticipate all the variables a pilot might encounter. Each provides only guidelines and food for thought. In the final analysis, a pilot's ability to cope with communications failure depends not only on his knowledge of the regulations, but also on his ability to improvise a plan of action and carry it out with a minimum of risk.

―――――――――――――― COMMUNICATING FOR SURVIVAL

Communication is the fundamental tool used by man to build an advancing society. Without it, there would not be antibiotics, footsteps on the moon, or supersonic flight.

It seems incongruous, therefore, that one of aviation's most pressing problems is the often unacceptable quality of this vital necessity. I am not referring to receiver quality or static-free reception. Rather, I'm referring to the breakdown in communications caused by confusing terminology and misinterpreted procedures. Occasionally these cause the link between controller and pilot to stretch to intolerable limits. Once in a while, it snaps.

One example of this type of accident occurred some years ago when an airline flight was "cleared for an approach" to Runway 12 at Dulles International Airport near Washington, D.C. The captain interpreted this to mean that it was safe to descend to the lowest altitude published prior to the final approach fix; the controller thought otherwise and a communications gap occurred. The resultant tragedy clearly demonstrated (according to NTSB) that a major cause of the accident was a lack of understanding between pilot and controller.

Although it might be easy to condemn the captain for having descended prematurely, it is worth noting that the approach clearance had been misunderstood by the aviation community for years.

Prior to this accident, the U.S. Air Force had requested clarification of "cleared for the approach" as it pertains to terrain avoidance responsibility. At least one major airline echoed the need for definition. A satisfactory answer was not provided.

The FAA did respond, however, to the loss of 92 lives. A few months after the Dulles accident, FAR Part 91 was revised to state, in essence, that when a pilot is cleared for an approach, he shall maintain the last assigned altitude until established on a published route at which time he may descend to the applicable MEA.

Admittedly, no one has the foresight to devise procedures that anticipate all potential problems. Even if this were possible, the resultant body of law would be impractically voluminous. But when pilots wave a red flag and admit confusion regarding a specific procedure, someone in the bureaucratic hierarchy should have the common sense to pay attention. Similar misunderstandings between pilots still occur with alarming regularity.

One reason for the confusion is that controllers have a lexicon and a procedures manual that is not readily available to most pilots. Occasionally this creates an impossible situation and is like playing football with one rule book while the opposing team uses another. Pilots, however, have more than touchdowns at stake.

Even the NTSB contributes to confusion by misinterpreting certain terms. Two members of the board, for example, stated officially that the Dulles accident would not have occurred, "if the pilot had maintained the minimum sector altitude (MSA) as depicted on the approach plate." This is true but erroneously implies that when a pilot is on a radar vector and is cleared for an approach, he should not descend below the MSA. This is completely absurd.

Consider, for example, a pilot being radar vectored on a heading of 220 degrees for an ILS approach to Runway 25 at Ontario, California. Prior to localizer intercept and while maintaining an assigned altitude of 3,000 feet, he is cleared for the approach. The pilot determines from his approach plate, however, that the MSA (for the quadrant in which he is flying) is 11,900 feet because of mountains north of his position. According to NTSB's implication, a pilot should not be below the MSA. Is he expected, therefore, to climb to 11,900 feet? Obviously not.

The MSA is an emergency altitude to be considered only when a pilot is unable to determine an applicable safe altitude due to navigation or communications difficulties.

There are a host of other terms subject to misinterpretation. Take, for example, something as simple as a VFR, straight-out departure. Recently, a pilot requested and was cleared for a "straight-out." After tracking the extended runway centerline until well outside the traffic pattern (three miles), the pilot turned right to proceed en route. Shortly after turning, however, he had a near collision in midair with a helicopter.

A violation was filed against the pilot because he failed to make a straight-out departure from the airport traffic area, which had a five-mile radius. The pilot ultimately got off the hook because the FAA did not (and still does not) have an official definition for a straight-out departure.

There are numerous other terms taken for granted that are not officially defined.

Parenthetically, the Dulles accident discussed earlier probably would not have occurred were it not for something else that most pilots take for granted—the radar vector. Had the captain been allowed to navigate by following published routes, he never would have been in doubt as to the minimum en route altitude for any portion of his flight; MEAs are printed for each route segment and are not subject to misinterpretation.

Radar vectors usually are accepted graciously by most pilots because these presumably simplify navigation and allow additional time to prepare for an impending IFR approach. But some pilots are beginning to regard radar vectors with mixed emotions. By accepting a vector, navigation and terrain clearance responsibility shifts—at least partially—from the cockpit to the controller. For a variety of reasons, this can result in disaster. This is because aircraft occasionally are vectored into mountains.

Once an aircraft is removed from a published route by a controller, it can be difficult for a pilot to determine applicable minimum safe altitudes, especially when over unfamiliar, mountainous terrain. For this reason, some pilots attempt to refuse radar vectors. Depending on traffic volume, such a request is frequently honored. At other times, the confines of a holding pattern may be the undesirable alternative, but at least this affords a pilot the peace of mind of knowing precisely where he is at all times.

It can be discomforting to be vectored toward rising real estate. So rather than worry about being forgotten by the controller (it happens), do not hesitate to ask how long you can expect to be on the vector. In this way, a pilot has a form of "clearance limit" at which point he can ask for a new heading or, in case of a frequency jam and an urgent need, he can turn toward lower terrain (with or without permission).

Relinquishing navigational responsibility to a controller is one thing, but allowing him to crawl into the cockpit and fly the airplane is quite another. At airports surrounded by noise-sensitive neighbors, for example, it is not unusual to hear a tower controller advising a pilot to use the "maximum rate-of-climb for noise abatement purposes." Such an instruction is irritating because a traffic controller does not have the right to dictate flight technique, especially when using the wrong terminology, as in this case.

The controller would like the aircraft to be as high as possible above neighboring homes during the climb. But as every pilot knows, it is the best angle-of-climb that produces this result, not the best rate-of-climb. Instructing a pilot, especially a student, to climb at the maximum angle can result in tragedy. The salient point is that the pilot-in-command knows best how to fly his aircraft at any given time; he should not relinquish command authority to someone on the ground who is unfamiliar with both the experience level of the pilot and the operation of the aircraft.

Pilots also get into hot water and jeopardize their certificates by requesting a controller to waive a regulation. Recently, for example, a pilot advised the tower of his intent to perform aerobatics in the control zone. The controller simply acknowledged the pilot who interpreted this as tacit approval for what he was about to do. Chalk up one violation against the pilot. A *controller does not have the authority to waive any published regulation.*

There are numerous traps in the ATC system, and even the pros get caught making assumptions that can result in accident statistics. As procedures become more complex and communications become a battle of semantics, it behooves a pilot to question anything about which he is in doubt. For many, this is a difficult pill to swallow. It is a form of ignorance they are reluctant to admit. But unless a pilot thoroughly understands what is expected of him at all times, picking up the mike and requesting clarification can be one of the most important survival techniques he will ever use.

Pilots and controllers both are guilty of adding to confusion by using improper terminology. Pilots of jet aircraft, for example, frequently request descents at "pilot's discretion." The purpose of this is to remain high as long as is practical in an effort to save fuel.

As a result, you'll often overhear something like this: "Flight 760, descend to six thousand, pilot's discretion."

The pilot gets cute and responds, "Roger, six thou, Papa Delta."

"Papa Delta," of course, has come to unofficially stand for "pilot's discretion." The controller picks up on this jargon and uses it when controlling someone unfamiliar with the phrase. A Comanche, for example, was cleared to "four thousand, Papa Delta."

Before the confused pilot had a chance to respond, another pilot piped up with, "Center, this is November Four Papa Delta, did you call?" Nonstandard terminology is easily misinterpreted and using it is dangerous.

Misunderstood communications were responsible for the world's worst aviation disaster. This occurred at Tenerife in the Canary Islands on March 27, 1977, after a Pan American Airlines' Boeing 747 had been cleared to taxi across an active, fog-shrouded runway where the visibility was only 300 yards. In the meantime, a KLM Boeing 747 was lined up with the active runway awaiting clearance for takeoff. The following is a transcript of the subsequent communications:

KLM to tower: "KLM ready for takeoff."

Tower to KLM: "Maintain holding position."

Tower to Pan Am: "Have you left the runway?"

Pan Am: "No."

Tower: "Do so and tell me when you have done it."

Tower to KLM: "Stand by. I will call you for takeoff."

KLM to tower: "We are taking off."

Less than a minute later, the KLM 747 plunged headlong into the Pan Am 747. Five hundred and eighty-two people were killed.

Pilots, especially those who are inexperienced, often are in awe of the faceless voices that boom from the cockpit speaker. They respond to controller's instructions as if they were commandments chiseled in stone by lightning from atop Mt. Sinai. These pilots are easily intimidated into doing something for which they are not prepared. Consider, for example, the pilot "cleared for an immediate takeoff" who is not quite ready. Because of his desire to comply, he goes anyway, but soon must abort because in his haste he forgot to secure the cabin door. Never allow a controller to talk you into something with which you are not totally comfortable.

Occasionally a pilot must take command of a situation and operate counter to the dictates of air traffic control. I learned this early in my airline career when flying with a crusty, veteran captain back in the 707 days. After being refused clearance to deviate left or right of course while approaching a thunderstorm (presumably because of parallel traffic on both sides of our aircraft), the captain picked up the mike and said nonchalantly, "Sir, we are now turning to avoid a cell. I'm afraid that you'll have to solve the traffic problem on your own."

It must be remembered that controllers are mere mortals and, like pilots, are capable of error and poor judgment. Consider also that the maximum hazard that a controller must face is falling off of his chair. Decisions affecting the safety of an aircraft must be made by the pilot-in-command. This is his moral and legal responsibility.

Sometimes an instruction from ATC must be placed in proper perspective. Take, for example, the case of a pilot about to execute a VOR approach. He is told by approach control to contact the tower "at the VOR." Passing the final approach fix (the VOR, in this case) is usually the busiest phase of a nonprecision approach, and the least important duty is to contact the tower. Communications should be delayed, therefore, until four of the "five Ts" have been satisfied: (1) Time (start stopwatch); (2) Turn (toward the final approach course); (3) Tuck (begin descent); (4) Tune (the proper radial); and, after these duties have been accomplished (5) Talk (to the tower). Numerous approaches have resulted in misses (and worse) simply because pilots were so unnecessarily anxious to report to the tower that they failed to properly exercise prudent IFR technique. Fly first; talk later.

Unintentionally and occasionally, controllers make requests or ask questions during critical phases of an approach or landing. If confronted by such a distraction, ignore the controller until you feel it is safe to take the time to respond.

Pilots readily complain about being mishandled by controllers, but there are equally valid complaints on the other side of this coin.

Controllers have one particular pet peeve that pilots frequently commit, and it is something that can lead to disaster. The scenario goes like this. The controller issues a clearance to a pilot, but pauses slightly before completing the transmission. Quick to respond, the pilot begins to transmit a reply without realizing that the controller has simultaneously begun to broadcast the remainder of the clearance. The controller releases his mike button in time to hear what he assumes to be an acknowledgement of the entire clearance when, in fact, a key element of the clearance was never received by the pilot.

Other incidents are caused by: (1) transmissions containing sound-alike words and aircraft identifications; (2) transposing numbers in transponder codes; (3) incorrectly copying a clearance containing a long string of numbers; (4) wrong aircraft acknowledging a clearance when this goes undetected by a busy controller; (5) a controller who forgets about an aircraft he has told to " standby"; and (6) incorrect clearance readbacks not caught by controllers.

The FAA is constantly attempting to resolve these and other communications difficulties by improving controller training programs. But the pilot's help is needed. The air traffic control system cannot work without mutual respect and cooperation. When in doubt about something, ask for a repeat or a clarification. Be alert for partially blocked transmissions. Don't hesitate to speak up when you overhear someone else make a mistake (such as when the wrong aircraft responds or when a controller fails to recognize that a clearance has been read back incorrectly).

Among other items, do not be overly cooperative by accepting dangerously fast approach speeds. Alert the controller when it appears that a radar vector for an ILS approach will not pro-

vide a satisfactory intercept or when a lower altitude is needed
to establish glideslope intercept prior to reaching the outer marker.

Pilots also can assist ATC by exercising tolerance and re-
straint. It is not unusual for a pilot to misinterpret the harried,
frenetic voice of a controller and take personal afront to what
appears to be a curt, overbearing attitude. Generally, when a
controller sounds rude it is because he is temporarily overloaded
with traffic. Pilots can help by being more considerate of a controller's problems.

Unfortunately, a few controllers do overstep their authority
and are unnecessarily demanding and dictatorial. Although it is
human nature to use the radio as the medium for a rebuttal,
this can only lead to distractions, misdirected traffic, and a generally hazardous environment. Pilots have a far more powerful
weapon to use against errant controllers—the pen. Simply state
your complaint and submit it along with the time of occurrence
to the branch chief of either ATC Evaluations or Operations at
the respective FAA regional headquarters. When your letter (or
phone call) is received, the tape of the conversation (which is
kept for only 15 days) will be consulted, and the misbehaving
controller will be put on the carpet.

Should a controller, however, require something that a pilot
considers unsafe and more immediate action is required, the
pilot can respond simply with "negative" or "unable." *A pilot is
not obligated to abide by a clearance until it has been accepted.*

The purpose of this discussion is not to induce confronta-
tions between pilots and controllers. Rather it is to point out
some major problem areas and emphasize that ATC consists
fundamentally of human beings, all of whom are fallible. The
common goal of safety requires alertness, honesty, and a clear,
understandable channel of communications between everyone
involved.

7

ADVANCED ADVENTURES

 **FLY TO EUROPE . . . YOURSELF**

Most general aviation pilots never consider flying a lightplane to Europe because of the seemingly vast distances involved. New York and London, for example, are separated by 3,000 nautical miles (nm). But crossing the Atlantic doesn't require the endurance to vault such an expanse.

Although long-range ferry tanks and navigation equipment are required to fly the 1,714-nm, nonstop leg from Gander, Newfoundland, to Shannon, Ireland, this equipment is not necessary when crossing the North Atlantic via the "ice route." Using Greenland and Iceland as stepping stones across the "pond," the longest leg of the flight can be reduced to 485 nm, a distance easily flown in many light twins and some singles, especially when long-range cruise procedures are employed. (Some pilots, however, prefer to install a small, supplementary cabin tank as a hedge against the unexpected.)

In addition to adequate fuel, a pilot accepting the challenge of an ocean should also carry appropriate survival equipment and possibly a long-range, high-frequency (HF) transceiver. These items (including the temporary installation of a cabin fuel tank)

can be rented from any of several fixed-base operators special-
izing in transoceanic equipment.

What cannot be purchased or rented, however, are the necessary IFR skills. Anyone not comfortable in the clouds should
not contemplate such a journey.

Much has been written about flying small aircraft across big
oceans and little can be added here to bolster the confidence of
those who feel that such a flight is beyond their limitations. No
one should be encouraged to fly the North Atlantic if he has
serious premonitions about it. But experience has proven that
modern aircraft and engines perform as well over the Atlantic
as over Atlanta.

Curiously, a flight via Greenland and Iceland can be safer
than a nonstop Atlantic crossing. Consider the takeoff weight of
a light twin burdened with sufficient fuel to make a direct shot
from Gander to Shannon. Occasionally this configuration so
overloads an aircraft that during the first few hours of flight, the
single-engine ceiling may be below sea level. This is a fact of
flight that ferry pilots have learned to accept.

Navigation via Greenland and Iceland requires no unusual
skill or knowledge. Anyone adept with ADF and dead reckoning
procedures should have no difficulty. To the delight of many
pilots, much of the route is defined by powerful radiobeacons
and VORTAC stations. Those flying aircraft equipped with loran,
of course, will have no more difficulty navigating across the
Atlantic than across the United States. Also, much of the northern route passes over snow-covered terrain or ice packs, both of
which can be more survivable than an oceanic ditching. And
considering the absence of sharks, some feel more comfortable
above the frigid Atlantic than the balmy Caribbean.

A pilot planning to fly across the Atlantic for the first time
will have to do some studying before departure. This is because
he needs to become familiar with regulations applicable to oceanic
operations (such as "VFR not allowed above 3,500 feet msl") as
well as the ICAO (International Civil Aviation Organization)
regulations applicable to those countries to be visited. He also

must learn the VHF and HF (high frequency) communications procedures and phraseology used outside the United States. ("Cleared to line up," for example, means "taxi into position and hold," and "cleared to the holding position" means "taxi to the run-up area and hold short of the runway.") Pilots also must become familiar with flight information regions (FIRs), VOLMET broadcasts (VOLMET is a French acronym that means "flying weather"), transition altitudes and levels, and TAFs (terminal aerodrome forecasts), a method of coding weather data that is used almost everywhere in the world except in the United States. To determine that pilots have done their homework, the Canadian government requires that first-time Atlantic fliers jumping off from Canada pass a written examination.

The major drawback to flying the Atlantic is weather. Anyone planning the trip (especially for the first time) should bring along a reserve of patience. Weather delays are common. Many crossings, however, have been conducted entirely in VFR conditions.

Most of the northern route lies within the semipermanent, low-pressure belt girdling the globe between 50° and 70° north latitude. During much of the year, a pilot can expect to rub shoulders with a polar front during at least a part of his journey. Although the associated weather is relatively calm and stratified compared to midlatitude fronts (there is much less cumulo-type cloudiness), it is known for widespread icing conditions in the low and middle levels. This implies that an aircraft should be equipped with anti-icing or deicing equipment although, with some patience, a flight can be planned around or above icing areas. Fortunately, thunderstorms are rare along this route.

It would be presumptuous to make any generalizations about North Atlantic weather because it is fickle. But one piece of advice can be relied upon: Inexperienced pilots should avoid the winter months. Meteorologists also advise caution during the early spring and late autumn. This is when North Atlantic weather is in a seasonal state of flux and when accurate forecasting is difficult. Summer months offer the best conditions.

Significant weather seems to move across the Atlantic in waves. A departure, for example, might be planned just prior to the forecasted arrival of a front or low-pressure system at Gander. The previous system will have had a chance to move eastward, leaving much of the North Atlantic undisturbed.

Careful planning is *extremely* important, especially with respect to navigation, weather, and aircraft performance. But it also is important (and convenient) to have some help along the way. For instance, when a pilot is about to undertake his first flight to Europe, he could arrange for assistance from any of several flight planning organizations (such as Houston-based Universal Weather and Aviation). Such an organization can plan on a pilot's behalf for ground transportation and aircraft service at each port of call. This includes arranging for fuel, maintenance, customs clearances, flight plan filing, weather portfolios, landing fees and permission, and so forth.

Gander, Newfoundland, is the most popular jumping-off point. This is not because the town is particularly alluring (it is not), but mainly because it lies approximately on the great-circle route from New York to London. Actually, Gander is not that far north. At 49° north latitude, it lies on the same parallel that defines the western U.S.–Canadian border.

Many light aircraft bound for Europe leave the United States from Boston. From there, Gander is 791 nm northeast. The maritime route over Nova Scotia (via Halifax) is quite scenic and provides an opportunity to get a last-minute check on fuel consumption, performance, and the status of all aircraft systems.

A pilot gets his first taste of overwater flying when he crosses a 139-nm chunk of the Atlantic, the Gulf of St. Lawrence, from Nova Scotia to the southwest coast of Newfoundland.

Approaching this landfall, the route passes abeam St. Pierre, a French-owned island where single-engine aircraft used to initiate Atlantic crossings. This was before the Canadian government gave its approval for these aircraft to use Canada as a jumping-off point.

Continuing northeast, the Victor airway leads over 143 nm of Newfoundland's rugged, lake-riddled terrain to Gander International Airport. Facilities here include an efficient and helpful meteorological staff claimed to have the most expertise in North Atlantic forecasting.

Gander's massive, architecturally impressive terminal building was constructed in the late fifties when piston-driven airliners made frequent, scheduled fuel stops en route to or from Europe. But when the carriers traded jugs for jets, Gander was left behind in a wake of burnt kerosene. Today it is used primarily as an alternate airport, receiving infrequent use except for a few Air Canada flights and transient general aviation aircraft bound for distant horizons.

The airport is reminiscent of a small, midwestern town bypassed by a new expressway. Restaurant and curio shop personnel stand by optimistically, waiting patiently for patronage.

The first leg across the Atlantic (see Figure 44) begins at Gander. Narssarssuaq, on the southern tip of Greenland, lies

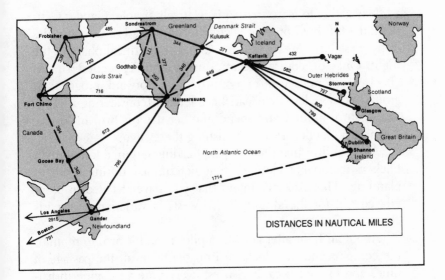

FIGURE 44

795 miles to the north-northeast. If forecasted winds or aircraft range make this long a leg inadvisable, a pilot can fly to Goose Bay, Labrador, 342 miles over land to the north-northwest. The distance from "Goose" to Narssarssuaq is only 673 miles, reducing the length of the first overwater leg by 122 miles.

The biggest potential problem of this leg is considered to be the occasionally moody weather at Narssarssuaq. The instrument approach there has fairly high minimums (1,500 feet and 3.7 miles) with the nearest alternate, Godthab, 250 nm to the north. Trouble is, the runway at Godthab is only 3,100 feet long, which makes it unsuitable for some aircraft. The best alternate for Narssarssuaq is Sondrestrom Air Base, which is 377 nm to the north. It is no wonder that an abundant fuel supply is a pilot's best insurance policy when flying the North Atlantic.

Immediately prior to leaving Canada, it is essential to reconfirm compass accuracy. This is done by lining up on Runway 9 (at either Goose or Gander) to insure that the compass is not being affected adversely by unknown quantities of magnetic deviation.

Navigating to Narssarssuaq is relatively simple. Gander Center and VORTAC provide vectors for the first 150 to 200 miles to help establish the desired track. This is a critical phase of the flight. Once on course and at cruising altitude, request a radar check of groundspeed to confirm your forward progress. If groundspeed is less than can be tolerated (considering fuel on board), turn around and spend another day (or two) in lovely, downtown Gander. (Summer fishing there is good.)

Also confirm that the compass heading required to maintain track is reasonably close to that determined during preflight planning. This also guarantees that you haven't failed to properly correct for the almost 40° of westerly variation that exists along this first leg.

About an hour after takeoff, a pilot is on his own to monitor the compass and the clock, to impatiently await the passage of time, and to have a cardiac arrest every time an engine instrument needle behaves erratically. He is all alone reflecting upon the smallness of his craft and the immensity of the sea.

But he doesn't have to be alone. A call in-the-blind on 121.5 is bound to result in a communications link with any of numerous jetliners crisscrossing the North Atlantic. These pilots are required to guard the emergency frequency and usually are more than willing to relay position reports. Many will have overflown southern Greenland and offer first-hand observations of the weather there.

These pireps (pilot reports) usually can be obtained prior to reaching the halfway point to Greenland and provide another opportunity to reverse course, if necessary.

Eloquent passages have been written about finding the Tunugdliarfik Fjord, the only fjord that leads from the Greenland coast to Narssarssuaq. But this really is not particularly difficult because the Danish government has installed a radiobeacon on Simiutak Island near the mouth of the fjord.

On a clear day, the precipitous walls can be overflown by homing in on the NA NDB (on the airport), 45 nm inland from Simiutak. But those who have flown the fjord route recommend that this entrance to Greenland be used whenever the weather is good (4,000 feet and five miles for newcomers). Flying between 3,000- to 5,000-foot-high cliffs rising from the frigid, blue-black waters is a majestic, awesome sight not to be missed.

To find the right fjord, depart Simiutak on a magnetic track of 091 degrees using pilotage and ADF skills to a maximum. Every rock on the surface must be related to its counterpart on the chart. The entrance to the proper fjord is 22 miles from the SI NDB and is identified positively by another beacon (NS). About 12 miles and numerous icebergs later, the fjord bends left.

At this point, it would be wise to reduce airspeed and extend partial flaps even though the airport is not yet in sight. When the last corner is rounded, the runway will appear only a few miles ahead. An unprepared pilot with an excess of airspeed and altitude could easily overshoot the airport and have to maneuver within the limited confines of a granite-and-ice cul-de-sac.

Narssarssuaq—or Bluie West I—is a classic one-way airport. The single, 6,000-foot-long runway dead-ends at the base of the Greenland Ice Cap. To make matters worse, the runway slopes from an elevation of 11 feet at the west end to 112 feet at the east. Consequently, landings are made on Runway 8 and departures from Runway 26, no matter which way the cold wind blows.

If, prior to departing Gander or Goose, it appears that Narssarssuaq weather will be inadequate, a pilot can use the alternate route via Frobisher Bay on the eastern edge of Canada's Northwest Territories. Although well off the beaten path, Frobisher has a long runway served by an ILS and plenty of fuel.

From Frobisher, a pilot can head for 485-mile-distant Sondrestrom Air Base at Sondre Stromfjord, which is across the Davis Strait on the east coast of Greenland. Most of this leg can be conducted by VOR navigation.

Sondrestrom (which offers precision and surveillance radar approaches) has been known to be unfriendly, but only to those who arrive unexpectedly. Prior permission to land there is required, but is not difficult to obtain. Scandinavian Airlines personnel are available to tend to your overnight needs. (Those arriving at Sondrestrom without prior permission can expect to pay a stiff fine.)

The next leg of the flight stretches across southern Greenland and another chunk of the Atlantic to Reykjavik Iceland, 649 miles ENE of Bluie West I. Since Narssarssuaq has no runway lights and its flare pots are not lit unless someone is expected, the departure should be planned at a time that would allow an unanticipated return to be made before sunset. But since southern Greenland is only 300 miles south of the Arctic Circle, summer days are very long (almost 20 hours in June) and winter days very short (less than 4 hours in December).

After a downhill (and usually downwind) departure from Narssarssuaq, it is necessary to climb in lazy circles to 11,000 feet before crossing the 100-mile-wide ice cap. The terrain across the cap reaches up to 9,000 feet but, because of snow and ice, very little of it can be seen.

After crossing Greenland's east coast and marveling at the glacial tongues of ice lapping at the sea, it's time for almost 450 miles of dead reckoning to the transmission fringes of the Keflavik VORTAC on the southwestern tip of Iceland.

"Kef" is a major international airport with all facilities, but anyone planning on spending time in Iceland (you should) would be better off landing at Reykjavik, which is the capital city. (Those who want or need to break up a trans-Atlantic crossing into the smallest possible bites can land at Kulusuk on Greenland's east coast when flying from Narssarssuaq or Sondrestrom to Iceland.)

The final leg across the Atlantic depends on the pilot's ultimate destination and usable fuel. The shortest leg is to Vagar in the Faroe Islands, 432 miles east-southeast of Keflavik, which can be flown almost entirely by radio navigation. More convenient, however, is Stornoway, Scotland, 582 miles southeast of Keflavik, which requires about 250 nm of dead reckoning. It is always wise to avoid dead reckoning over large bodies of water when strong cross-track winds are forecast. Otherwise, however, it is fairly difficult to drift so far off course as to miss a landfall that has a VOR waiting to greet you. To miss the Stornoway VOR after 250 miles of dead reckoning, for example, would require drifting steadily off course at more than a 25-degree angle.

Ultimately, the VOR comes alive and, shortly thereafter, a pilot is gazing at one of the British Isles on the distant horizon. It is a sight to be frozen in memory, a thrill never to be forgotten, an adventure never to be duplicated.

DITCHING

Ditching is a precautionary or forced landing of a landplane in water. The mere mention of this sort of an emergency procedure usually triggers thoughts of small airplanes crossing large oceans or of pilots who intentionally fly beyond gliding distance of land while crossing channels, lakes, or bays.

Certainly these pilots need to be familiar with ditching procedures, but they are not the only ones. Of the 30 to 40 general aviation ditchings that occur in U.S. coastal or inland waters each year, many are performed by pilots who usually do not venture over water. Sometimes it is unavoidable, such as when operating IFR between coastal airports. Arrival and departure routes for these areas frequently require pilots to fly beyond gliding distance of land for uncomfortably long periods of time.

There also are occasions when pilots opt to land in the water because this appears safer than landing on a crowded or rocky beach. Consider, for example, the dilemma faced by Takis Hinofotis, a flight instructor based in Santa Monica, California. While flying along the coast of Malibu one September, the engine of his Piper Turbo Arrow IV failed catastrophically because of a shattered connecting rod. The beach was crowded with sun worshipers, Highway 101 was choked with traffic, and the rugged, coastal palisades were even less inviting. With time and altitude in short supply, Hinofotis opted to ditch in the Pacific.

The procedure was performed well enough, for both the instructor and his student survived without a scratch. After they swam to shore, the aircraft drifted toward the beach and was tugged onto the sand by helpful onlookers.

Consider also the pilot of a Cessna Skylane who was crossing the Rocky Mountains on a VFR flight between Spokane, Washington, and Cut Bank, Montana. Certainly, he had no reason to be concerned with ditching. Yet that is exactly what he did shortly after his engine failed. Instead of trying to find a soft spot in the granite, he landed in a mountain lake and survived unscathed. (Since he had broadcast his predicament and location prior to losing much altitude, the pilot and his family ultimately were rescued by helicopter.)

Although total power failure (usually caused by fuel exhaustion) is the most common reason for pilots having to ditch, there are a host of other reasons why a water landing may be necessary. Oddly, the need to ditch often is not recognized or accepted soon enough and this can be the most hazardous factor in the overall operation. Assuming a splashdown is unavoidable, take advantage of all available time and altitude to prepare for what may be the most dangerous landing you ever will make.

As in any emergency, the pilot first must control the airplane. If the need to ditch is caused by an engine failure, pilots tend to establish a normal glide. But unless attempting to reach land, there usually is no reason to maximize glide range. After all, the water ahead usually is no different than the water below. Instead, fly the aircraft at the minimum-sink speed (about halfway between stall and normal glide speed). Although this reduces glide range, it also reduces sink rate and increases substantially the time required to lose altitude and the time available to prepare for the landing itself. When 1,000 feet above the water, normal glide speed should be resumed because maneuvering may be required.

One exception to this is when a maximum-range glide is needed to reach a distant surface vessel, which is the best assurance of assistance if a landing cannot be made close to shore. An attempt should be made to ditch ahead of the ship to increase the probability that someone on board will see you. Also, land to one side of the vessel, not directly in front of it—a large ship may not be sufficiently maneuverable to avoid collision.

While still at altitude, attempt communicating with any ground facility or even another aircraft. It is imperative to alert someone who can initiate an immediate rescue operation. Additionally, activate the emergency locator transmitter (ELT), if possible, and transmit the emergency code (7700) on the transponder, even if you believe the aircraft is too far from land to be detected. In certain areas, long-range radar extends 1,000 miles seaward.

During extended overwater operations, a pilot may recognize the eventual need to ditch even though he still can remain airborne for some lengthy period of time (such as when he knows insufficient fuel is available to make landfall). At such a time, he might be able to communicate (via relay) with a Coast Guard or Air Force Rescue Coordination Center. A rescue center usually can provide nearby ship positions and recommend ditch headings based on forecast wind and sea conditions. With enough warning, a rescue center even can launch an escort aircraft to provide navigational assistance (if a pilot is lost), illuminate a ditch area at night, drop survival equipment, and provide a plethora of advice and moral support.

While time still is available (during a glide, for example), be certain to review with passengers the use of emergency exits and insist that evacuation not begin until the aircraft comes to rest. Although life jackets should be put on as soon as possible, they should not be inflated until outside the aircraft. This is because an inflated life jacket hampers an escape from tight quarters and is prone to puncture by a sharp piece or corner of the aircraft structure.

Anyone who has seen a late-night rerun of *The High and the Mighty* probably knows the rest of the drill: Loose objects that could become missiles during a crash landing should be stowed or thrown overboard, collars and neckties should be loosened, shoes should be removed (to facilitate swimming), dentures and eyeglasses also should be removed, lap belts and shoulder harnesses should be cinched tightly, and cushioning material (such as jackets or pillows) should be placed so as to provide maximum cranial protection during the landing.

When approximately one minute from touchdown, each rear-seat passenger should be instructed to assume the crash position: cross forearms, grab and hold onto the top of the seat immediately in front, and rest forehead on arms. (A front-seat passenger can do the same using the top of the glare shield.) Finally, the pilot should remove his headset to prevent becoming entangled in wire during evacuation.

One final preparatory item is the subject of some controversy. Many argue that the cabin door should be kept closed during ditching to keep the cabin as watertight as possible. The

Coast Guard points out, however, that structural distortion of the fuselage and door frame might occur during a water landing and jam the door permanently. Unless other exits are available, the occupants could become entombed.

Others argue, therefore, that the door should be opened when on final approach and kept ajar by jamming a shoe or other article between the door and its frame. This, of course, will sacrifice some buoyancy.

Another subject of controversy is the relative seaworthiness of high-wing versus low-wing airplanes and fixed gear versus retractable gear. Most pilots contend that the ideal airplane for ditching is a low-wing aircraft with landing gear retracted. Statistics, however, do not substantiate this. Aircraft geometry and landing-gear configuration do not appear to affect survivability appreciably.

Although low-wing aircraft do offer superior planing and buoyancy (especially with empty fuel tanks), they should not be landed in water with flaps fully extended because this can cause pronounced nose-down pitching and make the aircraft behave like a submarine. Also, flaps hanging from a low wing may be torn away during touchdown, which might create gaping holes in the wings and have a disastrous effect on buoyancy. Consequently, low-wing airplanes land faster, increasing the probability of damage and injury.

Since the flaps of high-wing aircraft are less susceptible to water damage, they should be used to the maximum extent possible to reduce impact speed.

Another significant disadvantage of a low-wing configuration is that it is easier to dig a wingtip into a rolling sea during initial touchdown, which can result in a lethal cartwheel, Also, the ailerons on high-wing airplanes are most effective in maintaining lateral control because they are kept "high and dry" throughout most of the landing rollout.

The Coast Guard does recommend that a ditching be made with the landing gear retracted, but this should not be construed to mean that retractable-gear aircraft are more suitable for ditching than fixed-gear aircraft. Just the opposite may be true. Of the 104 ditchings made in U.S. waters during a recent three-year period, half were made in retractable-gear aircraft, yet these accounted for two-thirds of the fatalities that occurred during splashdown. This apparent paradox, however, does not suggest extending the gear for a ditching. What the statistics probably indicate is that, since retractables generally have higher stall speeds than fixed-gear aircraft, they usually are landed somewhat faster and subjected to greater deceleration forces.

Landing with the gear down can result in violent, destructive impact forces. The wheels should be kept in their wells, particularly when ditching high-performance aircraft. When touching down with a smooth belly, however, the aircraft tends to skip just the way a flat, spinning rock can when tossed toward a deep puddle at an acute angle. This initial touchdown generally is quite mild. But hang on; the second impact is likely to be much more severe, especially as the elevator loses effectiveness (because of airspeed decay) and the nose begins to dig in. Depending on many factors, this may even cause the aircraft to submerge. But, do not fret; it should bob to the surface quickly and provide sufficient time for evacuation before sinking.

Those who have ditched slow, fixed-gear aircraft, however, report that the main gear digging in during initial impact prevents the aircraft from skipping and subsequently striking the water in a stalled, nose-low attitude. The aircraft simply decelerates rapidly with the nose burrowing only slightly. Fixed-gear proponents claim this is safer than risking the secondary, nose-low impact frequently associated with retractables.

Considering all of the arguments, experts have yet to decide the optimum aircraft for ditching except perhaps that it should have STOL characteristics, be built of wood, and be stuffed with Ping-Pong balls.

When ditching in a lake, a pilot obviously should plan to land into the wind. Should a river be his goal, the landing should be made downstream (to reduce impact speed) unless a strong wind dictates otherwise. But when landing in the ocean, much more thought must be given to the safest landing direction.

The surface of an ocean almost always is characterized by long, parallel swells. These large undulations are caused by distant storms and are not wave irregularities caused by local winds. It is important that a landing be made parallel to these swells because landing into the face of one can be like flying into the side of a mountain. Although water often is regarded as a soft substance, it can be as hard as granite when struck head on at landing speeds (as anyone who has done a belly flop from a lofty diving board can attest).

Unfortunately, it is very difficult to detect swell movement when below 2,000 feet. The state of the sea must be assessed from a higher altitude and even this is not particularly easy unless the swells are pronounced. Learning to recognize swell direction, however, is one aspect of ditching that can be practiced during routine flights along a shoreline.

The Coast Guard often refers to secondary swells that also may influence the direction of landing; but since these usually are visible only to the trained eye, any further discussion of them is only of academic interest, except for one point. Occasionally, major and minor swell systems interact (even in rough seas) to form areas of relatively smooth water. This occurs where the peaks of one swell system fill the valleys of another. So, if time and altitude permit, execute a shallow, 360-degree turn to see if such an oceanic oasis can be found.

Although it is tempting to disregard swell movement and land directly into the wind, this must be avoided. Landing into the face of a well-developed swell can be catastrophic unless the wind component across the swells exceeds one-third of the touchdown speed. In this case, the pilot probably should compromise between landing parallel to the swells and into the wind. If the crosswind component exceeds half the landing speed, it might be wiser to land into the wind as long as the touchdown can be made in a valley between swells or on the backside of a swell. To this must be added, "Good luck."

The Coast Guard recommends that high-wing aircraft be

landed with full flaps and that low-wing aircraft be landed either with the flaps retracted or extended only slightly. Although the initial touchdown should be at as low an airspeed as possible, a full-stall landing is dangerous because of the possibility of striking the water nose-first. Instead, fixed-gear aircraft should touch down in a 10- to 12-degree, nose-high attitude; retractables should use a 5- to 8-degree attitude. These target attitudes are considered critical because if the aircraft lands with the nose too high, the tail may strike first and force the nose down too rapidly; if aircraft attitude is too flat, the nose may dig in prematurely.

After initial contact with the water, apply maximum up-elevator (assuming it is still attached) to keep the nose out of the water and work feverishly to keep the wings parallel to the surface; do not lower a wing to compensate for a crosswind. Otherwise a wingtip may dig in and cause total loss of control.

The aircraft most likely will come to rest in a nose-down attitude because an airplane's center of gravity usually is ahead of its center of buoyancy. Immediate evacuation is imperative even if the aircraft appears to be floating well. The typical general aviation aircraft will flood and submerge in about one minute.

If the door cannot be opened because of water pressure from outside the cabin, open a window and wait for water entering the cabin to equalize the pressure. The door should then open quite easily. If it still cannot be opened because of structural jamming, someone should crawl into the back of the cabin (where a pocket of air usually can be found), place has back against one side of the cabin, extend his legs and push out a window on the other side with his feet.

Although one-fourth of all ditchings involve fatalities, the U.S. Coast Guard points out that most of those who perish usually survive the procedure itself. Many of the fatalities occur after evacuation and are due to drowning because flotation equipment is unavailable. On occasion, life jackets are on board but are out of reach, are damaged during evacuation, or fail to inflate.

Another major threat—especially in winter—is hypothermia, a disabling condition in which the temperature of the human body drops below normal (98.6°F). Hypothermia occurs most rapidly when the body is immersed in cold water because water carries off body heat much more rapidly than does air.

When body temperature drops to 96°F, shivering becomes uncontrollable; below 90°F, shivering gives way to muscular rigidity and impaired mental acuity. With a body temperature of less than 80°F, the average person loses consciousness and eventually experiences heart failure.

Although the ability to endure hypothermia varies among individuals and circumstances, the U.S. Navy claims that no one can survive in 32°F water for more than one hour. As water temperature increases, however, the likelihood of survival increases dramatically. But hypothermia can occur eventually even when the water is relatively warm.

If possible, either swim to shore or have an inflatable raft readily available. In water temperatures of less than 35°F, pilots have reported such a rapid onset of hypothermia that they did not have the strength to swim to a nearby raft.

Ditching is a complex subject that has had experts debating for years. A pilot, however, has only one shot at perfection, with lives hanging in the balance. Preparedness is the key to his survival.

FORMATION FLYING

Not long ago, two Piper singles were heading north. The occupants, who included children, were returning from a sun-soaked vacation in Florida. But the flight ended abruptly and prematurely. The probable cause of the midair collision was revealed by film recovered from cameras found in the wreckage. The pilots apparently were more concerned about air-to-air photography than the safety of their families. Although the color prints turned out reasonably well, no one on board survived to see them.

Sadly, this tragedy could have been averted by applying the

fundamental rules either of formation flying or of common sense and self-restraint.

The need for airplanes to travel and maneuver in formation originated in military aviation. Bombers or fighters amassed in a disciplined cluster represented an awesome concentration of fire power. At the target, a formation of bombers could decimate a wide swath of terrain, a technique known as saturation bombing. Also, a damaged aircraft could be maneuvered into a formation and protected by others against further attack.

General aviation does not have such an imperative need for formation flying. The technique, however, is useful for air-to-air photography and when the pilot of a damaged or malfunctioning aircraft needs another to fly alongside and analyze a problem (such as when a landing-gear leg is suspected of not being fully extended). Otherwise, formation flying usually is done only for fun. If a pilot does not know and abide by the rules, the fun may be short-lived.

To the casual observer, formation flying appears deceptively easy, a tribute to those who have mastered the skill. Unfortunately, it often seems *too* easy and tempts unqualified pilots to try the same without being aware of the hazards involved.

The best way to learn formation flying is from an experienced instructor. But unless he has had military training, an instructor is not likely to know much more than his student. Consequently, formation flying in civilian airplanes is often self-taught. Although the procedure can be hazardous, a disciplined, cautious approach can eliminate much of the risk.

Safe formation flying begins on the ground where the pilots must discuss an impending flight and agree on a set of operating rules. First, determine who is to be the leader. He must be intimately familiar with the aircraft in the formation so as never to exceed the capability of the other craft and pilot (the wing man).

It is then necessary to agree to fly a specific cruise speed during the formation, one that can be maintained easily by both aircraft. Too great a speed makes it difficult for the wing man to catch up should he fall behind; too low an airspeed results in poor control responsiveness, making it laborious for the wing man to maintain position relative to the leader. If the flight is to include altitude changes, the leader may need to use less than maximum climb rates so that the chase pilot will have reserve climb performance should he need to catch up.

The method of rendezvous, route, altitude, and projected performance should be thoroughly planned to keep in-flight decisions and adjustments to a minimum.

Communications between pilots is critical. Plan to use an air-to-air frequency, but consider that it may be unusable because of saturation by other pilots. At such times, pilots flying in formation need to use a set of easy-to-understand hand signals.

It is impossible to create a sign language that covers all needs, but you can anticipate the important ones. Signals should be developed for such messages as widen formation, tighten formation, climb, descend, break formation, and return to base.

The importance of good communications cannot be overstressed. Nothing is more hazardous than confusion when attempting to fly in formation.

Some pilots claim that the formation leader requires the least flying skill—his role is simply to maintain straight-and-level flight at a specific altitude and turn, climb, or descend as necessary. In a way, he simply goes about the business of flying as though he were alone. But he also must be highly disciplined and hold altitude and heading with absolute precision. He must concentrate on flying and resist the urge to look back at the chase plane. Nothing makes a wing man more nervous than a leader looking over his shoulder, an indication that he is not concentrating on the precision required of him.

A leader must have faith in his wing man and virtually ignore the presence of the second airplane. A pilot unaccustomed to such discipline might consider having another pilot fly with him, someone who can keep an eye on the chase plane and also serve as a lookout for other traffic.

The wing man is the worker, the slave of the formation. He

must join the leader and maintain the desired separation and relative position. Any movement of the lead aircraft requires an equal response from the wing man, otherwise the formation falls apart. The wing man focuses his concentration on the lead airplane and uses it as a form of attitude indicator, faithfully following and reproducing its every movement. He manipulates aircraft and engine controls only in direct response to the lead airplane, without reference to his own instruments. He must trust the leader not to place him and his airplane in jeopardy. (Unfortunately, wing men have been known to follow their leaders into the ground.) A wing man uncomfortable with this role also might consider carrying another pilot to act as a lookout and, perhaps, to handle communications. (If the formation is for air-to-air photography, a third man is essential; a pilot flying in formation while trying to operate a camera is the seed of disaster.)

Establishing a formation is particularly challenging for the novice because he usually does not appreciate how rapidly the *apparent* rate of closure can increase as one aircraft closely approaches another. Seeing the lead aircraft suddenly blossom in his windshield can be unnerving to a wing man and cause him to break away and try again.

The first rule of establishing a formation suggests that the wing man exercise patience in closing the gap between aircraft. Second, he should approach the leader from below so that the worst consequence of an overshoot is sliding beneath and not into the other aircraft. Third, the leader must resist helping the wing man establish formation; only one pilot can do the maneuvering. Two aircraft maneuvering independently toward one another has been an ingredient in midair collisions.

Figure 45 shows the six basic formations, any of which can be stacked. This means that the aircraft in each formation may be flown at the same altitude, or their altitudes may be progressively staggered up or down. With just two airplanes, however, only three formations are possible: abreast, in trail, and echelon (right or left). Inexperienced pilots are discouraged from at-

FORMATION FLYING

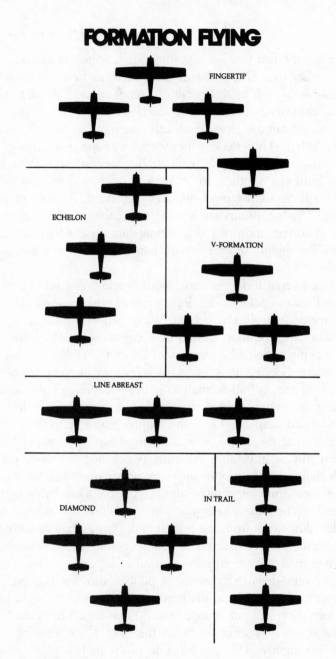

FINGERTIP

ECHELON

V-FORMATION

LINE ABREAST

DIAMOND

IN TRAIL

Figure 45

303

tempting the first two because these are the most hazardous.

A wing man flying abeam must twist his head excessively, making it more difficult to control aircraft attitude. Another factor to consider is aerodynamic interference. If the wingtips of the two aircraft are close, each can interrupt the wingtip vortex of the other. The effect is increased lift of the inside wings in the formation, creating a tendency for the two aircraft to roll away from one another. Inexperienced pilots may overcompensate for these rolling moments and increase the chance of collision. This phenomenon is most noticeable when airspeed is low. (The reduction of induced drag can make a tight, abreast formation slightly more efficient than airplanes flying independently.)

The in-trail formation also requires additional skill because it is difficult to detect a developing rate of closure when viewing an airplane from directly behind. Wing men who insist on flying the six-o'clock position should fly above or below the leader to avoid being buffeted by prop wash. Given the choice, fly below the leader because it is easier to keep him in sight. Another hazard of the in-trail formation is the possibility of the leader having an engine failure, resulting in a simultaneous loss of altitude and airspeed. From the trailing pilot's perspective, this appears as if the leader were backing down and toward him. When this or any other difficulty is detected by either pilot, each should break away in opposite, prearranged directions.

Aerodynamic interference also plays a role when flying tightly in trail. When the chase pilot slips in below and behind the leader, downwash from the lead aircraft's wings may be partially interrupted by the chase plane. Consequently, the lead airplane behaves as if it were entering ground effect and tends to pitch slightly nose-down. (Experienced pilots claim that this can be so noticeable as to signal the presence of someone trying to join the formation without being detected.) Downwash from the lead airplane also may strike the tail of the chase plane, causing it to pitch up slightly. This combination of the high airplane pitching down and the low airplane pitching up has led to collision.

The third, safest, and easiest formation to achieve and maintain is the right or left echelon (a left echelon is shown in Figure 45). The wing man is afforded a better perspective, a "sight picture," of the leader that enables him to detect quickly any relative motion between the two aircraft and to correct for it. Although aircraft in an echelon may be at the same altitude, most wing men usually find it easier to be slightly above or below the leader for a view of his upper or lower wing panels. This adds to the lead airplane's visibility and further improves the wing man's ability to maintain a precise formation.

Usually, it does not matter whether a formation of two is stacked up or down—that should be determined by whatever position seems most comfortable for the wing man to maintain. At times, flying high or low may be dictated by cockpit visibility and aircraft geometry. A pilot flying an airplane with a high wing that interferes with upward visibility may find it easier to keep an eye on the leader by staying above him. The opposite may be true in a low-wing airplane.

Many pilots assume that a right echelon is easier to maintain because the wing man, seated on the left, has a better view of the leader. But this is not necessarily true. When flying in a left echelon, a pilot looking across his cabin can frame the leader in his cockpit window. This may make it easier for him to detect relative aircraft movement.

When first practicing formation flying, keep the formation fairly loose (for obvious reasons). As skill develops, gradually close ranks. Though there is less margin for error as the distance between the aircraft shrinks, the exercise becomes less difficult. This is because a larger visual target makes it easier to detect and to correct for relative movement between the aircraft. (A tight formation also is less likely to be upset by turbulence because both aircraft are bounced in unison, but I do not recommend putting this theory to the acid test.)

When in formation, do not stare at any one point on the lead airplane because such a fixation makes it more difficult to detect relative movement.

Although this may sound heretical to some purists, it is much easier to stay with the leader by using power to vary airspeed and elevator to control altitude, than vice versa. Slight heading changes that may be required to remain in position with the leader should be made *very* gingerly. (It is okay to change heading a degree or two by yawing the airplane with a touch of rudder.) Remain alert, and correct any change in relative position as soon as it occurs; once established in formation, do not allow the "weave" to tighten or unravel. Under no circumstances should the wing man ever pull ahead of the leader or allow one airplane to overlap the other. *Any* situation that could lead to compromising safety dictates a mandatory dismantling of the formation. Lives hinge on the observance of this ironclad rule. (In a left echelon, the wing man breaks to the left and the leader breaks right, and vice versa.)

Entering and recovering from climbs and descents must be done very gradually and, of course, are the responsibility of the leader. Since the wing man attempts to copy his every move, the leader's maneuvering must be smooth. Rapid or jerky maneuvering must be avoided.

Turning in formation requires considerable practice and introduces a few unique problems. First of all, the wing man must not try to maintain the same altitude as the leader because this causes his relative position and sight picture to change, as shown in Figure 46. Instead, he must remain in the *same* position relative to the leader and maintain the same view of him whether in straight-and-level or turning flight. Consequently, the wing man in a left echelon is at a lower altitude than the leader during left turns (as shown in Figure 47) and above the leader during right turns.

Assume the leader of a left echelon initiates a right turn; the wing man must simultaneously turn, gain altitude, and increase airspeed (because his circle will be larger and require him to cover more ground).

Now consider this problem. The wing man maintains the

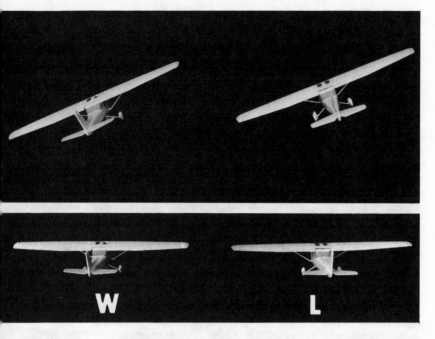

FIGURE 46

same bank angle as the leader (a necessity of formation flight), but he is flying faster. This results in the leader having a greater rate of turn than the wing man. (Remember the basics: Rate of turn for a given bank angle decreases as airspeed increases.) To fly the same circle as his leader in the same time, the wing man must increase his turn rate by adding slight bottom rudder.

When entering a turn in the opposite direction, the wing man (now on the inside of the turn) must lose altitude, reduce airspeed, and induce a slight slip to decrease his turn rate. (Skilled aerobatic pilots often share these chores; the leader contributes in this case by climbing a few feet, increasing airspeed, and adding slight bottom rudder. Considerable teamwork obviously is required.)

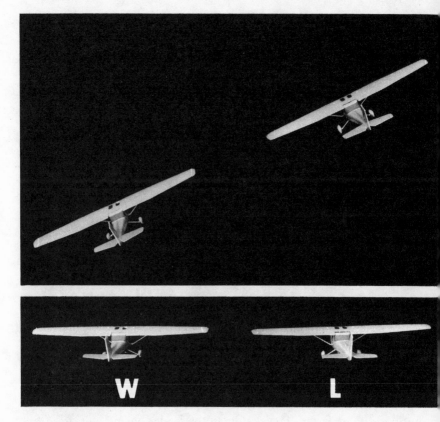

FIGURE 47

While turning, the wing man may find it necessary to steepen or shallow his bank angle to stay with the leader. This may result in a wing temporarily blocking his view of the leader. Should this occur, break formation immediately.

This discussion has described not only the fundamentals of formation flying, but also many of the hazards. If this causes you to be discouraged from attempting to fly in formation without adequate training, then my purpose has been genuinely served.

How to Set a World Aviation Record

It is natural to ask why anyone would want to establish an aviation record. For some, the answer is simple. Record setting is one way for a government to demonstrate technological advances or supremacy or for a manufacturer to promote and publicize its product. For others, it may be a burning desire to do what no one else has ever done. Dick Rutan and Jeana Yeager, for example, were willing to risk life and limb when they flew Burt Rutan's unorthodox and spindly *Voyager* around the world nonstop, without refueling. The nine-day flight was as much a psychological and physiological test as a technical one.

Why others seek to establish records is not as easily explained. One can wax mystical and compare the challenge to that of the mountain towering above the climber. But there are other reasons that motivate people to accomplish what others do not. For one person it might be ego, pride, recognition, or the thrill of an adventurous undertaking. For another, it might be the satisfaction of earning a place among the other 1,200 current record holders who have carved a place—however small or large—in the log of aviation history. Consider these world-record performances:

- Max Conrad's 4,668-mile, nonstop flight from Casablanca, Morocco, to Los Angeles in a Piper Comanche;
- Willard Macfarlane's climb from a standing start to 39,370 feet (12,000 meters) in 59.4 seconds in a McDonnell Douglas F-15 Eagle;
- Bob Harris's climb to 49,009 feet msl in a Burkhart Grob G-102 sailplane;
- Francesco Agello's 1934 speed mark over a three-kilometer course of 441 mph (383.21 kt) in a piston-powered Fiat seaplane, which was faster than any landplane of that era;

- Ben Abruzzo's 5,209-mile, nonstop flight from Japan to California in a balloon;
- E. Andreev's parachute jump that included a free fall of 80,360 feet; and
- Commander M. D. Ross's ascension to 113,740 feet in a balloon.

During aviation's early years, it was almost impossible to verify record claims. A stream of performance claims poured in from around the world. Many were accurate, but others were blatant exaggerations or examples of wishful thinking. It became obvious that some orderly method was needed to verify and maintain a record of performance developments.

In 1905, representatives from eight countries (including the United States) formed an organization to create rules governing world record attempts. Thus was born the Fédération Aéronautique Internationale (FAI). (The federation is headquartered in Paris and now includes 73 member nations.) The first world records established under the auspices of FAI were set in 1906 by Alberto Santos-Dumont: speed—25.7 mph (22.33 kt); distance—722 feet; and duration—21.2 seconds.

Although FAI approves and documents all successful record attempts, the task of timing and supervising world-record flights is delegated to the national aero club of the country involved. The United States's FAI affiliate is the National Aeronautic Association (NAA) in Washington, D.C. In the Soviet Union, pilots are under the jurisdiction of the Federatsia Aviatsionnogo Sporta. The rules, however, are the same for *all* pilots, which allows for worldwide competition on a common ground.

World records are grouped according to classes so that sailplane pilots do not have to compete against astronauts, for example. Airplanes are subclassed according to weight and type of powerplant (piston, turboprop, jet, and rocket). There is no distinction between turbocharged and normally aspirated engines nor between single- and multiengine airplanes.

At one time, the record book contained the names of aviations' most heralded pioneers, but over the years, their feats have been eclipsed. For instance, Charles Lindbergh's 90-mph (78.2-knot) record flight from New York to Paris no longer stands. This record now resides with Patrick Fourticq and Henri Pescarlo of France, who flew a Piper Malibu between the same cities at an average speed of 258.6 mph (224.7 knots).

Gone, too, are the around-the-world records held by Wiley Post and Howard Hughes. Modern aircraft have enabled pilots to circumnavigate the globe substantially faster than Post's 83 mph (72.1 knots) or Hughes's 161 mph (139.9 knots).

However, neither of these pioneering efforts would qualify, according to present rules. Previously, any route around the world would suffice. But someone eventually asked if he could break the record by using the North Pole as a pylon. Technically, this wily pilot could make a "360" around Santa's house and fly "around the world" in seconds. Therefore, it was decreed that an official record attempt must be made by flying a route that is at least 22,859 miles long (the circumference of the Tropic of Cancer). Since Post and Hughes flew northerly routes (both overflew the Soviet Union), the distances flown were only 15,596 and 14,284 miles, respectively.

The rules also have been changed to disallow stunt flying. At one time, FAI condoned endurance flying. This was during an era when substantial skill was required to keep an engine running for more than a few hours. But as powerplant reliability increased, these flights only tested pilots' abilities to endure prolonged periods of fatigue. Eventually, some aviators collapsed behind the wheel, with catastrophic results. This is why the 65-day, nonstop flight of Robert Timm and John Cook in a Cessna 172 (1958 and 1959) never received official world-record status. (Refueling was accomplished by handing a fuel hose to one of the pilots as they flew low and slow over a pickup truck.)

Duration records, however, still are allowed in balloons, airships, model aircraft, man-powered aircraft, and spacecraft. The longest flight in a balloon, for example, is 137 hours, six minutes—the time required for Ben Abruzzo, Maxie Anderson, and

Larry Newman to fly Double Eagle II from Maine to France in 1978.

(Do not take lightly the notion of world records for model aircraft. This is a highly competitive field, as is supported by some remarkable performances. A Russian enthusiast, Alexandre Smolenstev, kept his radio-controlled glider aloft for more than 33 hours. Z. Taus of Czechoslovakia launched a glider in *free flight* that soared for a straight-line distance of 193 miles. The speed record for powered models on a control line in circular flight is 245.7 mph, held by Leonid Lipinski of the USSR.)

NAA annually publishes *Aviation and Space Records*, a fascinating book for any flying enthusiast. Included in the book are all official world and national records for spacecraft, balloons, airships, landplanes, seaplanes, amphibians, rotorcraft, gliders, motorgliders, air-cushion vehicles, parachutes, hang gliders, man-powered aircraft, and model aircraft.

Not all record flights are included in the book, however. Although the *Guinness Book of World Records* states that Al Yates and Bob Phoenix made 193 takeoffs and daylight landings at unduplicated airports in a Piper Seminole in 14 hours and 57 minutes, this (and other such records) is unofficial because they did not comply with FAI rules.

In order for a flight to qualify as a world record, prospective pilots must conform to the specific and stringent requirements published in FAI's *Sporting Code* (also available from NAA, 1763 R Street, N.W., Washington, DC, 20009). Also, new speed and distance records must exceed previous performances by 1 percent. Altitude and climb records require a 3 percent improvement.

Some of FAI's rules are quite interesting. For example, when an attempt is made to break a speed record over a three-kilometer (1.62-nm) course, the flight must be conducted at no more than 100 meters (328 feet) agl. Diving into the starting gate is *verboten*. To negate the effects of wind, flights must be conducted in both directions along the course. The speeds then are averaged to obtain a final result.

Although the altitude restriction associated with a three-kilometer speed run prevents taking full advantage of turbocharged engines, there is no altitude limit when flying longer closed-circuit courses. Attempts at records for speed over these courses may be conducted at any altitude, as long as the altitude at the end of the speed run is not lower than the altitude at the beginning of the run.

Even though it might seem that Donald Taylor should have been able to fly around the world faster than 16.86 mph (14.65 kt), consider that time on the ground is counted as time in the air. Although Taylor took 60 days to complete the "round-robin" flight from Oshkosh, it *was* the first time a homebuilt airplane had been flown around the world. (*Voyager* was the second.)

Time-to-climb records are interesting in that the time required to reach a given altitude begins as the aircraft begins its takeoff roll.

Although it helps to fly downwind when attempting to break the record for distance in a straight line, calm conditions are best when attempting to break a record for distance or speed in a closed circuit. This is because a round-trip always takes longer *with* wind.

The records for piston-powered light airplanes are impressive, but the absolute records for airplanes (irrespective of weight or type of powerplant) are even more so. Consider these limits to which man and his flying machines have ventured:

- Distance in a straight line (without midair refueling): 25,012 statute miles in the Rutan *Voyager*.
- Heaviest aircraft ever flown: A Lockheed C-5B Galaxy that tipped the scales at 922,000 pounds.
- Altitude: 123,524 feet in an E-226M (a rocket-boosted version of the MiG-25 Foxbat).

- Altitude of an aircraft launched from a carrier airplane: 314,750 feet in a North American X-15-1.
- Speed over a straight course: 2,193 mph (1,905.66 kt) in a Lockheed SR-71A Blackbird.

Absolute records for piston-powered airplanes include:

- Distance in a closed circuit: 25,012 miles in the Rutan *Voyager*. (A nonstop, unrefueled flight around the world qualifies as a closed-circuit course if the takeoff and landing are made at the same point, which—in this case—was Edwards Air Force Base in Southern California. (Had pilots Rutan and Yeager looped *Voyager* as they passed over Edwards AFB at the end of their around-the-world marathon, they could have laid claim to the largest figure eight ever performed in an airplane. On the other hand, they did perform an outside loop of global proportions.)
- Altitude: 56,046 feet in a Caproni 161 biplane. (While setting this 1938 record, the pilot wore a primitive, water-filled pressure suit, and the engine was *not* supercharged.)

The World Record Experience

The 1974 advertisement in *Pilot* magazine aroused our curiosity. It said that the 271-knot Aerostar was the world's fastest piston-powered business airplane. Quite a claim, we thought. My close friend, Hal Fishman, the news anchor for KTLA-TV in Los Angeles, checked to see if any other lightplane could fly as fast. Apparently not. We then referred to NAA's *World Aviation & Space Records*. World speed marks at that time for class C-1.d aircraft (piston-powered landplanes weighing 3,858 to 6,614 pounds) were held by Y. D. Forestenco and Nicolay Golovanov of the Soviet Union. Using a single-engine 1,000-hp, Yak-11 "Moose," the comrades had flown 500- and 1,000-km closed-circuit courses

at 292.8 mph (254.5 knots) and 274.8 mph (238.8 knots), respectively.

If the claim made about the Aerostar was serious, it apparently would have no difficulty capturing these Soviet-held records. Would Aerostar designer and manufacturer Ted R. Smith be interested? He did not hesitate, and he even offered to supply us with a new Aerostar 601A (N90377) to fly, in order to prove that his airplane was undeniably the world's fastest.

Before we could assault the Russian records, however, we had to be sure that a coincidental and similar effort was not being conducted elsewhere. So, we applied to NAA for a sanction guaranteeing us a 90-day window during which no one else would be allowed to compete for the Yak-11 records. After that followed meetings with NAA officials to ensure that our plans would conform to international requirements.

The flights were to be conducted at 25,000 feet, because this is where the turbocharged Aerostar 601A performs best. The minimum flight time required to fly a closed-circuit course (a round-trip between two points) occurs when the wind is calm. Since such a condition rarely exists at that altitude, we had to select courses that were perpendicular to the winds aloft that morning. (This condition is less detrimental than flying with a tailwind in one direction and against a headwind the other.)

Because FAI rules allow an aircraft to be modified, we saw no reason not to take advantage of this. First, we had the manifold pressure relief valves removed (with Lycoming's approval) so that the engines could produce an extra 2.5 inches of manifold pressure. Since the induction system of almost every turbocharged engine has some air leakage, we also had the airboxes sealed. Finally, the turbochargers' wastegates were adjusted so that they would close completely. (To prevent sticking, the butterfly valves normally are set so as not to close completely.)

Prior to weighing the aircraft (in the planned takeoff condition and under NAA supervision), all unnecessary equipment (such as extra seats) was removed.

On January 22, 1975, I climbed into the left seat and nervously prepared for the 500-km flight. Fishman rode shotgun and later would command the 1,000-km effort. NAA timer Earl Hansen sat in back. Air traffic control was ready, too, with a chunk of airspace blocked for our exclusive use.

As we streaked over the starting point (a VOR) at Flight Level 250, the clicking sound of Hansen starting his dual chronometers sounded like a blast of TNT. The turbochargers and the adrenal glands were pumping at their maximum allowable limits. The head temperatures were a bit toasty, but there was no danger of detonation.

As we approached the second VOR, I mentally reviewed the technique for executing the pylon turn. It involved a compromise between turn radius and airspeed loss. Too shallow a bank angle would add excessive distance and too steep an angle would sacrifice too much airspeed.

The trickiest part was to begin the turn at the proper distance prior to reaching the VOR. If turn entry was delayed until passing the turn point, time and distance would have been added to the flight and reduced average speed over the course. Conversely, if we began the turn too soon, the flight path would have passed inside the pylon and invalidated the record attempt.

Luckily, the course reversal worked out well. We headed back toward the starting gate, which had to be crossed at the same altitude at which the record attempt began.

At the end of the day, Fishman and I had established new world speed records for the 500- and 1,000-km courses that were both fractionally close to 305 mph (265 knots). (The true airspeed of 278 knots experienced during both flights could not be achieved as end results because of the detrimental effects of the 50-knot wind, the airspeed loss during the pylon turns, and the added circumferential distances required to make high-speed, 180-degree turns.)

NAA cabled our provisional claims to FAI in Paris and prepared the dossiers containing all required documentation. We reveled in the glory, but it was not to last. Several months later, the experimental Bellanca Skyrocket, flown by John P. Harris, shattered the Aerostar's speed marks. Harris's record-breaking speeds for the 500- and 1,000-km closed-circuit courses were 326.5 mph (283.7 knots) and 313.9 mph (272.8 knots), respectively. Oh, well. Records—they say—are meant to be broken.

- Speed over a 15/25-kilometer course: 517 mph (449.26 kt) in the P-51D "Dago Red."
- Time-to-climb to 3,000 meters (9,843 feet): one minute, 31.9 seconds in a Grumman F8F2 Bearcat.

The typical general aviation pilot might believe that a world record is beyond his reach. This is not necessarily true. If he does not have access to an aircraft capable of out-performing one of the major world-class records, he might consider a speed record between major cities. Although some of these records would be difficult to break (such as Mark Patiky's dash between St. Louis and Washington, D.C., at 383 mph [332.6 kt] in a Mooney 252), others are not insurmountable (such as John Leggatt Jr.'s flight from Palm Springs to Phoenix in a Citabria at 99 mph [86 kt]). Many other city-to-city records are there for the taking, simply because they have yet to be established. Current rules, however, require that cities within the same country be at least 500 kilometers (310 sm) apart.

If a world record is not in the cards, a pilot might consider a national record. NAA supervises and grants U.S. records to some performances that do not otherwise qualify for international recognition. For example, NAA awarded a national record to R. Stephen Powell, who made 2,315 consecutive loops in a Bellanca Decathlon. Russel Saunders broke a U.S. record for the longest flight (680 miles) below sea level. (He flew a closed-circuit course in a Cessna 140 over Death Valley, California.) Other American records include "longest flight in an open-cockpit airplane" (2,740 miles), "first transcontinental flight made solely on auto fuel," "first family to fly over the Magnetic North Pole" (the Branstetter family in a Piper Cherokee 180), and "most different aircraft flown in one day" (65).

Anyone interested in attempting a world or national record should obtain NAA's Record Attempt Kit, which contains all the forms and information necessary to begin planning. According to NAA, "Anything goes as far as a national record is concerned, as long as the flight has merit."

BRAINTEASERS

It has been said that history is a body of myths commonly agreed upon. Aviation has a similar body of mythology, with roots that stem from when man first dreamed of flight.

One of the earliest and most popular myths is the Greek tale about the Athenian architect, Daedalus, and his foolhardy son, Icarus. It was believed for centuries that Icarus plunged to his death in the sea because he had flown too high, too near the sun, causing his waxen wings to melt. Daedalus, who flew lower and farther from the sun, survived.

The passage of time and the expansion of knowledge destroy many such myths, but others, presumably based on more scientific thinking, evolve to replace them. What follows are some challenging—and, I hope, entertaining—brainteasers based on commonly held misconceptions and little-known facts of flight. I hope you enjoy the stimulation they are intended to provide.

———•———

Murphy's Law claims that whenever something can possibly go wrong, it will. There are, of course, numerous corollaries to this adage, but one of concern to pilots states that headwinds occur more frequently than tailwinds.

In a way, the statement is accurate, especially with respect to round-robin flights. Given any specific wind direction and speed, a round-trip takes longer than when the wind is calm.

For example, assume that a pilot is flying due east from A to B, a distance of 300 nautical miles. With a calm wind and true airspeed of 150 knots, the round-trip (600 miles) would require exactly four hours (excluding time lost during climb, departure, and arrival maneuvering).

But now introduce a 50-knot westerly wind. The 300-mile outbound flight would be flown with a 200-knot groundspeed and require only one hour and thirty minutes. The groundspeed for the return leg, however, would be only 100 knots and require three hours en route. Total time for the round-trip would be four hours and thirty minutes, half an hour longer than had there been no wind at all.

The reason for the additional flying time is that the aircraft spends more time under the influence of a headwind than it does benefiting from the tailwind. Consequently, the average groundspeed is less than had the wind been calm.

With respect to round-robin flights, therefore, it can be said that *any* wind is an "effective headwind" because flight time is prolonged.

But what about one-way flights? Does Murphy's Law affect these, too? Do headwinds really prevail over tailwinds? Logic suggests that for any given flight, the odds in favor of a headwind are equal to those in favor of a tailwind, Right? Wrong! Sad to say, Murphy is once again correct. Headwinds do prevail, but not simply because the contrite, Irish gentleman has a vendetta against pilots. The reason is a bit more obscure.

Figure 48 shows a compass rose about an airplane, a diagram used commonly in textbooks to describe the effects of various wind directions. For example, winds blowing toward the airplane from the directions encompassed by the shaded area are headwinds, while those blowing from the lower two quadrants define tailwinds. Do you agree? Well, you shouldn't. This popular presentation is inaccurate.

The diagram implies that a crosswind from either 90 or 270 degrees has no effect on groundspeed. In other words, these crosswinds would be neither headwinds nor tailwinds. Not so.

In order to correct for a crosswind and maintain the desired true course, it is necessary to establish a wind correction angle, or crab. But the act of crabbing necessitates turning *into* the wind. The result? A loss of groundspeed. The stronger the crosswind, the greater the loss. In other words, a direct crosswind also is a headwind.

The table in Figure 48 provides the groundspeed loss due to crabbing into a crosswind for various true airspeeds (knots or mph). For example, if a 160-knot airplane is required to crab

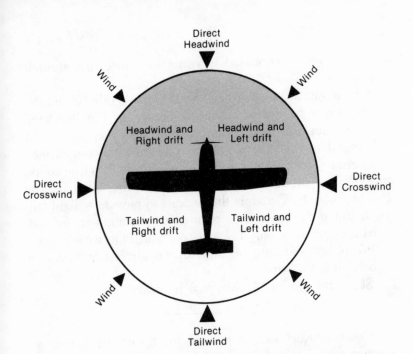

		WIND CORRECTION ANGLE (CRAB)				
		10°	15°	20°	25°	30°
TRUE AIRSPEED	80	–1	–3	– 5	– 7	–11
	100	–2	–3	– 6	– 9	–13
	120	–2	–4	– 7	–11	–16
	140	–2	–5	– 8	–13	–19
	160	–2	–5	–10	–15	–21
	180	–3	–6	–11	–17	–24
	200	–3	–7	–12	–19	–27
	220	–3	–7	–13	–21	–29
	240	–4	–8	–14	–22	–32

FIGURE 48

20 degrees into a crosswind to maintain course, the ground-speed loss is 10 knots.

Very strong winds that blow from even slightly behind the aircraft may appear to be beneficial, but by the time the wind correction angle is applied more groundspeed may be lost (by crabbing) than would be gained from the tailwind component.

Consider, for example, a pilot who wants to fly a true course of 360° in a 140-knot airplane. The prevailing wind is from 260° at 60 knots. Certainly this appears to provide a slight tail-wind. But if the problem is resolved on a computer, ground-speed is found to be only 137 knots. Although this wind provides a 10-knot tailwind component, 13 knots are lost by having to crab 25° into the wind.

So, to the glee of Mr. Murphy, headwinds do prevail.

———————————•———————————

Comrade Kochinko, a pilot in the Soviet Air Force, was given a most unusual flight assignment. He was told to fly to any point of his choosing in the Northern Hemisphere and, once there, perform the following navigational exercise:

"Fly a true course of 360° for 500 nautical miles, turn right and maintain a true course of 090° for another 500 nautical miles, and then turn so as to track along a true course of 180° for an additional 500 nautical miles."

This didn't sound particularly difficult until Kochinko read the final requirement of his flight orders: "After flying each of three 500-nm-long legs, the aircraft must arrive at the same point from which the first leg started."

Initially, Kochinko was much concerned about this seem-ingly impossible assignment because he knew that failure to comply would result in a Siberian vacation. Eventually, how-ever, the Soviet pilot realized that, yes, he could perform such a mission.

If *you* were Comrade Kochinko, how would you resolve this dilemma? Remember, the entire flight occurs within the Northern Hemisphere and the equally long legs must be flown in the designated sequence: north, east, and then south. So that you are not tempted to peek, the solution has been placed at the end of this chapter.

———•———

Perry Schreffler, a retired TWA captain, claims to have collected innumerable beers by wagering that, from within the cockpit, he can back a B-17 into a parking space. Considering that this four-engine, World War II taildragger does not have reversible-pitch propellers, the boast does seem hollow. But do not underestimate this bet.

Schreffler manages to perform the seemingly impossible by locking the left brake and pouring the coal to the number one engine, which is outboard (to the left) of the left main landing gear. As a result, the left wingtip moves forward. Since the left wheel is locked, the right main wheel is forced to roll slightly backwards. Schreffler then stomps on the right brake and advances the number four throttle to force the left wheel back. Alternating in this manner, it is indeed possible to "walk" a Flying Fortress backward.

———•———

Instrument pilots appreciate how serious a static-system failure can be. If the system were to fail, the altimeter, the airspeed indicator, and the vertical speed indicator (VSI) would be affected adversely. Unless the airplane is equipped with an alternate static source (many are not), the pilot is left with only one option: break the glass face of the VSI. This allows ambient pressure, only in an *un*pressurized cockpit, to flow through the instrument case and into the static system, returning the affected instruments to service.

Some time ago, I spoke to a pilot who claimed to have performed this emergency procedure. She cautioned that, when breaking the glass, one should be careful not to damage the indicator needle so as to preserve VSI indications. The pilot stated that, after resorting to this measure, all three instruments behaved normally.

From what she said, it is clear that the experience was fabricated. Do you know what gave her away?

During normal operation, changing air pressure is sensed by a diaphragm within the instrument case of a VSI. While descending, for example, increasing static pressure enters the system, forcing the diaphragm to expand and causing the VSI needle to dip. But, if the increasing pressure encountered during a descent enters the system through the instrument face rather than through the conventional static source, the diaphragm is compressed and produces a climb indication.

The result is that breaking the glass face of a VSI does provide reasonably accurate vertical speed indications, but these are out of phase with reality. Descents are indicated by climb, and vice versa. Quite obviously, the VSI does not "behave normally," as claimed.

To avoid being confused by such contradictory flight data, some experts recommend either covering the instrument or breaking off the needle. In any event, the instrument will require repair.

———•———

A pilot flying in turbulence usually is preoccupied with preventing his machine from going topsy-turvy and pays little attention to the airplane's behavioral traits. This, of course, leads to a question bound to make a hit with aeronautical trivia buffs, those masters of minutiae who know more about things than others care to know.

When an airplane encounters an updraft, does it pitch up, pitch down, or does it maintain its original attitude?

Since the nose often is the first part of an airplane to arrive at the scene of an updraft, it would be logical to conclude that it pitches up. However, it would be an incorrect assumption.

Regard an airplane as an overgrown weather vane; it always

tends to align with the relative wind. Consider the taxiing tail-dragger that stubbornly attempts to yaw into a crosswind. Similarly, an airplane in flight tends to head into assaulting gusts of air. When encountering an updraft, therefore, the nose tends to pitch earthward. Conversely, a downdraft results in a temporary pitch up.

———————•———————

Perhaps the best way to cope with truly strong and blustery winds is to shackle your airplane to the tarmac and head for the nearest watering hole until conditions improve.

While you are comfortably ensconced, however, assume that your tricycle-gear airplane, which has a 50-knot stall speed, is resting in the chocks while pointing directly into a 55-knot wind. Can this wing develop sufficient lift to levitate the airplane against the tiedown chains?

Although some are bound to respond affirmatively, the answer is resoundingly negative. This is because the wing's angle of attack is too small to generate the lift necessary for flight. At such a low airspeed, the wing requires a much larger angle of attack, which explains why an airplane must be rotated for take-off.

———————•———————

A long-standing controversy involves the notion of flying an airplane on the step, a procedure that presumably allows an airplane at cruise to pick up a few extra knots.

Proponents claim that this can be achieved by climbing a few hundred feet above cruise altitude and then entering a shallow dive to capture the target altitude with an excess of airspeed. According to this theory, the wing's angle of attack at such a relatively high airspeed will be slightly smaller, resulting in somewhat less drag. Consequently, the airplane will not decelerate to the normal cruise speed. Instead, it will maintain a slightly higher airspeed.

On the other side of this controversial coin are those who

disagree, claiming that step flying is little more than aerodynamic alchemy.

Anyone serious about investigating the subject easily can find convincing arguments (and altercations) to support both points of view. But, most important is: Can an airplane really be made to cruise faster by flying on the step? Those pragmatists who believe only what they see ultimately conclude that step flying is blarney, that there simply is no credible evidence to support the claim.

First of all, the technique of climbing above and then returning to cruise altitude is sloppy during VFR flight and intolerable when flying IFR. There is a much neater way to accomplish the same thing. Upon reaching the desired altitude, do not retard the throttle. Simply allow climb power to accelerate the airplane *beyond* the normal, indicated cruise airspeed. To maintain altitude at such a speed, a pilot must trim the airplane into a slightly more nose-down attitude than normally is required. The result is the same as diving to cruise altitude. Then, simply adjust the engine to cruise power.

Anyone who does this in a variety of airplanes will notice that the airspeed of each eventually settles down to what normally is expected. I have attempted to place a number of airplanes on the step (ranging from Cessna singles to Boeing jets) and have yet to confirm the presence of a step. If there were such a way to increase cruise speed, without burning additional fuel, the airlines certainly would have discovered it by now.

Some theoreticians attempt to mathematically prove the existence of an efficient step for cruising an airplane; but if the results cannot be detected on an airspeed indicator, either the proof is fallacious or the benefit is too subtle to be of significance.

I flew with several pilots who believed in step flying. Each claimed to achieve higher-than-normal cruise speeds, but after observing their techniques, it became obvious to me why they were so firm in their conviction.

When leveling off at cruise altitude in a conventional manner, not using the step entry, each pilot prematurely retarded the throttle from climb to cruise power. In other words, they never gave their airplanes a chance to fully accelerate to normal cruise in the first place. Diving to cruise altitude naturally resulted in a somewhat higher airspeed than their poor technique of establishing cruise flight would otherwise allow. Once these pilots accepted the suggestion of using climb power to accelerate to cruise speed (as always should be done), there was no apparent difference between the end results.

———•———

During the Rutan *Voyager's* historic, nonstop, unrefueled flight around the wold in 1986, pilots Richard G. Rutan and Jeana Yeager were uncertain how much fuel remained available as they neared the halfway point of their incredible journey. Knowing that climb performance varies with gross weight, they performed a series of flight tests over East Africa. The results of these tests enabled them to calculate the approximate gross weight of the spindly craft. Once gross weight was determined, it was a simple matter for them to estimate the weight of fuel on board.

Suppose, however, that Rutan and Yeager had wanted to determine the location of *Voyager's* center of gravity. Without knowing the amount of fuel in each of the 17 fuel tanks, CG location certainly could not have been calculated. Is there a way that they—or any other pilot, for that matter—could have pinpointed the CG without using numbers or mathematics?

A clue to the solution of this perplexing problem lies in the fact that the axes of motion of an airplane pass through the center of gravity. Bringing the control wheel aft, for example, results in the aircraft's pitching about a lateral axis that passes precisely through the CG. In other words, that portion of the aircraft ahead of the CG pitches up while that portion of the structure aft of the CG rotates downward. All that is required to determine CG location, therefore, is something that accurately senses aircraft movement about any of the three axes (lateral, longitudinal, or vertical). One item that does this quite nicely is a hand-held slip-skid ball (inclinometer), the instrument normally associated with a turn indicator or coordinator.

Figure 49 shows how the slip-skid ball behaves during a left skid. As expected, the ball responds to left-rudder deflection by sliding to the right. This movement of the ball, however, occurs only when the instrument is forward of the center of gravity. If the instrument was aft of the CG during a left skid, the ball would move left (in response to the tail swinging to the right), as shown in Figure 49. If the ball moves opposite to skid direction when ahead of the CG and toward the skid when aft of the CG, it is obvious that the ball would not move at all when placed at the CG. The precise location of the center of gravity can be determined, therefore, by holding a slip-skid instrument in your hand and moving it fore and aft until it fails to respond to gentle rudder deflection (in either direction).

Locating the CG in this manner and during different loading conditions is a fascinating, easily performed experiment that

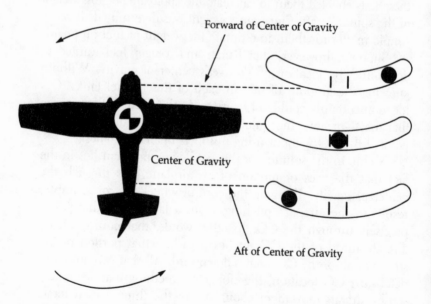

Forward of Center of Gravity

Center of Gravity

Aft of Center of Gravity

FIGURE 49

allows a pilot to visualize a principle of flight that ordinarily is accepted only on blind faith. Assume that a pilot determines— for a given load distribution—that the CG of his aircraft is exactly midway between the front and rear seats. Does this mean that all passengers would be equally jostled when flying through turbulence, or would the aft passengers be affected differently from those riding in front? During a skid, for instance, it would appear from our previous experiment with the slip-skid ball that ride quality worsens as distance from the CG increases. After all, the passengers are subjected to the same forces that move the ball in its glass tube. In this case, then, it would appear that those in front are affected as much by turbulence as those in back. (Passengers seated at the center of gravity do get the most comfortable ride.) But all is not always as it appears because the movement of the slip-skid ball—as shown in Figure 49—reveals only part of the story.

As left rudder is applied (or the aircraft yaws left because of a gust from the side), the slip-skid ball aft of the CG slides left because of the ball's inertia; as the tail swings right, the ball "attempts" to remain in position by moving left in the glass tube. Eventually, though, the centrifugal force developed during a left skid overcomes the ball's inertia and forces the ball to the right. In other words, the ball ahead of the CG moves only one way (to the right) during a left skid entry, but the ball aft of the CG moves left and then right. Similarly, those seated aft of the CG get shoved twice, first toward one side and then the other. This is why, for any given distance from the CG, rear-seat passengers are treated twice as harshly as those in front, something that pilots often fail to consider when gauging the effect of turbulence on their passengers. This explains also why those seated in the rear are most prone to airsickness.

———●———

Several years ago, an airline ground instructor posed a brain teaser to a large group of pilots to test their knowledge of basic meteorology. Unhappily, only a few could solve the problem. Feel like putting your expertise to the same test?

Figure 50 shows two pressure systems; one is a high, the other is a low. Both of the airports shown are at sea level and observers at each report identical weather conditions: clear skies, light winds, and standard atmospheric conditions (59°F, dry air, and an altimeter setting of 29.92 inches of mercury).

Each of two pilots flying identical light airplanes departs simultaneously from each of the airports shown. Everything else being equal, above which of the two airports will one pilot encounter better climb performance than the other?

Most pilots recall early lessons that teach how air circulates clockwise about a high-pressure system and counter-clockwise about a low (in the Northern Hemisphere). But most seem to forget that a high-pressure system consists also of subsiding (descending) air. Conversely, air rises from within a low.

This helps to explain why there generally is so much more weather in a low-pressure system as compared to a high. Rising

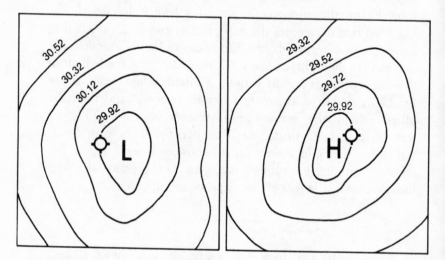

FIGURE 50

air condenses to form vertically developed cloudiness and precipitation.

Being aware of this basic information provides the solution to our problem. The pilot climbing within the low experiences the best performance because his plane is assisted by rising air—a spritely climb because of a "vertical tailwind." This does not refer to local vertical movements such as thermals. Rather, this refers to a huge mass of slowly rising air.

Conversely, the pilot flying in the high-pressure system must climb against subsiding air, which is much like fighting a vertical headwind. This condition has been known to evoke a comment such as: "This thing doesn't seem to be climbing very well today; we must be flying through *dead* air."

Most pilots solve the stated brain teaser incorrectly because they conclude that an airplane performs better in high pressure than in low. Quite true. But recall that the problem stated that the atmospheric pressure at each airport was identical (29.92"). The only difference is the pressure *surrounding* the two airports; one is *in* a high while the other is *in* a low.

———•———

Solution to Navigation Problem

Figure 51 is a polar (top) view of the Northern Hemisphere. The geographic North Pole is in the center of the "chart" and the large, outer circle represents the equator.

As one proceeds north from the equator toward the pole, the circles (parallels) of latitude become progressively smaller. If you proceed far enough, you eventually reach a circle of latitude that has a circumference of exactly 500 nautical miles. At a north latitude of 89°, for example, the circumference of that parallel is only 377 nautical miles.)

Comrade Kochinko simply began his flight assignment at a point 500 miles south of the circle of latitude that has a circumference of 500 miles. He then flew due north for 500 miles, turned eastward and flew around the pole in a 500-mile circle. At the end of his circumpolar leg, Kochinko turned south and flew for another 500 miles until arriving over the starting point.

(For the technically oriented, a circumpolar track of 500 miles occurs at 88° 40.4′ N. Kochinko began his flight assignment 500 miles south of this parallel, or at 80° 20.4′ N.)

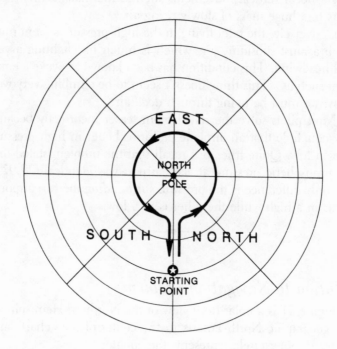

FIGURE 51

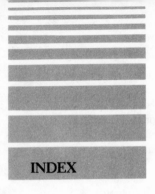

INDEX

ABOUT THE
AUTHOR

Barry Schiff has achieved international recognition for his general aviation expertise. An award-winning author, Schiff is a veteran captain for TWA and a contributing editor for *AOPA Pilot*. He has almost every FAA category and class rating. These include single- and multiengine (land and sea), helicopter, gyroplane, glider, and lighter-than-air (free balloon). He is one of very few flight instructors with all seven ratings.

Schiff also is an FAA-designated flight examiner and a general aviation test pilot with 20,000 hours in 225 types of aircraft. He has an aviation teaching credential issued by the California Department of Education, a ground instructor's certificate with all ratings, and holds eight world records in propeller and turbine airplanes.

Dedicated to aviation safety, Schiff has written several books (including two novels) and 500 articles for aviation publications all over the world.

His contributions to aviation have earned him numerous honors including the Louis Blériot Air Medal (France), the Gold Proficiency Award (Switzerland), and a U.S. congressional commendation.

Fly safely and skillfully—fly with Macmillan! These books are available at your local bookstore or by mail. To order directly, fill out both sides of this coupon and return to: Macmillan Publishing Company, Special Sales Department, 866 Third Avenue, New York, New York 10022.

Line Seq. No.	Qty.	ISBN	Title/Author	Price
1	____	0025271504	**Air Crashes** Collins	17.95
2	____	0025273108	**Flight Level Flying** Collins	18.95
3	____	0025271601	**Instrument Flying Refresher** Collins	17.95
4	____	0025271903	**Flying IFR** Collins	18.95
5	____	0025272209	**Dick Collins' Tips to Fly By** Collins	11.95
6	____	002518220X	**Art of Flying** Buck	17.95
7	____	0025182609	**Flying Know-How** Buck	19.95
8	____	0025180207	**Weather Flying** Buck	19.95
9	____	0025272403	**Takeoffs and Landings** Collins	18.95
10	____	0025272500	**Thunderstorms and Airplanes** Collins	14.95
11	____	0025272004	**Flying the Weather Map** Collins	16.95
12	____	0026071509	**Proficient Pilot** Schiff	18.95
13	____	0026071517	**Proficient Pilot II** Schiff	19.95
14	____	0026115204	**Defensive Flying** Slepyan	19.95
15	____	002611500X	**Crises in the Cockpit** Slepyan	19.95
16	____	0026185024	**Design for Flying** Thurston	22.50
17	____	0026185016	**Design for Safety** Thurston	22.50
18	____	0026166208	**Instrument Flying** Taylor	22.50
19	____	0026166607	**Understanding Flying** Taylor	22.50
20	____	0026166305	**IFR for VFR Pilots** Taylor	18.95
21	____	0026167301	**Fair-Weather Flying** Taylor	19.95
22	____	0025465708	**Positive Flying** Taylor/Guinther	18.95
23	____	0025816209	**Stalls, Spins, and Safety** Mason	19.95
24	____	0025045202	**Stranger to the Ground** Bach	15.95
25	____	0025046705	**Biplane** Bach	14.95
26	____	002504690X	**Nothing By Chance** Bach	16.95
27	____	0025406205	**Aircraft Versus Aircraft** Franks	19.95
28	____	068418835X	**On Extended Wings** Ackerman	7.95
29	____	0025793209	**Joy of Learning to Fly** Maher	17.95
30	____	0025403001	**Preflight Planning** Fowler	17.95
31	____	0025403508	**Flying Precision Maneuvers in Light Model Airplanes** Fowler	10.95
32	____	0025793500	**More I Learned About Flying From That** Moll	17.95
33	____	0020137001	**Weather and Forecasting** Dunlop/Wilson	8.95

Please add postage and handling costs—$1.00 for the first book and 50¢ for each additional book

Sub-total _____
Sales tax—if applicable _____
TOTAL _____

_____ Enclosed is my check/money order payable to Macmillan Publishing Company.

Control No [ ] Ord. Type [REG]

Lines Units

[ ]

For charge orders only:

_____ Bill my _____ MasterCard _____ Visa Card # _____

Expiration date _____ Signature _____

Charge orders valid only with signature

Ship to: _____

_____ Zip Code

Bill to: _____

_____ Zip Code

For information regarding bulk purchases, please write to Special Sales Director at the above address. Publisher's prices are subject to change without notice. Allow 3 weeks for delivery.

FC #911